P9-DDQ-033

This book belongs to

____

...a young woman of
passion, prayer, and purpose.

The *Elizabeth George* Young Woman's Collection

HARVEST HOUSE PUBLISHERS
EUGENE, OREGON

Cover by Katie Brady Design and Illustration, Eugene, Oregon

THE ELIZABETH GEORGE YOUNG WOMAN'S COLLECTION

Published by Harvest House Publishers
Eugene, Oregon 97402
www.harvesthousepublishers.com

ISBN-13: 978-0-7369-2497-9
ISBN-10: 0-7369-2497-3

Compilation of

A Young Woman After God's Own Heart
Copyright 2003 by Elizabeth George
ISBN-13: 978-0-7369-0789-7
ISBN-10: 0-7369-0789-0

A Young Woman's Walk with God
Copyright 2006 by Elizabeth George
ISBN-13: 978-0-7369-1653-0
ISBN-10: 0-7369-1653-9

A Young Woman's Call to Prayer
Copyright 2005 by Elizabeth George
ISBN-13: 978-0-7369-1463-5
ISBN-10: 0-7369-1463-3

Printed in the United States of America

08 09 10 11 12 13 14 15 / LB-NI / 10 9 8 7 6 5 4 3 2 1

A Young Woman After God's Own Heart

Elizabeth George

HARVEST HOUSE PUBLISHERS
EUGENE, OREGON

Acknowledgments

As always, thank you to my dear husband, Jim George, M.Div., Th.M., for your able assistance, guidance, suggestions, and loving encouragement on this project.

A YOUNG WOMAN AFTER GOD'S OWN HEART

Published by Harvest House Publishers
Eugene, Oregon 97402

Library of Congress Cataloging-in-Publication Data
George, Elizabeth, 1944–
A young woman after God's own heart / Elizabeth George.
p. cm.
Summary: Inspirational chapters and bible study citations present a pathway to a closer relationship with God.
ISBN-13: 978-0-7369-0789-7 (pbk.)
ISBN-10: 0-7369-0789-0 (pbk.)
1. Teenage girls—Religious life—Juvenile literature. 2. Girls—Religious life—Juvenile literature. 3. Christian life—Juvenile literature. [1. Prayer books and devotions. 2. Christian life.] I. Title.
BV4551.3 .G46 2003
248.8'33—dc21

2002013479

Printed in the United States of America

Contents

This book is lovingly dedicated to
the "young women" in my life,
my cherished granddaughters,

~

Taylor Jane Zaengle
Katherine Elizabeth Seitz

~

May you walk in
all God's ways.

~ Proverbs 3:6 ~

A Word of Welcome

Dear Friend,

Without even meeting you, I can tell you are someone very special! Why? Because you're choosing to read this book. When you consider its title, it becomes pretty obvious that you desire to become a woman after God's own heart. This book is packed with information and how-to's that will show you how to fulfill the desires of your heart—how to become a woman after God's own heart. As we begin our journey together, a few things will make it even sweeter.

Open your book... and enjoy it! Everything you need is here. I've tried to make it convenient for you as a busy young woman. In my mind I've pictured you reading this book on your bed at home, in a bunk bed at camp, in the backseat of the car or on an airplane while on your family vacation, in a lounge chair sunbathing around a pool, even in the library after you've finished your homework. Enjoy your book, carry it with you, and let God's Word instruct you.

Open your heart... to your friends. Encourage them to get books too. Then you will each be growing, which means your friendships will be growing in the right direction—in the things of the Lord. A godly woman needs other godly women as friends. So invite them to join you.

Open your heart... and look around. Are there any girls you don't know very well at school, or in the neighborhood, or perhaps where you work, that you can invite to join you in your study? Girls who need the Savior? Who need some guidelines for their lives? Who need a friend? Whisper a prayer to God, be bold, and reach out and invite someone you'd like to know better to get together.

Open your heart... to the priorities and topics covered in this book. They are tailor-made just for you. They'll give you God's wisdom and guidelines for the major areas of your life.

Open your heart... through prayer to the Holy Spirit. Ask Him to illuminate His Word, to help you understand God's plan and priorities for your life, and to transform your heart.

Open your heart... and dream! Dream of the woman you yearn to be—a woman after God's own heart.

And now let's put feet on those dreams! It is the prayer of my heart that the contents of this special book will encourage you, excite you, instruct you, and inspire you to follow after God's own heart even more passionately.

In His great and amazing love,
Your friend and sister in Christ,

Elizabeth George

Elizabeth George

Part One

The Pursuit of God

1

A Heart Devoted to God

But only one thing is needed. Mary has chosen what is better, and it will not be taken away from her.

Luke 10:42

Have you ever felt nervous…fidgety…on edge…cranky? Sort of like your life was falling apart and you were losing control? And even though you knew it and you didn't want to act the way you were, you kept on stomping through your day, lashing out at anybody and everybody who crossed your path—your parents, your brother or sister, your friends, a salesperson?

Well, my new friend, you are not alone! This happened to a woman in the Bible—a woman just like you and me—who got too worked up. In fact, she was a wreck! Her name is Martha, and Martha was a friend of Jesus.

What Happened?

What happened to put Martha over the edge? In a few words, Jesus and His disciples were coming to her house.

Wow! Now *that* should have been the best day of Martha's life! But Martha went into a tailspin. Why? Because Martha got too involved in the activities of her life—activities like…

serving Jesus and

working for Jesus.

And in all her serving and working, Martha failed to just…

stop and enjoy Jesus and

worship Him.

And how did Martha's busyness and the neglect of her spiritual life show? You guessed it—she got nervous…fidgety…on edge…cranky. And then she fell apart and lost control. Not only was Martha stomping through her day, but she was stomping through the kitchen, the dining room, and the family room. She even lashed out at her younger sister, Mary. And then (horror of horrors) she lashed out at Jesus!

What Was Wrong?

Martha was definitely out of control. And that led to her saying things she shouldn't have said, to blaming others for her awful condition, to bossing everyone around (even Jesus!), to comparing the amount of work she was doing with the amount of work her sister was (or wasn't!) doing, to complaining, to emoting…. Well, I'm sure you get the picture.

But, what was wrong?

✎ *From God's Word to Your Heart...*

Looking at the Bible's account and what it tells us about both Martha and Mary will answer all our questions. Read it below. It's what I call "the tale of two sisters." And while you're reading, notice what Jesus said was wrong in *Martha's* heart. Notice, too, the words the Bible—and Jesus—uses to describe Martha's conduct. And don't fail to catch how *Mary* is described and what good thing Jesus had to say about her.

> *As Jesus and his disciples were on their way, he came to a village where a woman named Martha opened her home to him. She had a sister called Mary, who sat at the Lord's feet listening to what he said. But Martha was distracted by all the preparations that had to be made. She came to him and asked, "Lord, don't you care that my sister has left me to do the work by myself? Tell her to help me!"*
>
> *"Martha, Martha," the Lord answered, "you are worried and upset about many things, but only one thing is needed. Mary has chosen what is better, and it will not be taken away from her"* (Luke 10:38-42).

What Made the Difference?

As we learn from these two sisters, we mustn't miss the fact that *both* of them loved Jesus (see verses 38-39). Both loved our Lord, and both served Him. But in this scene there was a great difference in their behaviors, which revealed something about what was going on in their hearts at the time.

You see, Mary not only loved serving the Lord, but she loved *listening* to Him. I mean, the split second Jesus started talking, Mary stopped! Her service came to a screeching halt, and she stopped, set her serving dishes aside, and took a seat at Jesus' feet. Why? So she could listen *to* Him—not just do *for* Him! After all, *He* had "the words of eternal life" (John 6:68).

So our dear Mary demonstrated a heart devoted to God by hearing His words and by worshiping Him. She was obsessed with Jesus. My guess is that Mary also loved the quieter disciplines of the Christian life—like sitting down in a favorite place to meditate on Scripture, to pray to God, and maybe even write in a journal or a diary. Whether this is true or not, we do definitely know that Mary knew when and how to make the choice to stop all the busy-ness of life and spend time with God.

And here's another point we don't want to miss. Surely Mary did her work. But Mary made sure her choices gained her the all-important time she needed to take care of her devotion and commitment to God. Yes, hers was a heart devoted to God.

What Is a Heart Devoted to God?

Because Mary was a woman after God's own heart, her heart was devoted to Him. She was preoccupied with one thing at all times—Him! As I said above, Mary was obsessed with the Lord. Therefore Mary consistently made one choice, one decision, that caused Jesus to speak of her as He did. And what was that one choice? Mary chose to spend time hearing God through His Word and worshiping God in her heart. In other words, Mary chose to spend some of her precious time with the Lord.

Time spent in this way, dear one, is the kind of time that is never wasted and can never be taken away from you either (see verse 42). Why? Because it is time spent in eternal pursuits, time that results in both daily and everlasting blessings.

Yes, But How?

I know you want to be a woman after God's own heart too, just like Mary was. So *how* can you move in that direction? Consider these three tried-and-true ways.

1. *Choose to spend time with God*—Here's how one woman after God's own heart put it: "I don't want to be robbed of even one of God's riches by not taking time to let Him invade my life. By not listening to what He is telling me. By allowing the routine, pressing matters of my minutes to bankrupt me of time for the most exciting, most fulfilling relationship in life."[1]

   Now, how can you make time in your busy day for "the most exciting, most fulfilling relationship in life"? For listening to God? For spending time with Him? For letting Him invade your life?

Listen to what my daughters' high school pastor told their youth group about spending time with God. He asked them, "Would you be willing to go on a bit of a fast each day, a *time* fast? Would you be willing to...

...say *no* to some time watching TV,

...say *no* to some time on the telephone,

...say *no* to some time with friends,

...say *no* to some time in the mall, in order to

...say *yes* to some time with God?"

And now the question is, would *you?*

2. *Choose God's ways at every opportunity*—"In all your ways acknowledge him, and he will make your paths straight" (Proverbs 3:6) could be the theme verse of this entire book—and of life! This well-loved verse describes a two-step partnership with God. *Our part* is to stop and acknowledge God along the way. *God's part* is to direct our paths and make them straight. This means that we are to consult with God regarding our every decision, word, thought, and response. This means that *before* we move ahead or *before* we react to someone or something, we need

to stop and pray first, "God, what would You have me do—or think or say—here?" If you do this you'll find the principles in this poem to be true for you and the choices you make.

> Good, better, best,
> never let it rest
> until your good is better,
> and your better best.

Don't you think this practice of stopping and consulting God *before* acting (and re-acting) like Martha did would help you and me to make the good, better, and best choices in the situations that we confront each day? Don't you think this habit would make us more like Mary?

3. *Commit yourself to God daily*—In Romans 12:1, the apostle Paul says "to offer your bodies as living sacrifices, holy and pleasing to God—this is your spiritual act of worship." As we consider our desire to commit ourselves to God daily, I want you to begin a new practice this week based on Romans 12:1. I want you to begin committing yourself to God daily. And how could you do that? Here's how one man did it. He wrote down a list of what he called "his rules to live by every day." And what was #1 on his list?

> Make a daily, definite, audible dedication of yourself to God. Say it out loud—"Lord, today I give myself anew to you."[2]

Why not make such a commitment to God daily for a week? And then why not seek to make it a habit for life?

4. *Cultivate a hot heart*—God has a few things to say to us in Revelation 3:15-16 about our heart condition. Read it for yourself:

> *I know your deeds, that you are neither cold nor hot. I wish you were either one or the other! So, because you are lukewarm—neither hot nor cold—I am about to spit you out of my mouth.*

I think it's pretty obvious, according to this scripture, which heart condition God considers the worst! And it gets even more serious as we think about these bone-chilling facts:

- To be *coldhearted* means to be unemotional, unconscious of God. Imagine being unemotional about the things of God!
- And to be *lukewarm* means to be indifferent. Imagine being indifferent toward God!
- But the third heart temperature is to be yours as a woman after God's own heart. You are to

> be *hot-hearted.* That means that the heat of your heart and emotion reaches a high temperature. That means boiling over! And such high heat is usually paired up with violent activity, emotion, excitement, and passion. It's fiery! As I said, that's the heart of someone—you!—who's committed to God.

Now, what is your heart's desire…and your heart's temperature toward God?

Heart Response

Are you there, dear one? Is yours the fiery heart of devotion to God that's just been described? Oh, how I pray that it is! But if you're not there, or if you're unsure how to get there, consider these few actions that will most definitely turn up the heat of your heart.

Step One—Do you need to receive Jesus Christ as your personal Savior? This is the beginning step, you know, to becoming a woman after *God's* own heart. Perhaps you need to pray a heartfelt prayer similar to this one:

> God, I want to be Your child, a true woman after Your heart—a woman who lives her life in You, and through You, and for You. I acknowledge my sins and shortcomings, my

> failure to live up to the standards You have set in Your Word, the Bible, and I receive Your Son, Jesus Christ, into my needy heart, giving thanks that He died on the cross for my sins. Thank You for giving me Your grace and Your strength so that I can follow after Your heart.

Step Two—Do you need to be more faithful to set aside time each day to listen to God like Mary did by reading your Bible? By praying? This can and must be a first priority each day. That's how you and I, no matter what our age, make the choice Mary made. That's how we choose the *one* thing, the *good* part, that can never be taken away from us. As we choose to sit at the Lord's feet *regularly*, we cease to act like Martha—too busy, too bossy, too distracted to listen to the Master and linger with Him and delight in Him.

Now, what will *your* choice be today? Tomorrow? Each day? I'm praying for you!

Things to Do Today to Develop a Heart That Is Devoted to God

- Think of at least three ways you can make time in your busy day for "the most exciting, most fulfilling relationship in life." How can you ensure time for listening to God, for spending time with Him, for letting Him invade your life?

♡ Memorize the poem below and put it to use in helping you choose God's way in the situations you confront each day.

Good, better, best,
never let it rest,
until your good is better,
and your better best.

♡ Make a definite, audible dedication of yourself to God today and every day this week.

Would You Like to Know More? Check It Out

✓ Read Mary and Martha's story in Luke 10:38-42 in your Bible. Describe the scene. Note who was there and what was taking place.

✓ Next, do a character study on Martha. Circle or list the words that describe Martha's conduct. Also note her words—who she spoke to and what she said.

✓ Then do a character study on Mary, noting the words that describe her conduct.

✓ Compare the two sisters. What differences do you notice in their words, actions, attitudes, posture, and interaction with Jesus?

✓ Then ask yourself, Am I busily "serving" Jesus…or sitting at His feet? Am I lashing out at others…or am I listening to my Savior? Am I worrying about life…or am I worshiping the Lord? Am I restless…or am I resting in God? What changes must I make to develop a heart that is devoted to God?

✓ What does Proverbs 31:30 say about the importance of maintaining your relationship with God?

2

A Heart That Loves God's Word

[You] will be like a tree planted by the water
that sends out its roots by the stream.
JEREMIAH 17:8

I can still remember the day my husband, Jim, and I planted 13 ivy vines in our backyard with the hopes that these baby plants would one day grow strong enough and full enough to cover our bare and oh-so-ugly(!) cement block walls.

Well, about three months later, my dream was coming true…except for one of the ivy plants. It was absolutely dead! So Jim went to work. He purchased a new replacement plant, got out his shovel, bent over the dead vine, and to his surprise, it slipped right out of the ground. In a glance Jim could see what was wrong. This one plant had failed to grow because there were no roots! Although the plant had enjoyed all the right conditions above ground, something was missing beneath the surface of the soil. It didn't have the root system that is vital for drawing the needed nourishment and moisture from the soil.

What a picture this is for you and me! As women after God's own heart we want to grow in Christ. But, just like any kind of plant, we must take care to nurture a healthy, powerful root system. Our heart's desire is…

> to flourish…not fail
>
> to thrive…not die
>
> to blossom…not wither

Therefore we must devote ourselves to developing a root system that is anchored deep in the Lord and in His Word, the Bible. We must willfully and purposefully spend time in God's Word—reading it, cherishing it, and (most of all) following it. This practice will make all the difference in your life, and in mine, too!

Roots Are Unseen

Where is a thriving root system grown? We know the answer, don't we? It's grown underground. So I want to challenge you to disappear from the public scene for a period of time each day. I want to encourage you to drop out of your friends' sight for a portion of your day. I want to invite you to withdraw from the distractions of TV and the Internet for a time of solitude. Why? So you can tend to your private life, your hidden life, the secret life you enjoy with God. When you and I are faithful to do this one thing each and every day, wow!, what a difference it makes.

But we get it all backwards. We think that the Christian life is made up of people, people, and more people! In fact, it seems like we're always with people—people at home, people at school (and after school), people at church.... On and on the people list goes. Yet, here's the truth:

> The greater the proportion of your day—of your life—spent hidden in quiet, in reflection, in prayer, [in study,] in scheduling, in preparation, the greater will be the effectiveness, the impact, the power of the part of your life that shows.[3]

Roots Are for Taking In

What happens when you and I do slip away to be with God in study and prayer? We receive. We take in. We are nurtured and fed. We ensure our spiritual health and growth. When we spend time with Christ, He supplies us with strength and encourages us in the pursuit of His ways.

I call this time with God "the great exchange." Away from the world and hidden from public view, I exchange...

> my weariness for His strength,
> my weakness for His power,
> my darkness for His light,
> my problems for His solutions,
> my burdens for His freedom,
> my frustrations for His peace,
> my turmoil for His calm,
> my hopes for His promises,

my afflictions for His balm of comfort,
my questions for His answers,
my confusion for His knowledge,
my doubt for His assurance,
my nothingness for His awesomeness,
the temporal for the eternal, and
the impossible for the possible!

Roots Are for Storage

Roots serve as a reservoir of what we need. As we stop (like Mary did in the previous chapter) and regularly send down our roots into God's Word, into His springs of living water, we begin to collect His life-giving water. Then what happens?

God's Word begins to create in us a reservoir of hope and strength in Him. Then, when times are rough and things get difficult (like when your classmates make fun of your commitment to God…or when you are tempted to give up—or give in to sin…or when a friend turns on you or gossips about you…or when there is tension in the home), you and I won't be depleted. We won't dry up, disintegrate, or die. We won't run out of strength, collapse in exhaustion, or give up.

And here's another wonderful thing that happens. Because of the reservoir, when problems come (and Jesus said they will—see John 16:33!), we can simply reach down into our hidden reservoir of strength and draw out from what God has given us. What's needed is available right at that moment! Like the psalmist wrote about God's people, we will be able to go from "strength to strength" (Psalm 84:7). Yes, roots deep into God's truth are definitely needed when times get rough.

Roots Are for Support

Here's another reason to make sure you spend time in God's Word. Without a well-developed root system, you and I can become top heavy. "Top heavy" is a vivid term used to describe a plant that has lots of leafy, heavy foliage above the ground but nothing to support it from underneath. In other words, there are only a few scanty roots but not enough to hold it up. So, when times get tough (and remember, they will!) and the winds of adversity begin to blow (and they will!), we topple. You see, without a network of strong roots, we have to be staked up, tied up, propped up, and straightened up...until another wind comes along, and over we go again!

Do you want to stand strong in the Lord? Then you must cultivate a strong and healthy root system. Here's what I want for you and me.

> In bygone days a process was used for growing the trees that became the main masts for military and merchant ships. The great shipbuilders first selected a tree located on the top of a high hill as a potential mast. Then they cut away all of the surrounding trees that would shield the chosen one from the force of the wind. As the years went by and the

winds blew fiercely against the tree, the tree only grew stronger until finally it was strong enough to be the foremast of a ship.[4]

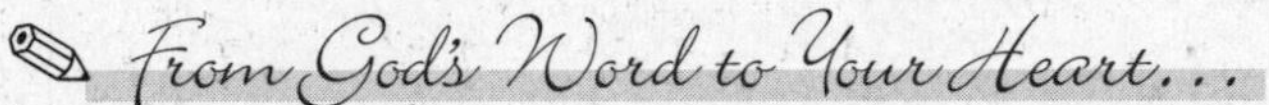

Let's pause now and read the verses below. Several describe the characteristics of a plant—or in our case, a woman—whose heart is rooted in God's Word. As you read, be thinking about several things that stand out in your mind and heart from these picturesque verses and the stamina portrayed in each.

> *Blessed is the man who does not walk in the counsel of the wicked or stand in the way of sinners or sit in the seat of mockers. But his delight is in the law of the LORD, and on his law he meditates day and night. He is like a tree planted by streams of water, which yields its fruit in season and whose leaf does not wither. Whatever he does prospers* (Psalm 1:1-3).

> *Blessed is the man who trusts in the LORD, whose confidence is in him. He will be like a tree planted by the water that sends out its*

roots by the stream. It does not fear when heat comes; its leaves are always green. It has no worries in a year of drought and never fails to bear fruit (Jeremiah 17:7-8).

The L*ORD will guide you always; he will satisfy your needs in a sun-scorched land and will strengthen your frame. You will be like a well-watered garden, like a spring whose waters never fail* (Isaiah 58:11).

We are hard pressed on every side, but not crushed; perplexed, but not in despair; persecuted, but not abandoned; struck down, but not destroyed (2 Corinthians 4:8-9).

Yes, But How?

Now, *how* does a woman draw near to God's heart? *How* can you and I put ourselves in a position where God can grow each of us into a woman of remarkable endurance?

1. *Develop the habit of drawing near to God*—Notice the habits of these men of remarkable endurance. Think about what you can learn from each of them.

    Abraham—*Early the next morning Abraham got up and returned to the place where he had stood before the* Lord (Genesis 19:27).

    David—*In the morning, O* Lord, *you hear my voice; in the morning I lay my requests before you and wait in expectation* (Psalm 5:3).

    Jesus—*Very early in the morning, while it was still dark, Jesus got up, left the house and went off to a solitary place, where he prayed* (Mark 1:35).

    Now for you, my friend. Can you say that your habit of drawing near to God is deeply ingrained? Or is it somewhat regular, merely in-the-making, or needing to be improved?

2. *Design a personal time for drawing near to God*—If you're like most busy women—young or old—your time with the Lord could use a little help. So let's set about to design a better time. (Remember? "Good, better, best....")

   When? Did you notice that the three men above had a *time* when they met with God? As you review your daily life and look into your heart, what would be the best time for you? Or put another way, when would you like it to be?

   Where? And did you notice that each of these people of God had a *place* for meeting with God? Do you have a place? If not, where would you like your place to be?

   What tools? The right tools will make your *time* with God in your *place* more productive, more efficient, and more meaningful. For instance, I take my Bible, my pink highlighter, and my personal journal to my *place* at my *time*. Sometimes I take my favorite devotional book along with me. And sometimes I even use a textbook to look up certain kinds of information (a dictionary, a Bible reference book). Think about how you will stock your *place* so that the next *time* you land there for your devotions, everything you need will be handy.

3. *Detail your daily progress*—One picture is truly worth a thousand words! So I'm asking you to do what I do. Start today to use the chart in the back of your book, "Quiet Times Calendar," to keep track of your all-important devotional life. Simply color in or shade in the days you meet with God and read from His Word. Then a quick glance will tell you how well you're doing in your pursuit of becoming a woman who loves God's Word. (You'll find this chart on pages 218-19.)

Heart Response

Here's something else to think about as you seek to love God's Word even more—if someone asked you to describe the quiet time you had this morning, what would you say?

This is exactly the question Dawson Trotman, founder of The Navigators ministry organization, used to ask young men and women applying for ministry work. In fact, he once spent five days interviewing candidates for overseas missionary service. He spent a half hour with each one, asking specifically about their devotional life. Sadly, only one person out of 29 interviewed said his devotional life was a constant in his life, a source of strength, guidance, and refreshment. As Trotman continued to probe into the lives of those men and women planning a lifetime of service for God, he found that never since they had come to know the Lord had they ever had a consistent devotional life.[5]

Now, my cherished reading friend, how would *your* interview about *your* devotional life go? What answers would *you* be able to give? Ask your heart Mr. Trotman's question now.

And, if your answer isn't all that great, what can you do right this minute to set your life and the pattern of your days in a new direction, a direction that will ensure that you grow in your love for God's Word? After all, as the old saying goes, "Every journey begins with a single step." And that includes your journey to becoming a woman after God's own heart!

Things to Do Today to Develop a Heart That Loves God's Word

- ♡ Did you choose a time to be with God yet? If not, do it now. Then pick a place to be alone with God.

- List the tools you will need for your place. Then place those tools in your place so that tomorrow you are ready to meet with God.

- If you don't know what to study, may I suggest one of the studies in my A Woman After God's Own Heart® Bible Study series? These fun studies were created for busy women (like you!) to be completed in about 15 minutes a day. Every one of them was selected because it focuses on being a woman, on the lives of the women of the Bible, and on our roles as women. You'll find a list of these studies on the last page of this book.

Would You Like to Know More? Check It Out

✓ Read Psalm 1:1-3. Make a list of the actions of the man or woman whose heart is rooted in God's Word. Note what she does not do and what she does do. What are the results of such a love for God's Word? Are there any changes you must make today?

✓ Do the same for Jeremiah 17:7-8. Here is a picture of spiritual health and growth. Write down the actions of the person who is blessed. Note the hard conditions and the signs of health and strength. Then list the indicators and benefits of spiritual health and growth. Are there any changes you must make today?

✓ Read 2 Corinthians 4:8-9. The apostle Paul was a man after God's own heart who continually drew strength from God when the pressures of life built up. Yet Paul, like the great ship's mast described earlier, stood firm. Because of God's Word, God's truth, God's strength, and God's grace to him, what was Paul able to testify? Are there any changes you must make today to root your heart and life in God's Word so that you can tap into this same kind of strength as you walk through life?

3

A Heart Committed to Prayer

Part 1

Then Jesus told his disciples a parable to show them that they should always pray and not give up.

Luke 18:1

I wish I knew more about you, my precious friend! I wish I knew where you live, what your room (and your *place* where you meet with God) looks like, what *you* look like, what your family is like, what some of your favorite things to do might be.

But right this minute, I wish I knew how old you are. Why? Because I made a very important choice in relation to becoming a woman after God's own heart when I was 38 years old, and I'm praying that you are *way* ahead of me in making such a decision! Yes, I'm glad that you're much younger than I was, and I hope you're much further along in your spiritual growth than I was at that time.

Anyway, I made the significant choice on my tenth spiritual birthday. (And, again, I hope you're *way* ahead of me!) On that day I was having my quiet time, my time alone with God. After spending some time thanking Him for His Son and for His salvation of my soul, I dared to turn my thoughts forward. I prayed, "Lord, what do You see missing from my Christian life? What needs attention as I begin a new decade with You?"

Well, before I got the question mark tacked onto my heart-searching prayer, God seemed to respond immediately by calling to my mind an area of great personal struggle and failure—my prayer life!

Oh, I had tried praying. I knew God's Word said I should. But each new effort lasted, at best, only a few days. And then I was back where I started, mumbling something like, "God bless me and my family today." Oh, yes, I had tried praying!

But on that tenth spiritual birthday, I wrote out the following commitment to God:

> I dedicate and purpose to spend the next ten years (Lord willing) developing a meaningful prayer life.

My dear friend, these words, poured out of an earnest heart, launched a complete make-over of my whole life—every part and person and pursuit in it! And I want to share with you just a few of the blessings of prayer that became mine. And take heart! They're blessings that can become yours as well.

Blessing #1: A Deeper Relationship with God

When you and I spend regular, daily, unhurried time in prayer with God, we experience a deeper relationship with Him. And we grow spiritually in a multitude of ways. Here are just a few examples.

Prayer increases faith—I had heard that a good way to grow in faith in God was to keep a prayer list. And so I began to write out a prayer list. With my list in hand, I began taking my concerns for family, friends, and myself to God each day. I was awed as, for the first time ever, I paid close attention to how He answered item after item! And, of course, with each day, each prayer time, and each answer, my faith in God grew.

Prayer provides a place to unload burdens—What is your #1 problem today? And what are the other pressing problems of your life? Today, right now in fact, one of my best friends is having cancer surgery. I am a thousand miles away, unable to be with her or help in any way. My heart is heavy and anxious! But through prayer I am doing what the Bible tells you and me to do—I am "casting" my problem and my burden on my heavenly Father (1 Peter 5:7). I know when I do this, when I do what God says to do with the cares of my life and the cares of my friend's life, I'm putting my impossible problems into His able hands. God will take care of them…as only He can.

When you and I begin each day by giving all the cares of life to God in prayer, we can then rise up relieved, freed from many heavy weights. Author and fellow pray-er Corrie ten Boom offers a vivid image of this privilege. She writes,

As a camel kneels before his
master to have him remove his
burden, so kneel and let the
Master take your burden.[6]

I also like this advice given by a poet in a scene between the Lord and one of His children. I don't know who wrote it, but it says it all!

But this you must remember,
This one thing you must know...
I cannot take your burden
Until you let it go.

Prayer teaches us that God is always near—What can you do when trouble strikes? I mean trouble like a tragedy, a catastrophe, a disaster? Well, my friend, I had the opportunity to find out on January 17, 1994, at 4:31 in the morning, when a devastating 6.8 killer earthquake struck our home in California. I was home alone and can only remember trying to save my life by getting out of the house. And, as I cried out to God while staggering toward the front door, with our house literally buckling and cracking beneath my bare feet, from the depths of my heart and soul came God's reassurance of His presence. And it came from a passage out of the Bible (Psalm 46:1-2) that I had planted there by memorizing it.

God is our refuge and strength,
an ever-present help in trouble.
Therefore we will not fear...

(And, by the way, the rest of this passage and the next verse just happens to go like this: "...though the earth give way and the mountains fall into the heart of the sea, though its waters roar and foam and thc mountains quake with their surging"! Sounds like an earthquake to me!)

Beloved young sister, the more you and I pray, the more we are reminded of God's powerful presence in time of need! One man put it this way: "The purpose of prayer is to reveal the presence of God equally present all the time in every condition."[7]

Prayer trains us not to panic—Jesus said we shouldn't give up, give in, or panic. No, He said we should pray instead (see Luke 18:1). In other words, we are not to give in, cave in, or collapse under pressure. Instead we are to persevere. Turning to God for every need during your regular daily prayer time will ingrain in you the habit of prayer, which can then replace your natural tendency to panic at the first hint of any problem.

Prayer changes lives—You've probably heard that "prayer changes *things*." But, dear one, once you develop a more regular prayer life you'll discover that "prayer changes *you*"!

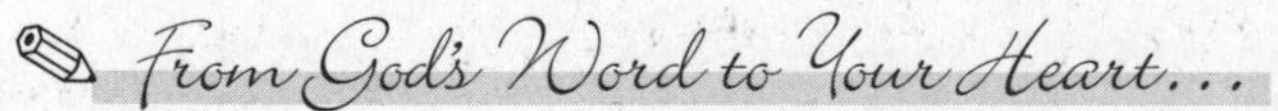

Wow! Look at all the ways you and I grow in our trust in God and in our knowledge of God when we pray! What good news! But now I want you to see for yourself what

God has to say about enjoying a deeper relationship with Him through prayer. Interact with these teachings from the Bible. Note the instructions they give you…right from God's Word to your heart. And while you're at it, think about something you can do to put these powerful truths and promises into action concerning the issues of your life today, tomorrow, and all your future tomorrows.

> *Then Jesus told his disciples a parable to show them that they should always pray and not give up* (Luke 18:1).

> *Cast all your anxiety on him because he cares for you* (1 Peter 5:7).

> *God is our refuge and strength, an ever-present help in trouble. Therefore we will not fear* (Psalm 46:1-2).

> *I lift up my eyes to the hills—where does my help come from? My help comes from the Lord, the Maker of heaven and earth* (Psalm 121:1-2).

> *Call to me and I will answer you and tell you great and unsearchable things you do not know* (Jeremiah 33:3).

Thanks for taking the time to look at the verses above. I hope (and pray!) these scriptures gave you a better idea of what I've been saying about the blessing of a deeper relationship with God through prayer. We are indeed blessed to enjoy the privilege of prayer, of conversing with almighty God. May your heart be encouraged to pray. And may your prayers be ever lifted to our great God so that…

> you are growing in faith,
>
> you are handing off your burdens,
>
> you are more aware of the presence of God,
>
> you are less likely to panic when troubles arise, and
>
> you are being changed and transformed into the image of God's dear Son and your Savior, Jesus Christ!

Heart Response

I know we took a long time on this one blessing (a whole chapter, in fact!). But wasn't it eye-opening to drink in just these few ways that the one discipline of praying daily can help us to grow spiritually? And don't you agree that your relationship with God is vitally important? After all, you, like me, desire to be a woman after *His* heart. And it's truly incredible and unbelievable that you and I can enjoy a relationship with the God of the universe! It's truly by His grace!

So now, dear heart, I am inviting you to make a commitment similar to the one I made. And while you're at it, thank God profusely that you're not 38 years old like I was when I made my commitment! That means you have a 20- to 25-year head start on me. I'm deliriously happy for you!

And I have more good news for you. When I decided to learn more about the awesome privilege of prayer, I fully expected drudgery and joyless labor. But as I moved ahead on my commitment to develop a meaningful prayer life, I was surprised by the blessings that began to blossom in my heart. As a favorite hymn tells us, "Count your blessings, name them one by one." And dear one, as I said, these are just a few!

Now, write out your own personal commitment to develop your prayer life. Then let's look in our next chapter at even more blessings that come our way as we pray.

My Commitment to Pray

Things to Do Today to Develop a Heart Committed to Prayer

- Did you make your personal commitment to prayer? If not, why not? It's not too late to do it. Just remember that *desire* is half the victory, and your prayer of commitment is an expression of your desire to become a woman of prayer.

- Now that you've made that commitment (you did make it, right?), take a sheet of paper—maybe a page in your personal notebook or planner—and list the people you want to pray for. The next time you pray, read each person's name aloud to God. Then say what's on your heart about each dear person. Keep moving right on through your list as time permits.

- Begin another prayer list of your own personal concerns—your #1 problem, some decision you must make, some behavior you should change, some fear that tends to rob you of your joy in the Lord. Then pray...instead of giving in to these pressures.

Would You Like to Know More? Check It Out

✓ What does Matthew 7:7-8 tell you to do, and what does it promise as a result?

✓ When it comes to prayer (and hope and patience), what does Romans 12:12 advise?

✓ How can you have peace and live a life that is free from anxiety, according to Philippians 4:6-7?

✓ How faithful should Christians—and you—be in the area of prayer, according to Colossians 4:2?

✓ For the recipe to a wonderful life, see 1 Thessalonians 5:16-18!

✓ What does Hebrews 4:16 say your attitude should be as you pray...and what are the blessed results?

✓ In case you are hesitant to pray, what assurance is noted in 1 Peter 3:12?

4

A Heart Committed to Prayer

Part 2

The prayer of a righteous man
is powerful and effective.
James 5:16

Even though we've never met, I have *so* enjoyed praying for you, my unseen friend! Do you realize what an amazing person you are? That *you* hold the keys to the future of Christianity (humanly speaking, that is)? That you are one of the significant godly young women of today who will become the godly women (and possibly wives and mothers) of the years to come? And I know that you care about your spiritual growth because you've chosen to work your way through a book like this one. Oh, how I thank God for *you*. And I thank Him that you truly desire a close relationship with Him.

There's a young woman in the Bible who reminds me of you. She's Mary, who became the mother of our Lord Jesus Christ. Maybe you already know that Mary was about 14 years old when God sent His angel Gabriel to speak to her (Luke 1:26-38). What do we know about Mary at that point in her life? We know that...

> she was completely committed to God's will for her life (verse 38).
>
> she was highly favored by God (verses 28 and 30).
>
> she was a virgin (verses 27 and 34).

One thing I really love about Mary is her prayer life. In fact, her prayer life was so stunning that God has used Mary—a 14-year-old, a teenager!—to teach all Christian women down through the centuries how to pray. You see, Mary truly had that deeper relationship with God that we talked about in our last chapter. And surely that relationship was partly developed as she prayed to her heavenly Father. You and I can learn much about prayer by reading what is called "Mary's Magnificat" or "The Song of Mary" in Luke 1:46-55. The first thing that impresses us in Mary's Song is that when Mary opened her mouth to pray, the first words that rushed forth were, "My soul glorifies the Lord and my spirit rejoices in God my Savior" (verses 46-47).

And now it's our turn, dear one. It's time for us to learn more about prayer and about how to further develop a heart that is committed to prayer. To review, we've already discussed that Blessing #1 is a deeper relationship with God. Now let's go on and look at even more of the blessings that are ours through prayer.

Blessing #2: Greater Purity

In our last chapter I mentioned that prayer changes us. And now I want to point out that one major change prayer brings about in us is greater purity. Becoming more like Christ is a process of spiritual growth that requires dealing with sin. And taking the confession of sin seriously during prayer time moves that process along, causing us to purge our life of practices that are not pleasing to God.

I certainly know this to be true in my life. How? Because I was able to pinpoint a serious sin area in my daily life, a habit that I *knew* went against God's Word. In both 1 Timothy 3:11 and Titus 2:3, God says—in black and white!—that His women are not to gossip. And (you guessed it!) I had a terrible problem with gossip.

But there's good news, too! Real change began when I started to not only pray about gossip, but to confess it as sin each time I did it. I began to acknowledge to God (and admit to myself!) that this practice went against His Word, that it was harmful to His people and to others, and that it had no place in my life as a child of God. Now, don't get me wrong—I still have my struggles. But believe me when I tell you that I am not the same gossiping woman I used to be! Purification—purging my life of a major sin—took place, in part, because I faced my sin regularly in prayer. In other words, the conviction of sin led to confession...which led to purging...which led to greater purity.

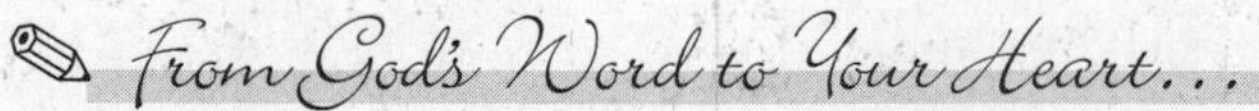

Now that I've told you a little about one of my problem areas, let's see what God's Word says about purifying ourselves of practices that are not pleasing to Him. Note what this verse teaches us as women after God's own heart about greater purity.

> *If we confess our sins, he is faithful and just and will forgive us our sins and purify us from all unrighteousness* (1 John 1:9).

Now, do what I did (and still do). Pinpoint one practice in your life that you know is not pleasing to God, a practice or habit that is, in fact, directly opposed to His Word. Put that sinful action at the top of your prayer list. Then pray about it—every day. (Pray about it every *minute* of every day, if you have to!) And confess it to God when you fail. Ask God to help you create a plan of action to radically remove it from your life. Be severe! Be decisive! Be whatever you must be and do whatever you must do to move toward purifying yourself of this one area. It'll be tough, but cry out to God for His help and for His grace to do battle and to get a grip on this area of your life. A woman after God's own heart willingly sacrifices her favorite sins for greater purity!

Blessing #3: Confidence in Making Decisions

How do you make decisions? If you're like most women, you make them based on how you *feel* at the moment some opportunity comes along. In other words, you make *physical* decisions and *emotional* decisions—not *spiritual* decisions. You tend to make decisions that are based on your physical and/or emotional state at the moment rather than waiting to make decisions that are spiritually made through—and after—prayer.

Well, dear one, I just described me! Here's a typical scenario from my life (before I began to pray about my choices). If some opportunity came up, and I was tired at the moment, guess what my answer was? *No!* Or if I felt frayed and frazzled around the edges, like I just couldn't handle one more thing, again, my answer was *no!*

But I learned to follow a three-step pattern that has helped me make better decisions. (Remember? "Good, better, best....") I learned to...

1) *wait* to make decisions so that I could

2) *write* them down on my prayer list and then

3) *wait* on God for direction.

As a result, I came up with this prayer principle for my decision making (which I gladly pass on to you!):

~ *No decision made without prayer!* ~

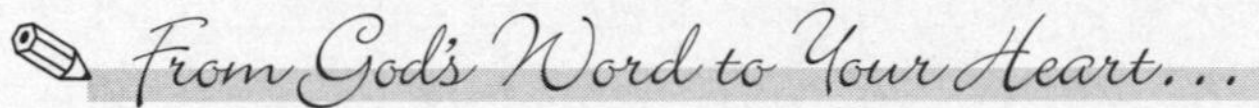

We want to be women after God's own heart, right? So let's note what these scriptures teach us about the lives and hearts of two of God's devoted servants.

Hear God's report of King David's heart—*After removing Saul, [God] made David their king. He testified concerning him: "I have found David son of Jesse a man after my own heart; he will do everything I want him to do"* (Acts 13:22).

Hear the heart cry of the apostle Paul—*"What shall I do, Lord?"* (Acts 22:10).

Now, how do you think 1) *waiting* before you make a decision so that you have time to 2) *write* down the decision(s) you must make and then 3) *waiting* on God's direction through prayer would help you make good, better, and best decisions? And how do you think the prayer principle *no decision made without prayer* would help?

Blessing #4: Improved Relationships

What a blessing prayer is! Prayer results in better relationships with people—*all* people! How can this be? Because as you pray for others, you find these prayer principles to be true.

- *You cannot think about yourself and others at the same time.* (Praying for others forces you to think of others.)

- *You cannot hate the person you are praying for.* (Prayer is an act of love that changes your heart.)

- *You cannot neglect the person you are praying for.* (Prayer causes you to care more about others as you carry them in your heart.)

From God's Word to Your Heart...

While we're thinking about our prayer life, let's touch on friendships and relationships for a minute or two. I know that every teen struggles with friends—with making and maintaining friendships. As a Christian woman I know you want healthy personal relationships. And that includes your relationships with your parents and brothers and sisters. Plus we all have relationships to nurture beyond the family circle, relationships with not only our best friends but also with those who are unkind. And then there are "boy" friends!

But as we pray about these relationships—about all our relationships—we witness many improvements. Here's a list of the major categories of relationships that probably fill your life. Note what the Bible says about them and how you can pray accordingly.

Parents

Children, obey your parents in the Lord, for this is right. "Honor your father and mother"—which is the first commandment with a promise—"that it may go well with you and that you may enjoy long life on the earth" (Ephesians 6:1-3). *Children, obey your parents in everything, for this pleases the Lord* (Colossians 3:20).

Friends

Do not be misled: "Bad company corrupts good character" (1 Corinthians 15:33). *A man of many companions may come to ruin, but there is a friend who sticks closer than a brother* (Proverbs 18:24).

Boyfriends

An unmarried woman or virgin is concerned about the Lord's affairs: Her aim is to be devoted to the Lord in both body and spirit (1 Corinthians 7:34). *It is God's will that you should...avoid sexual immorality; that each of you should learn to control his own body in a way that is holy and honorable.... For God did not call us to be impure, but to live a holy life* (1 Thessalonians 4:3-4,7).

Enemies

Love your enemies, do good to those who hate you, bless those who curse you, pray for those who mistreat you (Luke 6:27-28).

Whether we are praying for our loved ones, our friends, or our unloved ones(!), a heart that is committed to pray for others makes a difference in those relationships. I once heard about a teacher who assigned her students the following project: They were to select the person on campus they disliked the most. Daily during the coming month, they were to pray for that person and then go out of their way to do some act of kindness for that person. Here's what one young woman wrote after the month was up:

> By the end of the month my dislike of [the girl selected] had been replaced by a growing compassion and understanding....[This assignment] helped me see things about myself—my unfriendliness, my lack of compassion, my

> judging without first trying to understand the causes of behavior I disliked.

Let's ask God to help us have greater love and compassion for others. Let's pray for others.

Blessing #5: Contentment

Oh, wow, is this ever an area for prayer! Why is it that we are rarely satisfied? That we worry about our lives? That it seems like everyone else has what we want? That we're on the slow track to popularity, achievement, development, relationships, growth? The list of our discouragements could truly go on and on!

Well, thank the Lord that contentment is ours...when we pray! Before we dive into what God tells us about how to grow in contentment, think a minute about the things you worry about. If you want to, jot them down here.

✎ *From God's Word to Your Heart...*

Now let's see how God's guidelines for contentment can help you and me not to worry.

> *Do not worry about tomorrow* (Matthew 6:34).
> *Do not be anxious about anything, but in everything, by prayer and petition, with*

> *thanksgiving, present your requests to God. And the peace of God, which transcends all understanding, will guard your hearts and your minds in Christ Jesus* (Philippians 4:6-7).
> *I have learned to be content whatever the circumstances....I have learned the secret of being content in any and every situation....I can do everything through him who gives me strength* (Philippians 4:11-13).

Look at your own list of "worries." How will you put these principles to work the next time you worry?

Yes, But How?

I know we've covered a lot in this chapter! And I don't want to leave you without giving you some very practical ways to get started on your commitment to pray.

1. Start a prayer log to record requests and responses as you travel your own personal journey of prayer.

2. Set aside time each day to linger with the Lord in prayer and remember that *something is better than nothing*. Begin small—and watch for the mighty effects!

3. Pray always (Ephesians 6:18) and in all places, enjoying God's presence with you wherever you go (Joshua 1:9).

4. Pray faithfully for others, especially your parents and brothers and sisters. And don't forget to pray for your enemies (Luke 6:28)!

5. Take seriously the powerful privilege of prayer.

Heart Response

When it comes to my prayer life, I have a saying that helps me each day—*First things first*. I try to make my quiet time with God the first thing I do each morning. Somehow, dedicating my fresh new day to God in prayer first thing makes a tremendous difference in that day. It reminds me who I am (His child) and who I am to serve (Him!) and what I am to do with my day…and my life (glorify Him). And as I pray for the people in my life, the very act of prayer amazingly changes my heart toward them as God gives me His love and His wisdom for living out these relationships in a way that causes Christ to shine through me.

And now I have a question for you: Do you think praying—even for just five or ten minutes a day—could change your life? I believe it can! Lingering in God's presence will increase your faith, provide a place for you to unload your burdens, remind you that God is always near, and help you not to panic when troubles come. When you accept God's invitation to pray, He will transform your heart and change your life.

Now *that's* exciting! All this…and more!…is available to you, my friend, as you nurture a heart committed to prayer. What will your first step be?

Things to Do Today to Develop a Heart Committed to Prayer

- ♡ Make a prayer sheet for each member of your family and begin praying daily for them. Ask each family member what needs you can pray for.

- ♡ Begin a prayer sheet for listing the decisions you must make. Be faithful to bring them to God in prayer each day. Ask Him for His wisdom.

- ♡ Pick out the person you dislike the most and pray daily for her or him for one month.

Would You Like to Know More? Check It Out

✓ In Luke 1:46-55, Mary pours out her heart in prayer. Write out how Mary referred to herself, and how she referred to God. List, too, her descriptions of God. What strikes you most about her prayer? What ingredients of her prayer can you include in yours?

✓ What do you learn about Jesus' prayers in Mark 1:35? What ingredients of His prayer life can you include in yours?

✓ What is said about Elijah and his prayer life in James 5:17-18? What ingredients of His prayer life can you include in yours? (Notice what James 5:16 says—"The prayer of a righteous man [or woman!] is powerful and effective.")

5

A Heart That Obeys

I have found David...a man after my own heart;
he will do everything I want him to do.

ACTS 13:22

We love God, don't we? And we love to read His Word and to pray to Him. But, oh dear, this next area of being a woman after God's own heart is hard!

I'm talking about obedience. And I can never think about the importance of obedience to God without remembering an evening when my daughter Katherine made brownies for the rest of the family...and left out the salt. Well, you know the results! We had to throw out the whole batch because an all-important something was missing and they tasted awful.

And beloved, just as a batch of brownies requires several ingredients to become what we intend it to be, several ingredients are key to our becoming women after God's own heart. We've already talked about devotion to God, devotion to His Word, and devotion to prayer. But one more ingredient—as important as salt in brownies—goes into making you and me women after God's own heart, and that ingredient is obedience. The heart God delights in is a heart that is teachable, willing, and responsive to Him and His commands. In short, it's a heart that obeys.

Two Kinds of Hearts

Just how did I come up with the title of this book, *A Young Woman After God's Own Heart?* Well, it's drawn from the Bible, from Acts 13:22. It's from a sermon preached by the apostle Paul. And in that sermon, Paul pointed out the lives of two different men who had two kinds of hearts. Here's what we know about these two men.

> *King Saul*—The first man was Saul, who reigned as king over Israel and God's people for 40 years.
>
> - Saul served himself and did things his way.
> - Saul's worship consisted of outward acts of sacrifice only.
> - Saul's heart was centered on Saul.
> - Saul's devotion to God was impulsive and irregular.
> - Saul was proud and relied on his own skill, his own wisdom and judgment, and his own physical strength.

King David—The second man was David, who served as king over God's people after God removed Saul as king.

- David's heart was willing to obey God.
- David served God, not himself.
- David was concerned with following God's will, not his own.
- David's heart was centered on God, not on himself.
- David, a mighty warrior, depended upon God for his victories and repeatedly declared, "The LORD is the stronghold of my life" (Psalm 27:1).

God gave both these kings opportunities to lead Israel, but in the end they walked down different paths—Saul away from God and David toward Him. These two men were like two different musicians, one who sits down at a piano and plunks on it, here a little, there a little (everyone can play "Chopsticks"!) and the other who sits for hours at a time, a disciplined, faithful, and dedicated student. The first creates immature, irregular, crude sounds that fade away, while the other learns, grows, excels, and lifts the hearts and souls of others as he fine-tunes his music—his life—to the Almighty. Saul's song—his walk with the Lord—was fickle, on again, off again, and undeveloped. But David, known as the sweet psalmist of Israel (2 Samuel 23:1 KJV), offered up to God pure melodies of devoted love and heartfelt obedience. Truly, his was a heart after God!

✎ *From God's Word to Your Heart...*

Now it's your turn to look at what God's Word has to say about these two men and their two kinds of hearts. As you read these verses, look into the mirror of God's Word and ask God and yourself, "Is mine a heart of obedience?"

As you read these verses, note the two men mentioned, what is said about each, and how God defines a man after His own heart.

> *"The Lord has sought out a man after his own heart and appointed him leader of his people, because you have not kept the Lord's command"* (1 Samuel 13:14).
>
> *After removing Saul, [God] made David their king. He testified concerning him: "I have found David son of Jesse a man after my own heart; he will do everything I want him to do"* (Acts 13:22).

As we've learned here, Saul was a man who simply did not care to obey God! He was not a man after God's own heart...and David was!

Yes, But How?

But more important to me than Saul's heart and David's heart is *your* heart! I think I can safely say that you wouldn't be reading this book if you didn't want to follow after God's own heart by faithfully following His Word and His will. So the question now becomes, *how?* How can we follow David's example in our devotion to God? And what can we do so that God can grow in us a heart that is committed to obedience? A heart committed to doing God's will is an important ingredient when it comes to living out our love for God.

Well, dear one, God calls us to take care of our hearts. God tells you and me to "guard" our hearts with all diligence, for it affects everything we do. He tells us to mark out the path of our feet, to look straight ahead, and not get sidetracked. Rather than turning to the right or to the left, we are to follow the ways that are established by God (see Proverbs 4:23-27).

And what is the key here? Answer: The key to living a life of obedience—a life that stays on God's path—is the heart. If we guard our hearts, if we diligently attend to them, then all the issues, the actions, the "on-goings and the out-goings" of life will be handled God's way.[8]

So how can you and I stay on God's path? Here are several proven guidelines—Five C's—for nurturing a heart that is responsive to God and His ways. These five guidelines, precious one, will help lead us to a life of obedience.

Five Guidelines to Obedience

1. *Concentrate on doing what is right*—When God looked into David's heart, He saw there what He wants to see in you and me, too. He saw a heart that will do His will. And that calls for a tender and teachable heart, a heart that will concentrate on doing what is right.

Many times we know exactly what the right thing to do is, don't we? But what about those times when we're unsure? I mean those times when, in your heart, you want to do the right thing, but you're just not sure what that right thing is? Well, take heart! Here are a few rules to live by when this happens to you.

- Don't do anything! To do what is right, you must take time to pray, ask God for guidance, think, search the Scriptures, and ask advice from someone more mature in Christ. Simply say to the person who is asking you to do something you're unsure of, "I'm going to have to give this some thought. I'll let you know later." Your best plan of action is to do nothing until you know what the right thing to do is. As Proverbs 3:5 instructs, "lean not on your own understanding"!

- Do acknowledge God. Instead of leaning on your own understanding, "in all your ways acknowledge him." Then what happens? "He will make your paths straight" (Proverbs 3:6).

- Do ask for wisdom. Again, the Bible is clear when it instructs that "if any of you lacks wisdom, he should ask God...and it will be given to him" (James 1:5).

- Again, don't do anything. The bottom line for you and me as women after God's own heart is this—when in doubt, *don't* (Romans 14:23)! Or, put another way, *when in doubt, it's out.*

2. *Cease doing what is wrong*—The split second you think or do anything contrary to God's heart, stop immediately! Just put the skids on the activity. If it's gossip, stop. If it's an unworthy thought, stop (Philippians 4:8). If there's a spark of anger in your heart, stop before you act on it. If you've spoken an unkind word, stop before you speak another.

3. *Confess any wrong*—When it comes to this principle from Scripture, I deal very bluntly with myself. When I do something against God's Word, I acknowledge in my heart that what I did is wrong. I say, "This is wrong! This is sin! I can't do this!" After all, as the Bible says, "if we claim to be without sin, we deceive ourselves" (1 John 1:8). So I call sin "sin," and by doing this I am actively training my heart to be responsive to God's convicting Spirit. So, you and I must...

   - Confess sin (1 John 1:9), and the sooner the better!

   - Forsake sin. God's Word calls us to confess *and* forsake our sins (Proverbs 28:13). Don't be like the farmer who said, "I want to confess that I stole some hay from my neighbor." When the clergyman asked, "How much did you steal?" The farmer declared, "I stole half a load, but make it a whole load. I'm going back to get the other half tonight!"

4. *Clear things up with others*—It's true that confession makes things right with God. But what if you've hurt another person? Then, my fine young friend, you must clear things up with that person, too.

   That's just what I had to do on the very first morning I sang in our church choir. As I walked into the choir room early that morning, a sweet, friendly woman stuck her hand out, smiled, and said, "Hey, are you one of the new guys?" I snapped back, "No, but I'm one of the new *girls*." Well, I knew immediately what I had to do. I took care of the sin of unkindness and cruel speech with God by a prayer in my heart. (And believe me, that was the easy part!) But...I had hurt a person! And she was one of God's precious children! So after the choir finished singing, I waited for this dear woman, stuck out my hand, and said, "I really have a smart mouth, don't I? I'm sorry I responded to your kindness with such a smart remark! Will you please forgive me?"

   God doesn't want us to offer anything to Him until we've made things right with our brothers and sisters. Then, *after* we've settled matters with others, we may come and offer Him our gift of worship (see Matthew 5:23-24).

5. *Continue on as soon as possible*—Have you ever done something wrong, confessed it to God, stopped

doing it, even made things right with others involved, but you just couldn't get over it? I call this behavior "wallowing." I mean, it's over…but I just can't seem to go on because I keep wallowing in what I did. I keep right on reliving my failure. I say to myself, "I can't believe you did that, said that, thought that, acted like that! How could you have done that? You're unworthy! You're totally unfit to serve God."

Well, whenever you and I play out this scene, we need to turn to another truth from God's Word and let it lift us up, dust us off, refresh us, and set us back on His path. God's Word directs us to stop wallowing and to be "forgetting what is behind" so that we can spend our energy "straining toward what is ahead" (Philippians 3:13-14). It's true that we must remember the lessons learned through failure. But it's also true that we must not fail to go on.

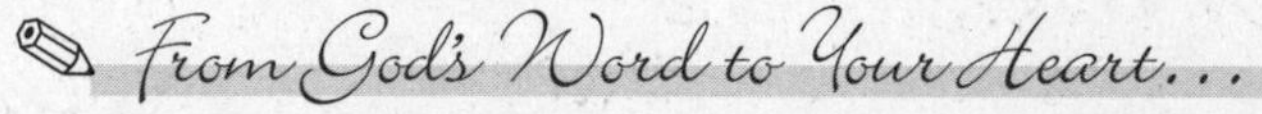

We've certainly covered a lot of ground in this lesson—important ground! But I don't want us to leave this section without seeing and handling the Scriptures ourselves. So I want you to read these powerful truths for yourself. They are truths that deal with cultivating a heart that obeys.

And as you're reading, notice what each of these Bible passages teaches you about living a life of obedience—a life that stays on God's path. What advice does each one give that would help you to live a life of obedience? And, if you're really brave, make note of any changes you need to make so that yours is a heart that obeys.

> *If any of you lacks wisdom, he should ask God, who gives generously to all without finding fault, and it will be given to him* (James 1:5).

> *If we claim to be without sin, we deceive ourselves and the truth is not in us. If we confess our sins, he is faithful and just and will forgive us our sins and purify us from all unrighteousness* (1 John 1:8-9).

> *He who conceals his sins does not prosper, but whoever confesses and renounces them finds mercy* (Proverbs 28:13).

> *But one thing I do: Forgetting what is behind and straining toward what is ahead, I press on toward the goal to win the prize for which God has called me heavenward in Christ Jesus* (Philippians 3:13-14).

Heart Response

Well, precious one, as we step out on the path to becoming a woman after God's own heart, it's obvious that obedience is a foundational stepping-stone on that path. And I know you'll want sure footing here. And such a step—the step of obedience—will prepare you to respond later to what God has to say about the other important areas of your life. So I have a few questions for you.

In Saul's day, God declared that He was looking for a heart that would obey Him, that would do all His will. Do these words describe your heart? Is God's desire your desire? Does your heart follow hard after God (Psalm 63:8 KJV), close to Him, on His heels, literally clinging to Him?[9]

If not, then I beg you to stop right now. Search your heart. Pinpoint any behavior that calls for a heart response of confession. Then make the confession, choose to cast off that behavior, and step right back onto God's path of beauty, peace, and joy, the path enjoyed by a woman after God's own heart, whatever her age. As you desire all that God desires, love all that He loves, and humble yourself under His mighty hand (1 Peter 5:6), then your heart will indeed be a heart after God. What a blessed thought!

Now, my precious friend, how's the recipe of your heart? Is anything missing? Any key ingredient like, say… obedience? Is yours a heart that obeys? A favorite line of poetry prompts you and me, "Little one, search that heart of thine." I'm searching mine. How about you?

Things to Do Today to Develop a Heart That Obeys

- Write out the "Five Guidelines to Obedience" on a 3" x 5" card. Over the next several days memorize them.

- List any issues where you are struggling with doing what is right. *Lay* your issues next to the guidelines, *pray*, and *obey* God's instructions.

- Do you need help with any of the guidelines? Don't turn the page until you've asked someone to help you do everything God wants you to do (Acts 13:22).

Would You Like to Know More? Check It Out

✓ Read Proverbs 4:23-27. Write down the references to the human body and God's instructions regarding each member of the body mentioned. What we love and what we do make all the difference in the world in how we live. Ask yourself, "Are the things I love leading me in the right direction—in God's direction?"

✓ Make a list of the principles taught in Proverbs 3:5-6 that can help you do what is right. Do the same with Psalm 37:3-5 and Psalm 1:1-2. Go a step further and make two columns—"What to do" and "What not to do," listing God's instructions under the appropriate column. Once again, are the things you love leading you in the right direction, on the path of obedience?

✓ See now what God says about our relationships with others in Matthew 5:23-24. How important are right relationships when it comes to your worship of God? What does God say to do about a broken relationship? What is on God's "to-do" list when it comes to our relationships with others and our relationship with Him?

Part Two

The Pursuit of God's Priorities

6

A Heart That Submits

Part 1

Children, obey your parents in everything, for this pleases the Lord.

Colossians 3:20

Whenever I'm asked to name the books I've read that have been the most life-changing for me, I always include *What Is a Family?* by Edith Schaeffer.[10] In fact, I've read it more than once…even more than twice. Through her wonderful writing and out of her large heart, the woman who wrote this lovely book was able to paint a picture of what God must have meant family life to be. I know my family life hardly measured up! And that may be true of yours, too.

But I want us to know what the Bible says about the individual roles of each member of the family circle. After all, we all live in families! And we all have parents. Plus most of us have a brother or sister…or two! So let's start with these core relationships and learn how to nurture a heart that submits when it comes to family.

Honoring Your Parents

You've probably heard of the Ten Commandments that Moses brought down from Mount Sinai. They were spoken by God to Moses, who delivered them to God's people. They were (and still are!) God's guidelines for how He wanted His people to live. They weren't God's Ten *Suggestions*. No, they were God's Ten *Commandments*, the law of God. And one of those commandments states this:

> *Honor your father and your mother, so that you may live long in the land the* Lord *your God is giving you* (Exodus 20:12).

My friend, as one writer exclaimed, this commandment regarding our attitude toward our parents is "a BIGGIE in the Bible"![11] Why? Because it's found in the Ten Commandments.

So what's a young woman after God's heart to do about this command? Well, as we learned in our previous chapter, we are to obey it. That's what a woman after God's own heart does. Remember? She fulfills all God's Word, keeps His commandments, and does everything He wants her to do. So, dear heart, you and I are going to honor our fathers and our mothers...as long as they are alive. This applies to you at your age. And it applies to me at my age (my mother just happens to be 93!). It's one of God's forever commandments.

Our next question has got to be, "What then does it mean to honor your parents?" I like this explanation. It may appear simplistic, but I think it covers about everything ...including our "Yes, buts" and our "But, what ifs."

> What does it mean to "honor" parents? Partly, "honoring" means speaking well of them and politely to them. It also means acting in a way that shows them courtesy and respect (but we are not to follow them in acts of disobedience to God). Parents have a special place in God's sight. Even those who find it difficult to get along with their parents are still commanded to honor them.[12]

Therefore, to obey God's commandment to honor your parents, you also need to obey your parents (except, as the statement above says, if they are asking you to sin against God). Such obedience calls for you to have a humble heart (1 Peter 5:5). I also think a better understanding of a few other teachings will assist you in your obedience. For instance, did you know that...

- Parents are commanded by God to teach their children (Deuteronomy 6:7)?
- Parents are commanded by God to train their children (Ephesians 6:4)?
- Parents are commanded by God to discipline and correct their children (Hebrews 12:7)?

I can tell you from experience that the hardest thing I've ever had to do as a woman after God's own heart was to follow through on God's command to me, as a young mom, to discipline my two little ones. And I suspect every other young mom has the same struggle! But I knew the Bible said that if I loved my darlings, I would discipline them (Proverbs 13:24). You see, when parents discipline their children, it proves their love. I'm sure I did it wrong a few times (maybe more!). But the Bible says when a child is left to himself, that child is not loved and will ultimately become a heartache to his or her parents (Proverbs 29:15). Therefore, with the encouragement of the Scriptures, with much prayer, and with many tears, I disciplined my children. (And now it's their turn with their five little ones!)

So why am I talking about mothering in a book written to you and your teenage friends who are not yet mothers? For two reasons. First, I want to let you know what God says to parents—*your* parents. And second, I want you to know how hard it is for parents to obey God. And it's hard, too, to be sure you are disciplining properly. But the bottom line is that if parents don't discipline, then there's a real mess to deal with later! Read on and see for yourself!

✎ *From God's Word to Your Heart...*

Meet Eli and his two sons. Eli was one of God's high priests who judged Israel. And, believe me, his story is a sad one! Why? Because he failed to discipline his sons. Rather than wholeheartedly taking on the God-ordered responsibility of a parent to correct his children when they sin, Eli did little or nothing. He let his sons get away with "murder"! Not literally, but his sons did take the best of the burnt animal offerings that the people gave to God and kept the meat for their own food. They were also guilty of blaspheming God and "slept with the women who served at the entrance to the Tent of Meeting" where the worship of God took place (1 Samuel 2:22).

We don't know what led up to Eli's failure in his important role as parent to his sons. The Bible doesn't say. Maybe he tried to discipline and correct his boys in their early years. Maybe he tried a few times with little or no results and then just gave up. Or maybe he tried and his sons refused to cooperate. Or maybe he just didn't take the time. Perhaps he just didn't want to be bothered with it or was just too busy with other "more important" things. But, in the end, the sons were wicked and God was displeased. God judged Eli, predicting the deaths of Eli's sons, and all three men—Eli and his two sons—died, Eli's sons in battle and Eli when he heard of their deaths (1 Samuel 2:12-36 and 4:12-18).

With this dismal tale ringing in our ears, let's look to God's Word for His plan for you to honor, respect, obey, and love your parents. As you read these scriptures, ask God to show you how you can do a better job in the submission department. Pinpoint areas that need immediate first aid.

> *Children, obey your parents in the Lord, for this is right. "Honor your father and mother"—which is the first commandment with a promise—"that it may go well with you and that you may enjoy long life on the earth"* (Ephesians 6:1-3).

> *Children, obey your parents in everything, for this pleases the Lord* (Colossians 3:20).

Yes, But How?

Okay. We now know that God's Word says to obey your parents and to honor them. Now the question is, exactly *how* can you follow through on God's Word as a young woman after God's own heart who does all God's will? How can you head down God's path of obedience in this vital area? Here are a few pointers. And I think that as you read them you'll find that a heart that submits boils down to paying attention to the little things...which add up to a big thing. What are some of these little things?

1. *Your attitude*—Here's a *big* little thing! Your attitude has to do with your moods. And your moods can be right and godly, or they can be sinful. Stop for a minute and think about your attitude. Is it generally cheerful, helpful, energetic, agreeable, positive, giving, respectful? Or do you tend to mope around, grunt and grumble, resent your parents, your family, your responsibilities, even your life as a teenager? Is your day (and your life) filled with anger? Do you seem to be stomping through your days, rolling over anyone and everyone who gets in your path? (Hmmm, is this sounding like the two opposite behaviors seen in Mary and Martha from chapter 1?)

   You and I both know where our attitude is born, cultivated, and maintained, don't we? It's in our quiet time, as God's Word fills our empty hearts and sets the direction for our day...and as we pray! God's Word points the way, and prayer to God joins our hearts in agreement with God's way. And we need a huge attitude adjustment each and every day. If we fail to have this all-important time with God, we are doomed for the day. And so is everyone else! They better beware, give us a wide path, and stay out of our way!

Now, think again...what is the title of our book? Right, it's *A Young Woman After God's Own Heart*. And such a woman seeks to walk with God and to walk in all His ways and to show forth the graciousness of Christ. So, purpose along with me to...

- seek the Lord's help daily through His Word and prayer
- seek an "I'm #3" attitude (with your father as #1 and your mother as #2)
- seek to put away self-*ish*ness and put on self-*less*ness.

2. *Your room*—We'll spend more time on this topic later, but for now think about your place, your room, your space. Wherever it is and whoever you share it with (you know, your sister!), realize that your room is a part of your parents' home. Sure, you're responsible for it, but it's not yours—it's theirs. It belongs to your parents. And realizing that should make a difference. You honor your parents as you honor their property.

So I want to encourage you to have an "extra mile" attitude (there's that word again!) when it comes to your room. Whatever your parents are asking of you in terms of neatness, cleanliness, noise, rules, guests, etc., go the extra mile and do it even better and with a cheerful spirit. It's just like Jesus said, "If someone forces you to go one mile, go with him two miles" (Matthew 5:41).

Heart Pause

I want you to take a break now—a pause. You've done a great job of hanging in there on a difficult but vital topic. Congratulations! I'm very proud of you in the Lord.

Submission certainly is a difficult area for everyone. What makes it difficult is that many times we think we know more or know better than the person we are to submit to. It's like this: I have no problem submitting to someone who is asking me to do something in an area where I know absolutely nothing, something like flying an airplane or going through a medical exam or procedure. But boy-oh-boy! do I have a hard time submitting in an area or to a person when I *think* I have some knowledge or understanding. That's where the struggle begins.

But, dear one, God calls us to be women after His own heart. And His high calling requires a heart that submits. Now...how are you doing so far?

Things to Do Today to Develop a Heart That Submits

♡ Before we go on, read again the definition of what it means to honor your parents. Then think of one thing you can do today to honor your father and mother. Follow through at your first opportunity. And don't forget to do the same tomorrow…and tomorrow…and tomorrow and.…

♡ Do an attitude check. How would you describe your general attitude around the house? (How do you think your parents would describe it? Your brothers and sisters?) Then do an attitude adjustment. What specific changes will you (not *could* you or *should* you, but *will* you) make? Don't forget to ask God for His grace in this matter!

♡ Quick…is there something, anything! you can do right this minute to take care of your room? Anything you've been neglecting, putting off, or just plain ol' rebelling against doing? Honor your parents by doing it now.

Would You Like to Know More? Check It Out

- ✓ Read 1 Peter 5:5-6. Here God describes the beauty of a heart of humility. Make two lists. In the first list note what your role is, and in the second note what God's role is. We know God never fails. Are you failing to obey in any way? What changes will you make?

- ✓ Read Luke 2:41-52. Jot down the details of this family scene—the people and places mentioned and what happened. In the end, what was Jesus' response to His parents? What do you learn from Jesus' example about submission to parents?

✓ What do these scriptures teach us about Jesus' submission to His Father's will?

Matthew 26:39

Matthew 26:42

John 4:34

John 6:38

John 15:10

Hebrews 10:7

Again, what do you learn from Jesus' example?

7

A Heart That Submits

Part 2

Honor Christ by
submitting to each other.
Ephesians 5:21 (TLB)

How's your heart coming along, my dear traveling companion?

Do you remember our "Heart Response" section in chapter 5? We discovered that developing a heart that obeys—that obeys God's Word—was the step on the path to becoming a woman after God's own heart that would be most meaningful on our journey. And it is soooo true! Obedience to what God says in His Word is what prepares us to respond now in this important area of submitting to parents.

And I pray that you are beginning to see the importance of submitting to your parents. Did you think *submission* was a passing phase in your life? Did you think, "If I can just grin and bear it, if I can just submit when it's convenient, then someday this 'submission thing' will be over and I'll be free to do anything and everything and act as I please"?

If you still feel this way, please forgive me. Perhaps I have failed to properly communicate the importance of submission as a lifelong process and as a lifestyle for all of God's children. Submission is the training ground for everything that is future in your (and my) life. And, as it's been said, "a child has to learn obedience in the home or he will never learn obedience to the Heavenly Father."[13]

Let's continue on now where we left off in our last chapter. Let's look at a few more of the little things you can do to train yourself in the heart and art of submission. So far we've considered *your attitude* and *your room.* Let's pick up at the "Yes, But How?" section.

3. *Your cooperation*—Have you ever been in a play? Or danced in a ballet? Or been on a sports team? As you well know, everyone had to cooperate to make the show or the game the best it could be. You all had to be a team, right?

   Well, it's the same way in a family. There are some things God wants of His families—to live together in unity (Psalm 133:1) and to glorify Him (1 Corinthians 10:31). Your parents probably want the same things for your family and are probably trying to move your family in that direction. And your job is to cooperate. True, it may at times seem strict, and it may at times be difficult, but you need to move along with them.

   So here's how it goes. If your parents want you or your family to go to church, you go. If they want to go back to church at night, you go. If they want to go to church on Wednesday night, you go. If they want to go to family camp (and it just happens to be the same weekend something great is happening at school), you go. If they need you to watch your little brother or sister while they run errands, you do it. If they need help around the house, you give it. If they are saving up for something special and have to cut the budget, you gladly give up a few trinkets or clothes or outings with your friends. In other words, you cooperate.

4. *Your help*—This may seem like a repeat of what's above, but it may just be my only chance to say this: Every person on the face of the earth yearns to hear these four little words—"How can I help?" So I encourage you at home and with your parents and family members to constantly be asking, "How can I help?" (And don't be afraid of what they may answer. For one thing, they'll probably fall off their chairs in disbelief!) As the Bible says, two are always better than one (Ecclesiastes 4:9). So offer your help.

5. *Your prayers*—Let's rewind for a second. Do you remember several chapters back when we talked about the importance of prayer? We agreed that prayer is important, that prayer changes things, and that prayer changes us. And that change includes our hearts. Well, it's pretty obvious, isn't it, that we must, must, *must* pray for our parents. Here's how it works: If your parents have an annoying habit or way of

dealing with things, pray for them. If they don't get along with each other, pray for them. If they pick on your little brother, pray for them. If they are stressed out, pray for them. You can never pray too much for your parents!

And keep on praying for yourself, too. If you think you don't even like your parents, pray for yourself. If you think they're stupid or dumb or out of it, pray for yourself. If you think what they're asking of you is unfair, pray for yourself. If you think your parents are too strict, pray for yourself. If you think they don't understand you, pray for yourself.

And what are you asking of God? Ask Him to soften your heart, to change your attitude (there's that word again!), to give you the special help of His grace, to give you a greater appreciation for your parents, to help you to submit, honor, and respect them. Ask God to work not only in your parents' hearts, but also in yours! That's what a woman after God's own heart does.

6. *Your submission*—As a Christian, you'll be hearing the word "submission" a lot! The Bible calls us to submit to about everyone you can think of—the government, bosses (1 Peter 2:13-18), the church (Hebrews 13:17), even to one another (Ephesians 5:21). But your home and your relationships there are the training ground for your submission to all others, including your future submission to a hus-

band (Ephesians 5:22). Therefore, you honor your parents and submit yourself to them.

Submission is a challenge straight from God to you. It's a measure of your spiritual maturity. Why? Because no one can make you submit to anyone else. You must choose to do it yourself. Your parents can't make you, your friends can't make you, and your youth leader can't make you. No, you have to decide to submit *yourself* to your parents. And here's the shocker—if you aren't submitting to your parents now, you aren't submitting to God, and you'll probably have trouble fulfilling God's desire for you to submit to your future husband's leadership. That's pretty far-reaching, isn't it?

7. *Your truthfulness*—Everyone wants to enjoy good communication with others. Well, good communication at home begins with your being truthful to your parents. An author I know and respect shared this story from her teenage days. Her friend received a new car for her sixteenth birthday and stopped by to take her for a ride. But somewhere during the course of their ride, another girl, who didn't have a driver's license, took the wheel and began driving. And, wouldn't you know it—there was a car wreck! At this point her "friends" asked her to lie about who was driving. Well, as the parents began to arrive on the scene of the wreck, the first words out of the mothers' mouths were, "Who was driving the car?" After my friend chose to tell the truth (and go against

the wishes of her cohorts), one mother said, "I've already talked to a neighbor who saw the three of you go by, and she told me who was driving. If you had lied to me, I wouldn't have trusted you again."[14]

Things get sticky in life. And sometimes we end up in situations we didn't choose, like this teenager did. But no matter what happens to you, you must always tell the truth. That's what a woman after God's own heart does. Why? Because, first of all, she shouldn't have anything to hide if she's walking on God's path of obedience. And second, truthfulness is the foundation of all good relationships...especially your relationship with your parents. So make it your habit to tell the truth. It's a habit of noble character.

8. *Your giving*—If I could wish one thing for you, if I could have one prayer answered for you as you read and complete this book, it would be this: I would pray that you begin today to go through life as a giver. You see, the world seems to be divided into two kinds of people—those who give and those who take. One, the giver, is *other*-oriented and the other, the taker, is *self*-oriented. Those who think of others are Christlike, and those who think only of themselves tend to lie and cheat, manipulate and connive. Their hearts are set on themselves and not on Christ or on others.

   So, my dear friend, I want you to be a giver! I want you to make a difference in the lives of other people.

I want you to join with me in my goal to better the life of every person God allows to cross my path. I want you to be constantly asking the Lord and your heart, "What can I give?" in every situation. And "every situation" includes first and foremost your situation at home. Why? Because *what you are at home is what you are.*

Here's a little visual aid. Imagine that you are the richest person in the world. It's in your power to bless everyone else in the whole world because you have so much to give and share with others. Then imagine yourself walking down a path or a road or a street (or a corridor at school). And there you are...literally throwing your riches away, exuberantly tossing them to everyone you meet. You smile! You greet them! And you give them something!

Oh, how I want this woman to be you! (And oh, how I want this woman to be me!) And if you think about it, we do have everything to give! We have life in Christ (2 Timothy 1:1). We have been blessed by God with all spiritual blessings in heavenly places in Christ (Ephesians 1:3). We even have God's love, joy, peace, patience, kindness, goodness, faithfulness, gentleness, and self-control (Galatians 5:22-23). We have soooo much to give! So let's start where it counts the most—right at home—and give to those at home first. Believe me, if you can do this at home, you can do it anywhere! (Oh yes, and while you are giving, remember this principle: *Give...expecting nothing in return!* (Luke 6:35).

Heart Response

You are so wonderful for staying with me through these important heart exercises! My heart is so full of the many wonderful things I want to share with you. I don't want you to struggle and fail, to suffer and flop around like I did when I was trying to grow into a woman after God's own heart. I want you to *know* what God's great plan is for your life as His woman. I guess I'm trying to give you some shortcuts to spiritual growth. My vision for you is large. It's grand! There is so much God desires for you. And I desire it, too!

Now, please, don't leave this chapter without making your own heart response to God's Word regarding a heart that submits. Check your heart. How's your attitude? What's going on in your room? Are you cooperating with your parents? Are you lending your help as well as your prayers? Is yours a heart of submission, of truthfulness, and of a sweet giving spirit? Pray along with David,

Search me, O God, and know my heart;
test me and know my anxious thoughts.
See if there is any offensive way in me,
and lead me in the way everlasting.

Psalm 139:23-24

Things to Do Today to Develop a Heart That Submits

- Practice saying "How can I help?" three times in front of your mirror. Then go to your mother and say it to her. (P.S., be prepared to catch her when she faints!)

- Think about your cooperation and your submission in your family. What are the three things you find most difficult to do in these areas of family unity? Put these three things on your daily prayer list for yourself…then pray to cooperate and submit the next time they come up.

- Determine—just for today—to be more giving to your family members. Determine to give away your smile, your warm greeting, your loving touch, your helping hand, and your kind words of encouragement. Do it…no matter what the response. Do as Jesus did—"He went around doing good" (Acts 10:38).

Would You Like to Know More? Check It Out

- ✓ Read Ephesians 5:21-24, listing the people mentioned and who they are to submit to and why. As a bonus exercise read verses 25-28 and do the same. What did you learn?

- ✓ Read 1 Peter 2:13-18. Again, list the people mentioned and who they are to submit to. What did you learn?

✓ Continue looking at God's plan for the family by reading Ephesians 6:1-4 and Colossians 3:18-21. List the instructions given to each family member. Did you find yourself here? And are you demonstrating a heart devoted to God by obeying God's instructions to you, or do you need to make some changes? What changes?

✓ Now prayerfully read 1 Peter 2:21-24. Write out how Jesus submitted to His Father's will for His life. Then write out a prayer of thanksgiving to God for sending His Son to die for sin—*your* sin—and for Jesus' obedience to His Father's will.

8

A Heart That Loves

A new command I give you:
Love one another...By this all men
will know that you are my disciples,
if you love one another.

JOHN 13:34-35

If you're like me, you admire the men and women of the Bible who exhibited great faith and hearts after God. Well, may I introduce you to three giants of the faith? Each of them loved God. Each of them obeyed God. And each of them served God to their last dying breath.

The first is probably the most well known. His name is Moses. Wow, what a man of God! In fact, he's been dubbed "the greatest Jewish leader."[15] Moses not only led the Israelites out of Egypt, but he was also the man who received the Ten Commandments from God. Moses had a pretty rough life, but he was devoted to God and ultimately became a prophet for God and the writer of the first five books of the Bible, called the Pentateuch. We can definitely say that Moses was "sold out" to God.

The second giant is Aaron. This godly man was the first high priest of God in Israel. Talk about a privilege! He was also the man God chose to communicate to the king of Egypt for Moses, to be Moses' right-hand man, and to speak for Moses. Aaron, too, was certainly sold out for God.

The third giant is actually a giant-*ess*, a woman. Her name is Miriam. This woman was a prophetess, a leader of women, a woman who wrote songs of praise to God and knew how to use her head under pressure. Miriam, too, was sold out for God.

Now, here's something else about this awesome threesome—they were siblings! They were two brothers and a sister that God used mightily. They were family.

Love Your Brothers and Sisters

It's sad to hear someone say that her brother or sister is her biggest headache in life. To quote the apostle James, "Surely, this is not right!" (James 3:10 TLB).

And it's not! God wants His families to love one another and to serve Him. And the Bible contains a good number of brothers and sisters who served God together as a team. For instance,

- Siblings Aaron and Moses and Miriam served God together.
- Brothers Peter and Andrew followed Jesus and became two of His twelve disciples (Matthew 4:18 and 10:2).

- Brothers James and John followed Jesus and became two of His twelve disciples (Matthew 4:21). In fact, Jesus nicknamed these two brothers "Sons of Thunder" (Mark 3:17).

- Sisters Mary and Martha and their brother, Lazarus, were devoted followers of Jesus. Together they faithfully cared for Jesus and His disciples (Luke 10:38; John 12:1-2).

Where, we wonder, is such dynamic teamwork born? Well, my friend, it's born in a home. It's born in a family. And it's born out of love—love for God and love for one another.

✎ *From God's Word to Your Heart...*

What is the secret to healthy relationships between brothers and sisters? In a word, it's love. Hear what our Savior and the apostle Paul had to say about love. As you read along, think about what these verses teach us about love. And think even more specifically about what they teach us about loving our brothers and sisters. Do you need to make any changes in your attitude toward your siblings, in your treatment of them?

> *A new command I give you: Love one another.... By this all men will know that you are my disciples, if you love one another* (John 13:34-35).

If anyone says, "I love God," yet hates his brother, he is a liar. For anyone who does not love his brother, whom he has seen, cannot love God, whom he has not seen. And he has given us this command: Whoever loves God must also love his brother (1 John 4:20-21).

When the Holy Spirit controls our lives, he will produce this kind of fruit in us: love...patience, kindness, goodness...gentleness and self control (Galatians 5:22-23 NLT).

Yes, But How?

There are many ways we show concern and demonstrate a heart of love when it comes to our family members. We discussed some of those ways in the previous chapter in the area of our relationship with our parents. But now let's turn our eyes (and hearts!) toward our brothers and sisters, whether older or younger. I'll share several important areas that speak loudly of love. Maybe you will think of others along the way. If you do, jot them down at the end of the chapter. Whatever you do, seek to develop a heart that loves, especially a heart that loves those in your family circle.

1. *Respect one another*—When you show respect for the territory, room, possessions, and privacy of another person, your relationship with that person will improve tremendously. And right away! You know how you feel when your privacy is violated, when others help themselves to your things without asking, when someone barges into your room without knocking or asking, when someone reads your personal journal or diary or mail...or email! Well, you need to respect the space of others exactly like you want your space respected. Even if you share your room with your sister, a part of that room is *her* territory. So why not begin improving your relationships with your family members by showing a greater respect for them by respecting what is theirs?

2. *Listen to one another*—In any friendship, communication is nine-tenths of the relationship. You know how it is with a best friend—you could talk to them for hours...which means you are listening for part of that time! So make it your goal to learn better communication skills inside your family. If you can talk to one another, you can become friends—even best friends! And listening is a large part of connecting with one another. So get creative. Reach out. Set up a regular Coke date with your brother or sister. When a sibling is swimming in the pool, join him or her and maybe just float along on a raft, talking, sharing, asking questions, catching up. If you share your room with a sister or two, get an update on

their lives after lights-out at night. And, by all means, pray with your brothers and sisters…and for them. It doesn't have to be anything long or heavy, just the heartfelt prayer of a loving sister. Don't worry if they think it's dumb or stupid. They'll get used to it and grow to appreciate it. And then don't be surprised if they start coming to you with their problems and asking you to please pray with them!

3. *Serve one another*—God has given us ears to hear and eyes to see (Proverbs 20:12). And it's hard to live under the same roof and not see and hear how your brothers and sisters could use a little assistance from someone…anyone!…even *you!* So ask God to make you more sensitive to the needs of your siblings, to serving them. Ask Him to open your ears and eyes (and heart!). For instance, when you see your sister or brother carrying a heavy load or backpack up the steps to the front door, jump up and say, "Let me get that door for you." Also, we all lose things (and you know how frustrating that can be!). So volunteer to help out in the search. And when you're doing your laundry and find your brother's or sister's laundry in the dryer, take it to them and say "Here's your laundry out of the dryer. Do you want me to help you fold it?"

4. *Help one another*—We covered this same point in our chapter regarding your parents, so hopefully this Christlike attitude is becoming ingrained in your

daily behavior. But do the same for your siblings. Ask them, too, "How can I help?" When they're stewing over their homework, late getting out the door, trying to learn their Bible verses for their Bible club meeting, lend a helping hand and an understanding heart. Be on the lookout for ways to help out. Everyone appreciates—and needs(!)—a helping hand.

5. *Share with one another*—When I say share with one another, I don't mean just clothes and things. I mean to also share ideas and dreams. If you can unlock another's heart, then you can be a better pray-er, encourager, supporter, and helper to that person...even if that person just happens to be your brother or sister! And while you're at it, don't forget to share the truths and the verses you are learning from the Bible. And share in worship together. You never know when one of these shared experiences will mark your sibling's life. You never know when the verse you passed on verbally or in a written note will be just what they needed to get through a rough day! The more you can share together, the better friends you become.

6. *Touch one another*—I have two things I want to say in this area of touching one another. The first is positive and the second is negative. So, first the positive. I love it when I see brothers and sisters walking arm in arm or with their arms around each other,

hugging, patting each other on the back, even giving high fives. Such affection is a privilege and an outworking of the natural closeness that comes with being a part of a family. In many ways, no one else has that privilege. So be generous with your hugs and genuine affection.

But then there is the negative. One day when my husband and I were checking into a hotel, a family was waiting behind us in the check-in line. During the entire time we were dealing with the hotel clerk, the three kids in the family (who were all in their teens) were kicking each other's bottoms, slugging each other in the arms, slapping at each other's faces, and doing a few other physical things to each other I won't even mention(!)...while the parents did nothing. It was clear that in this family physical "affection" and touching had gone way too far! I felt sorry (and angry) for the daughter/sister whose body and dignity were treated with such disrespect by her brothers. And I felt sorry (and angry) that the two cute teenage boys were allowed to treat their sister, a young woman, in such a disrespectful way. To think that these crude brothers were the future boyfriends and husbands of some other poor girls out there made me sick.

So I'm saying to you, regardless of where (or how low!) your "family standard" has fallen, of where your parents have or have not drawn the lines and set the boundaries, *you* must treat the bodies and persons of your brothers and sisters with utmost respect and dignity. *No inappropriate touching!* I'm sure you would want the same thing for yourself. So begin with yourself and "do to others as you would have them to do to you" (Luke 6:31).

7. *Pray for one another*—Here it is again! Prayer! You simply cannot pray for your brothers and sisters enough! And remember, too, that when you pray for others, God changes your heart, gives you His love and wisdom, and many times moves in the hearts of those you pray for. So think of the grandest thing you could ask of God for your siblings. Do they need to know Christ? Then pray! Do they need to get along better with Mom and Dad? Then pray! Do they need a friend, a job, better grades? Then pray! Are they trying to make an important decision, like whether or not to go to college, or which college? Then pray! Is one of them in a doubtful relationship with a boyfriend or girlfriend? Then pray! The Bible commands us to "pray for each other" (James 5:16) and assures us that God's ears are open to our prayers (1 Peter 3:12). So take the time to pray for your brothers and sisters. As someone known as "the kneeling Christian" once said, "Prayer is our highest privilege, our gravest responsibility, and the greatest power God has put into our hands." Who knows what God may do?!

8. *Encourage one another*—Everyone can use encouragement. All teens struggle with schoolwork and

grades, as well as with making friends and getting along. Yes, everyone can use a friendly word of encouragement from a sister who comes alongside them with cheerfulness. Everyone can use a "Way to go! Good job! Hang in there! You're the best! I'm so glad I'm your sister." And don't forget to encourage one another in the Lord. That's what two famous friends in the Bible did. Jonathan and David encouraged one another to "find strength in God" (1 Samuel 23:16).

As I said earlier, everyone yearns for a close relationship with someone who respects, helps, shares, encourages, and listens to them. And that includes your brothers and sisters! So why not be that someone in their lives? Why not put on a heart that loves and make loving those under your own roof your first priority in the love department?

Heart Response

We began this all-important chapter by looking at a team of two brothers and a sister who were mightily used by God. How refreshing! And how inspiring!

Unfortunately, however, the Bible also contains stories of siblings who are anything but what God desires. For instance, Cain killed his brother Abel (Genesis 4:8). Sisters Rachel and Leah hated and envied one another (Genesis

30:1). And Joseph's brothers hated and envied him so much that they sold him to slave traders (Genesis 37:26-27).

So I want to end our time discussing family matters with the greatest "how" of all when it comes to a heart that loves. It is God's commandment to us to *love one another.* Here's a definition of love that opened my eyes to what it means to love one another: *Love* is a feeling of the mind as much as of the heart; it concerns the will as much as the emotions; it describes the deliberate effort that we can make only with the help of God.

In short, love is not an emotion, but an action. Love is the things we do…and hold back from doing. And love is a decision. Love is an act of the will. Plus, praise God, we have His help in showing forth His fruit of the Spirit, His love, in our hearts and our lives when we look to Him (Galatians 5:22)!

So…let's push family quarrels aside and let the love of God reside in our hearts. Let's become *sisters* after God's own heart!

Things to Do Today to Develop a Heart That Loves

- ♡ Write a little note of encouragement to each brother or sister.

- ♡ Be on the lookout for ways to serve your siblings. Volunteer to help, too.

- ♡ Set up a page in your prayer notebook for each of your brothers and sisters. (And don't forget to pray!)

Would You Like to Know More? Check It Out

✓ The story of Miriam's love for her baby brother, Moses, can be found in Exodus 2:1-10. How does Miriam's helpfulness to her mother and her concern for her baby brother touch your heart?

✓ The story of Miriam, Aaron, and Moses' joint service to God is highlighted in Exodus 15:1,20-21 as they celebrate God's deliverance of His people. How does the example of this threesome challenge you in your relationship with your siblings?

✓ Sadly, the story of Miriam and Aaron's jealousy against their brother, Moses, darkens an otherwise good relationship (Numbers 12:1-16). How does their envy of their brother speak to your heart?

✓ God's Word defines "love" in 1 Corinthians 13:4-7. What areas do you need to work on in your relationships with your brothers and sisters?

9

A Heart That Cares

The wise woman builds her house.

PROVERBS 14:1

Having two daughters has provided me with one particular glad/sad occasion many times. That repeated occasion was the day each fall when I drove my girls and all their belongings to their college campus and helped them move into their dormitory rooms for another year of schooling. Of course I was glad that they were growing up, glad that they were taking on the challenge of attempting a college education, and glad for the many wonderful friends and adventures that awaited them. But there's no getting around it—it made me sad to say good-bye to my daughters, who were also my friends. And it especially made me sad to deposit them into a stark, bare, empty dorm room containing absolutely nothing but an exposed mattress. More than once, I cried my way home!

But soon that much-anticipated evening came—Parents Night—when Jim and I (along with all the other parents of collegians) were invited to tour the dormitories. Well, I just cannot describe to you the joy and surprise we received when we entered our daughters' cubicles! Their rooms had been miraculously transformed! What had once been forlorn was filled with the beautiful and the unique as Katherine and Courtney sought to express themselves in their individual rooms. There were ruffles and frills, dried flowers and ribbons, pictures and posters, tea sets and fish bowls, candles and baskets with live ivy plants. Music was playing and special lighting and lamps created a warm glow.

I'm sure I don't have to tell you that I left Parents Night with a much happier heart! Why? Because my girls now had a home away from home. But more amazing than what I saw was knowing that each of my daughters had done it herself. Each had taken her own "things" from her real home and used them to create a second home. In the end, they had turned nothing—barren look-alike dorm rooms—into something, beautiful expressions of their beautiful hearts.

Your Own Home-Sweet-Home

Just how did my daughters' abilities blossom? And just where did they learn to decorate, to "fuss," to express themselves, to feather a nest, to clean and organize, to make beautiful crafts, to create places that ministered not only to them but to the countless others who passed through their doorways in the college dorm?

Well, the answer is summed up in a single word—they learned these homemaking skills at *home*. And their learning experience was a co-partnership between my daughters and me. Here's how it happened.

I've said before that I did not grow up as a Christian. Therefore I started out as a baby Christian at age 28…and at ground zero in thc homemaking department! I was a remedial learner, one that was definitely behind and desperately needed help. But I was also an eager learner. Boy oh boy, did I ever have a need to know! I had been married eight years and had two tiny preschoolers and a pigpen for a home!

But as I began to read my brand-new Bible, I took a pink highlighter in hand and began to mark everything I read that had to do with being a Christian woman, wife, mother, and homemaker. As God spoke to my heart through His Word, my knowledge of who God wanted me to be and what God wanted me to do grew. And it wasn't long before my eager heart responded. It was then that I learned to build my own home-sweet-home so that my family could be blessed. I bought and read books, I met with older and wiser women, and I worked hard. But I finally "got it"!

Not wanting my Katherine and Courtney to suffer in ignorance (and sloppiness) as I had, I began teaching them what I was learning. Then, whatever I was doing to take care of my "house" (the entire house), my girls were doing in their "little house" (their room), in their own home-sweet-home.

✎ *From God's Word to Your Heart…*

Exactly what do you and I find in the Bible that tells us what God has in mind for us as women after His own heart in the area of our home-sweet-home? Here are a few key scriptures. As you read them, please think of things you might need to do to improve. Do you need an attitude change? Do you need better skills? Do you need help?

> *The wise woman builds her house, but with her own hands the foolish one tears hers down* (Proverbs 14:1).

> *By wisdom a house is built...through knowledge its rooms are filled with rare and beautiful treasures* (Proverbs 24:3-4).

> *[A woman of noble character] watches over the affairs of her household and does not eat the bread of idleness* (Proverbs 31:27).

> *The older women [are to]...train the younger women...to be busy [workers] at home* (Titus 2:3-5).

Yes, But How?

These verses paint a picture of what a woman of wisdom does—she builds and takes care of and watches over and works away at creating a home-sweet-home. As an unmarried woman, that home is wherever you happen to live. Whether you live in your own room in your parents' house or share it with a sister or two (I know of one family whose four girls share the same room!), whether you live in an apartment or a dorm room like my daughters did, the place where you live is yours to "build." It's yours to turn into your own home-sweet-home.

So here are a few how-to's on home-sweet-home building.

1. *Learn the basics*—There are only a handful of simple basics involved in taking care of your room. They are dusting, vacuuming, cleaning, doing laundry, and organizing. And like any skill, these are learned by repetition. The more you do anything, the easier it becomes...until soon you can almost do it without thinking.

   I taught my daughters these basics, and together the three of us did them over and over and over until we were all able to do them quickly. Then, miracle of miracles(!), a certain amount of joy set in as we admired our handiwork. Our faces shone (like our clean rooms) with a sense of pride in the end result and the rewarding feeling of accomplishment.

But here's the greatest blessing. When Katherine and Courtney got married, guess what? Homemaking was no big deal! Taking care of a "home" was no problem! Why? Because they had basically been doing it all their lives in their own little home-sweet-home, in their room. Their knowledge of the basics left them with only one new major assignment as newlyweds—learning how to be *wives!* And then along came the babies and another new major assignment—learning how to be *mothers!* (I'm sure you get the picture!)

2. *Do your share*—Wherever you live and whoever you share it with, whether family or roommates, be sure you do your part of the work. Don't try to get out of work. That's a bad habit to develop and a hard one to break! Instead make it a goal to do your part and to do it excellently! As the Bible says, "Whatever your hand finds to do, do it with all your might" and "Whatever you do, work at it with all your heart, as working for the Lord, not for men" (Ecclesiastes 9:10 and Colossians 3:23). This is also a good place to put Jesus' "extra mile" concept to work in your heart (Matthew 5:41) by doing *more than* your share!

3. *Volunteer to help*—If your mom's in the kitchen preparing a meal, volunteer to help her. You'll be amazed at what you'll learn. (I just heard a mother of six say that all her children learned to cook at age seven, that every one of her children could fix his

or her own food if it were necessary. She explained that they rotate nights cooking with her in the kitchen, but each fixes his or her favorite dishes. Now, that's motivating!) So volunteer! And don't forget how much everyone loves to hear those words, "How can I help?" Make it a point to be like Jesus, "who went around doing good" (Acts 10:38). Remember His words, how He said "It is more blessed to give than to receive" (Acts 20:35). And remember, too, that He told us to give "without expecting to get anything back" (Luke 6:35).

4. *Get help if you need it*—Like the instruction in Titus 2:3-5 said, women are to teach one another how to take care of their homes. So, if you need help, go get it. Ask for it. Whether that assistance comes from your mom or from someone else, seek help in this vital area of being a woman after God's own heart.

5. *Develop a heart that cares*—Did you notice the title of this chapter? I titled it "A Heart That Cares." And that's the key for both you and me when it comes to our place at home. We simply must care. And it helps me to care when I know that *God* wants me to care. And it helps me to care when I acknowledge that *what I am at home is what I am*. I'm either messy or I'm neat. I'm either buried under things or I'm on top of things. I'm either unorganized or I'm orderly. I'm either living in chaos or I have a plan that I'm following. I'm either a flake or I'm dependable.

So ask yourself (as I ask myself often), How am I doing when it comes to my place, my finances, my clothes? What character qualities are being evidenced by my care for my place? Your answers will tell the whole tale (and I'm hoping it's a good one!).

6. *Set aside time*—The biggest challenge to taking care of your home-sweet-home is always finding the *time!* So you must *make* the time. How? Each week take your calendar in hand and mark off an hour or two for taking care of your room. That's about how long it will take to run your laundry through the washer and dryer, to dust and vacuum your room, and arrange the contents of your drawers. Yes, you may have a little cleaning to do in your bathroom and on some trouble spots on your desktop and mirrors, but that will only take minutes. Then stick to your plan. If a friend calls, set another time to get together or have her come over *after* you've cleaned your room! What a nice reward for you...and what a nice treat for your friend (not to mention your family!). Which reminds me, don't forget that the place where you live—your room—really isn't yours. It belongs to your parents! So be sure to work at this next how-to.

7. *Follow these "Golden Rules for Living"*—They will not only help you build your own home-sweet-home, but they will help you get along with those you must share it with!

If you open it, close it.
If you turn it on, turn it off.
If you unlock it, lock it up.
If you break it, admit it.
If you can't fix it, call in someone who can.
If you borrow it, return it.
If you value it, take care of it.
If you make a mess, clean it up.
If you move it, put it back.
If it belongs to someone else, get permission to use it.
If you don't know how to operate it, leave it alone.
If it's none of your business, don't ask questions.[16]

Heart Response

Dear sister and friend, are you catching God's vision for you and your place? Do you see the value of learning to care about the place where you live? Of learning to do what it takes to take care of the place where you live?

Take an inventory of your own heart attitude toward that precious place you call home, the place where you live, your place. If you couldn't care less about the looks of your special place, ask God to perform open-heart surgery in you. Ask Him to open it up and give you a heart that cares.

We've talked about how your homelife is the training ground for your future relationship with a husband and children of your own (if the Lord wills). Well, dear one, home is also the training ground for your work ethic, whether that work ethic is used in the home as a homemaker, on a job, or on the mission field. If and when you get married, get a job, or serve on the mission field, you take yourself and the character qualities you've learned at home (by taking care of yourself and your room) with you. You will either be sloppy in your place of service, or you'll be meticulous. You will either be lazy and unreliable, or you'll be diligent. You will either be unimaginative, or you'll be creative. You will either be disorderly, or you'll be organized. You will either be haphazard and sporadic, or you'll operate on a plan and a schedule. You see, you will take what you *are* with you! *What you are at home is what you are!*

So what is it that will make the difference? The answer is found in the attitude you are developing right now at home. The care you take with yourself, of your own things and the things of others at home, and the effort you make at home today will extend into your future. *What you will be tomorrow, you are becoming today.*

Things to Do Today to Develop a Heart That Cares

- Make a list of all the "touches" and tasks that are needed to make your room a home-sweet-home.

- Are there any basics that you need help on? If so, who will you ask for help?

- Mark off some time on your schedule this week to begin working your way through your list.

Would You Like to Know More? Check It Out

✓ The many works of love done by the woman honored in Proverbs 31 prove her love for her home and her family. Read Proverbs 31:10-31. What strikes you most? And which of her efforts can you put into practice to better your life and the place that is your home-sweet-home?

✓ Regarding the Proverbs 31 woman, what character qualities are evident in God's description of her? Once again, what strikes you most? And which of her sterling qualities can you (or *must* you) seek to develop in your life and heart?

10

A Heart That Chooses Wisely

He who walks with the wise grows wise,
but a companion of fools suffers harm.

Proverbs 13:20

This past week I heard my sweet, kind, patient, understanding husband, Jim, on the phone with our cell phone service. It seems that I had gone over the number of minutes that we pay for every month on my cell phone account. I was horrified...because we already pay for quite a few minutes! But more? I knew that most of those minutes were spent talking to lots of people about lots of things that had nothing to do with friends and friendships. Yet I also knew some of those many minutes (how many, I wondered?) had also been spent talking to my friends.

My friends are important to me as I'm sure yours are to you. And, my dear friend, that's as it should be. You see, the Bible says you and I are created in the image of God

(Genesis 1:26). That means we resemble God in some very special ways. And one of those ways is that, like God, we are social beings. That means…

- *We have fellowship with God*—God created us to have fellowship with Himself. God doesn't *need* us as friends, but He *chooses* to be our friend and to fellowship with us, and

- *We have friendship with Jesus Christ*—God's Son, Jesus, has chosen us to be His friends. Jesus said, "You are my friends….I have called you friends" (John 15:14-15).

Understanding this very special relationship we enjoy with God and the friendship we have with Jesus points to yet another priority area for a woman after God's own heart—*she chooses her earthly friendships wisely.* Not only is her spiritual relationship with God important, but her physical, human relationships are also important.

The Bible gives us a perfect example of a healthy, biblical friendship in the lives of David and Jonathan. We'll look at their remarkable friendship later, but for now, understand that Jonathan was an extremely committed friend to David, and vice versa. In fact, Jonathan hung in there with David, actually helping David to escape the repeated attempts of murder by Jonathan's own father! David and Jonathan can teach you and me a lot about what it means to choose our friends wisely.

Finding a Friend

But how can you and I find a friend like a David or a Jonathan? Of course, the best first step (always and in all things) is to see what God says about friends in His Word, the Bible. Let's see what He has to say about friends and about how to choose wisely.

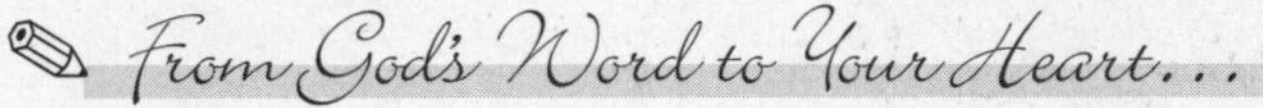

The Bible is very clear and specific when it tells us what kind of person to look for in a friend...and what kind to avoid like the plague! First let's look at God's list of people to reject as friends. As you read through these verses, make a mental note about the speech, character, and conduct of those who are most definitely *not* to be your friends. You can pray for them, and you should be friendly to them, but they are not to be your friends. What are the warning signals to beware of? (P.S., God's warnings apply to friends of the opposite sex as well!) (And another P.S.—in the Hebrew language, the language the book of Proverbs is written in, the word "friend" and "neighbor" are the same.)

> *Blessed is the person who does not walk in the counsel of the wicked or stand in the way of sinners or sit in the seat of mockers* (Psalm 1:1).

Do not set foot on the path of the wicked or walk in the way of evil men (Proverbs 4:14).

He who walks with the wise grows wise, but a companion of fools suffers harm (Proverbs 13:20).

A violent man entices his neighbor and leads him down a path that is not good (Proverbs 16:29).

Do not make friends with a hot-tempered man, do not associate with one easily angered, or you may learn his ways and get yourself ensnared (Proverbs 22:24-25).

Whoever flatters his neighbor is spreading a net for his feet (Proverbs 29:5).

But now I am writing you that you must not associate with anyone who calls himself a brother [a Christian] but is sexually immoral or greedy, an idolater or a slanderer, a drunkard or a swindler. With such a [person] do not even eat (1 Corinthians 5:11).

Do not be misled: "Bad company corrupts good character" (1 Corinthians 15:33).

Whew! That's quite a list, isn't it? But God cares for you and wants to protect you from those who will harm you and influence you away from God and toward evil. So now, how do you go about finding a friend? Take these scriptures to heart, for they lay the groundwork for successful friendships.

He who walks with the wise grows wise, but a companion of fools suffers harm (Proverbs 13:20).

Do not be yoked together [teamed up] with unbelievers. For what do righteousness and wickedness have in common? Or what fellowship can light have with darkness?... What does a believer have in common with an unbeliever? (2 Corinthians 6:14-15).

Yes, But How?

Did you notice the subtitle of this book? It's "A Teen's Guide to Friends, Faith, Family, and the Future." Well, here we are, dealing with the section about friends. Let's look at a few guidelines for finding a friend, being a friend, and building lasting and godly friendships.

1. *Follow God's rules*—God's rules will save you from a lot of heartache, mistakes, and regrets. Steer clear of people who fall on God's lists of "Do Not's" and actively seek out those who enhance your life as a Christian. And here's a hint—you'll usually find these people at church or in a Christian youth group.

   I like what one man said about friendships formed on the basis of a mutual love for God. He wrote these words to describe the qualities at the heart of the friendship between David and Jonathan: They...

   ...assented to the same authority,

   ...knew the same God,

   ...were going the same way,

   ...longed for the same things,

   ...dreamed mutual dreams, and

   ...yearned for the same experiences of holiness and worship.[17]

2. *Remember it's better to have no friends than to have the wrong friends*—There's nothing wrong with

being a late bloomer in the friendship department. *Hold on* to your innocence and character and *hold out* for friendships with those who make you a better Christian and a better person rather than grasping onto someone—anyone!—just to have a friend. And if you get lonely, God has provided friendships for you.

First, you have a friend in Jesus. As I said earlier, you can always turn to Jesus. Jesus said, "I have called you friends" (John 15:15). If you have a personal relationship with Jesus Christ, then, friend, you have a friend for life in Him! You are indeed His chosen friend…and His forever friend!

Second, you have friends in your parents. (Are you squirming yet? Are you wondering, "You can't be serious!"? Well, I am!) It's true! There's nothing wrong—and maybe everything right—with having your mom and dad as your best friends. It's not childish. And it's not stupid. They are God's gift to you. And believe me, no one loves you more or cares for you more deeply and genuinely than your very own mother and father.

And *third*, you have friends in your brothers and sisters. (And now are you wondering, "You must be joking now! Not my goofy brother!" No, I'm serious again!) The same thing is true of family. I can tell you from experience that your friends throughout life will come and go. You may stay in touch, talk on the phone, and email one another. But your friends will usually move on (maybe even literally moving on to another town). They will go to different colleges, get married, move away with their husbands, start their families, and...well, you get the picture. But your family will always be there, especially if you build and maintain friendships with them. As I write this, my father and my husband's parents have already died, and my mother, who suffers from Alzheimer's disease, has not known or recognized me for seven years. And guess what? We thank God every day that we still have our brothers and sisters. We delight in the anchor of these lasting family friendships.

So, dear sister, do your part. Of course you'll want to spend time with Jesus (after all, that's what we've learned that a woman after God's own heart does!). But also spend time with your parents and with your brothers and sisters. Be friends with them. Support them. Love them. You'll be building friendships that will last a lifetime.

3. *Be friendly*—I hope you've gotten the message from the Bible (and from me) about how important it is to protect yourself and to be wise when it comes to finding friends—the *right* friends. And I hope you're also understanding that you must be friendly to all, that you must be a friendly person. As a Christian woman, you have so much to give! And, as we've already learned, everyone needs a smile and a warm "hello" and a kind word, especially a word about

Jesus. You and I want to be like Jesus, who was a friend to sinners (Luke 7:34) and who "went around doing good" (Acts 10:38). So I want to end this chapter with these "Ten Commandments of Friendship."[18] Take them with you throughout your life.

- Speak to people—there is nothing as nice as a cheerful word of greeting.
- Smile at people—it takes seventy-two muscles to frown and only fourteen to smile!
- Call people by name—the sweetest music to anyone's ear is the sound of their own name.
- Be friendly and helpful—if you would have friends, be friendly.
- Be cordial—speak and act as if everything you do were a real pleasure.
- Be genuinely interested in people—you can like *everyone* if you try.
- Be generous with praise—cautious with criticism.
- Be considerate of the feelings of others—it will be appreciated.
- Be thoughtful of the opinions of others.
- Be alert to give service—what counts most in life is what we do for others!

Heart Response

There's no doubt that friends and friendships are important parts of your life! Friendships are part of God's plan and a major means of mutual growth, encouragement, excitement, learning, and love, not to mention witnessing and evangelism. Biblical friendships definitely bless us and build us up.

As we leave this discussion of God's guidelines for finding friends, I want to share this bit of wisdom for life with you: There seems to be three kinds of people in life—

> those who pull you down,
> those who pull you along, and
> those who pull you up.

Based on these three kinds of people, I strongly believe that your best friends should be Christians. Your best friends should be believers who pull you along and pull you up toward Christlikeness—like David and Jonathan did for one another. Your best friends should be soul partners—like David and Jonathan were. Your best friends should be strong, like-minded Christians who help you to think your best thoughts, do your noblest deeds, and be your finest self.

So as you go about the business of looking for a friend and making friends, have the highest standards possible—those we've been discussing from the Bible. First of all, have the highest standards for yourself. Don't sell yourself short. You *be* the kind of person who pulls others along and pulls them up toward the things of God.

But don't settle for anything less than God's highest standards for yourself in the "best friend" category. Those you spend your precious time and life with must love the Lord, first and foremost, in *their* hearts. And they must help *you* to love the Lord even more. *They* must possess a fiery passion for serving Jesus Christ, and they must fan the flames of *your* passion for serving Him.

Remember, when you pick your friends, you are picking your future! So choose your friends with care. You become what they are!

Things to Do Today to Develop a Heart That Chooses Wisely

♡ Review again the scriptures listed in the section titled "From God's Word to Your Heart." Summarize the teaching of each verse in a word or two. Then write out a list in your personal notebook of these guidelines regarding the kind of friend you want to be...and have. Look at it often—even every day!

♡ Make a list of your current "friends." Place these names next to your list of God's guidelines for friends. Do they all belong on your list of "best friends"? Why or why not?

♡ Make one more list—those you know who pull you along and who pull you up in your relationship with the Lord. How can you spend more time with them? (They just may be friends-in-the-making!)

Would You Like to Know More? Check It Out

✓ Read Proverbs 1:10-19, God's instructions written for the purpose of "giving...knowledge and discretion to the young" (Proverbs 1:4). What is the scene here, and what is the writer saying to his teenager in verses 10 and 15? What do you want to remember from this wise teaching?

✓ You'll love reading about the most famous friendship in the Bible, the beautiful relationship enjoyed between David and Jonathan, the son of King Saul, found in 1 Samuel 18:1-4; 19:1-6; and 20:1-42. It will take you a few minutes, but boy, is it worth it! Remember as you read the story of their friendship that King Saul was trying to murder David. We'll look at this friendship again in our next chapter, but for now, how did the friendship develop, and what was it based upon? What lessons in friendship can you take away from David and Jonathan?

11

A Heart That Is Loyal

A friend loves at all times....
There is a friend who sticks
closer than a brother.

PROVERBS 17:17; 18:24

It is such a joy to be the mother of two daughters. I have learned so much from my girls as we've gone through many of life's ups and downs together. And I can say that I *know*, from my own life as a teen and from witnessing, watching, worrying, and walking through the teen years of my daughters, that the whole area of friendships is vital...and volatile! It's vital in that everyone wants to have friends. And it's volatile in that friendships can blow up right in your face!

That's what one of my daughters found out...the hard way! When our family arrived back from the mission field, she was entering junior high school. And, because we had been gone, she had no friends. So as a family we began to pray for a friend for her. Well, soon we were all delighted when at last a friendship with another girl began to bud.

From a distance, it looked like all the ingredients were there for a godly "best-friend" relationship (like we learned about in the last chapter).

Well, one day after school my daughter ran through the front door at home wearing a necklace her new friend had given her. I'm sure you've seen one—the kind of necklace that has half a heart on it. It comes with two chains and two half-hearts, and each friend wears one. It's a friendship necklace. Needless to say, she was overjoyed! She had a friend! And her friend had gone so far as to purchase the two necklaces and to give my daughter one of them to wear, signifying their friendship. It appeared that our prayers had been answered.

But…can you guess the end of the story? It wasn't long before tensions set in, voices were raised, emotions ran high, and arguments began. And sure enough, the day arrived when one of these two "friends for life," these two "heart sisters," threw her half of the necklace at the other, and that friendship was shattered. It was over!…and we began to pray all over again.

Being a Friend

Have you had an experience like my daughter had? Then you know that finding a friend is not easy. No one ever said that it would be. And no one would ever say that being a friend is easy either. Being a friend—a friend like the scriptures at the beginning of this chapter describe, a friend who loves at all times and who sticks closer than a brother—is quite a challenge! But being such a friend is an important assignment God gives to you and me as women after His own heart.

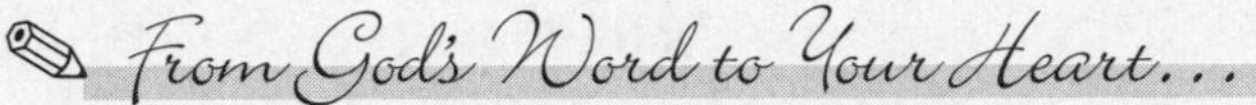

As always, God gives us our guidelines for life, and that includes our guidelines for being a loyal friend. As you read through these wise sayings from the Bible, formulate in your mind and heart what kind of friend you must be. Note, too, the things a friend does and does not do.

> *He who covers over an offense promotes love, but whoever repeats the matter separates close friends* (Proverbs 17:9).

> *A friend loves at all times, and a brother is born for adversity* (Proverbs 17:17).

> *A man of many companions may come to ruin, but there is a friend who sticks closer than a brother* (Proverbs 18:24).

> *Do not forsake your friend* (Proverbs 27:10).

Yes, But How?

Everyone has had experiences with flickering friendships that were short-lived, beginning quickly...and ending just as quickly. So how can we develop friendships that last? Obviously, we need to *find* the right friends to begin with. (That's what our last chapter was about.) But we also need to *be* the right kind of friend.

1. *Be loyal*—The most endearing and enduring quality between two friends is loyalty. We've all been hurt by a turncoat "friend." As we learned about David and Jonathan, true friends are equally loyal to each other. Their friendship wasn't one-sided or lopsided. Jonathan stood up to his father, King Saul, in defense of his friend David. And David kept his promise to Jonathan to look after his family members in the future. How loyal are you to your friends? Are you "a friend who sticks closer than a brother" (Proverbs 18:24)?

2. *Be understanding*—And don't keep score! Loyal love, according to 1 Corinthians 13:5, "keeps no record of wrongs." That means true friends don't get upset when a birthday is forgotten, when a phone call isn't returned, when time passes and there's no contact, when you don't get to touch base or sit together at church, when a friend spends time with someone else. Instead, true friends understand and support each other's commitments and responsibilities. They understand that family comes first, that

homework is important, that everyone is very busy. So pray for your friends, be understanding, and volunteer to help out when your friends are under pressure.

3. *Be respectful and sensitive*—For instance, when you call a friend, ask before you begin talking, "Is this a good time to talk, or do you want me to call back?" Also call and ask before you drop in or drop by for a visit. Don't forget...your friends have family responsibilities and relationships to take care of, chores, homework, piano practice, etc. Find out when the best time is for getting together.

4. *Be honest and be attentive*—One of the richest blessings of a solid friendship is honesty. The Bible says it this way—"Wounds from a friend can be trusted...and the pleasantness of one's friend springs from his earnest counsel" (Proverbs 27:6,9). Many people throughout your life will criticize you, but very few will be honest in their concern for you and speak to you face to face. That's one role of a true friend. You and a true friend should be committed to pulling each other along and pulling each other up toward God's goals for your lives as His young women. And don't forget, when your friend takes on this role to help you grow in an area where you need help, listen! Don't be proud. And don't be hurt. Thank your friend for caring enough to bring up a difficult subject (you can be sure it wasn't easy!), then

take it to the Lord in prayer. Examine your heart to see if what your friend said is true.

5. *Be careful with the opposite sex*—We'll devote time to this topic later in our book, but for now go back to the principles we learned from the Bible in the previous chapter. Be friendly to everyone, but be very cautious and take a *l-o-n-g* time when it comes to becoming friends with boys. The three things you'll really want to watch out for in your conduct and speech are being *too* friendly, being *too* flattering, and spending *too* much time talking. As I said, more later!

6. *Be witnessing in your encounters*—Those acquaintances in your life who are not Christians should be hearing you talk about Jesus, talk about God, talk about the Bible, talk about your church, and talk about your Bible study group. What happens when others hear you talk about these things (which, of course, are the most important things in your life, right?)? Those who hear you will possibly be put off by what you're saying and want nothing to do with you. Or maybe...just maybe!...they'll want to know more about your Savior, they'll want to go with you to church or to your youth group, and they'll want to do a Bible study with you. You see, *you* have the words of life—the gospel of Jesus Christ. And *you* have God's Word to give to all, "the holy Scriptures, which are able to make [others] wise for salvation

through faith in Christ Jesus" (2 Timothy 3:15). And God has placed these people in *your* life! So be bold for Jesus. And here's another huge benefit—when you speak up about your faith right away with a boy, it will let him know up front what you are all about. The boys in your life need to know right away that you are not interested in them if they are not passionate, active Christians.

7. *Be a constant encourager*—Let's go back a minute to the friendship between David and Jonathan. Their friendship, as we learned, was based on their love for God and on the things of the Lord. So how did they encourage one another? The Bible says that when it was evident David was targeted for murder, "Jonathan went to David…and helped him find strength in God" (1 Samuel 23:16). The best way to encourage your friends is in the Lord, with Scripture verses and through praying together. And when you give a compliment, be specific in your praise. Don't say, "Hey, that was great." Instead, say something like "I always appreciate the way you…." Take a few extra seconds to be specific. For instance, "I was watching you minister to that elderly woman, and you taught me a huge lesson by the way you…." Learn to praise conduct and character. It calls for a decision and some effort, but remember—your goal is to bring your friend along or up in her relationship with God. And with God, godly conduct and character count mightily!

8. *Be prioritizing your friendships*—You only have so much time in a day. So it's important that you identify who you are spending the bulk of your time with. And don't forget your family! They are the priority relationships God has given you. But after family, who are you spending time with, and how much? Is it those who pull you up and pull you along in your spiritual growth and walk with God? Is it those who help you to live out God's plan for your life with excellence? Who help you seek to set your heart and mind on things above, not on earthly things (Colossians 3:1-2)? Or is your time mostly spent with unbelievers or Christians who live on the edge or hang out on the fringe?

Don't get me wrong. Read number 6 again on pages 150-51. There's nothing wrong with giving of yourself to these acquaintances. But be sure they are not eating away your time, the time you could be studying the Word, being in a Bible study, being discipled, and being involved in a ministry at church. And be sure you are reaching out and ministering to these wonderful people. The best thing you can do for these friends is to find out (and that means listening!) the details of their lives, let them know how much you care for them and that you are praying for them, and continually ask them to come along with you to church or to your Bible study. Better yet, ask them to get together and have a Bible study *with* you! (And a word of caution here—you should *not* have a one-on-one Bible study with a boy. Leave that to your dad, an older brother, or a youth pastor! As I said, more on this later! But for now, trust me—don't do it!

9. *Be nurturing your friendships*—We never wake up in the morning and coldheartedly, calculatingly decide "I think I'll neglect my friends today." No, the neglect is more subtle. We just wake up in the morning and don't even *think* about our friends! Therefore, our friendships must be nurtured and developed. You and I have to make willful decisions about the keeping and growing of friendships—with both family and friends. And that takes time, care, and love…and maybe even a little money as you purchase a greeting card or small gift for a friend. The apostle Paul told his friends in Philippi, "I have you in my heart" (Philippians 1:7). Do you carry your friends in your heart?

10. *Be praying for your friends*—Dear one, we have no greater or finer (or more costly!) gift to give both our family and friends than to pray for them—faithfully, frequently, and fervently. Everyone struggles, and everyone faces trials and encounters crises. And we can be sure there are issues in our friends' lives that will never be shared with us. We'll never know all the battles that are being fought in another person's life. So, we pray.

    And for what do we pray? Pray for your friends' spiritual growth, for their schoolwork, for their responsibilities and relationships at home with the members of their families for their involvement at church. And pray for others to come alongside them and encourage them, too. I especially love it when someone tells me exactly what they are praying for me. So be specific about what you are praying for them. And share specific Bible verses that you think will encourage them. You never know when the verse you share just might be the perfect "word that sustains the weary" and strengthens your friend to get through a tough day (Isaiah 50:4). And you never know when *you* just might be the true friend whose faithful, frequent, and fervent prayers help another to excel in greatness...or make it through a difficult life! So, dear friend, *pray* for your friends!

Heart Response

Is your heart moved? Mine is! As I said before, God intended us to have friends and to be a friend. You and I as women are social beings. We long to love and to be loved. That's the way God made us. So I want to encourage you (again!) in all your relationships—be the best friend anyone could ever have!

But I also want to caution you that friendships—true friendships—come with a price tag. And that price tag includes *time*. It takes time to find a friend. It takes time to be a friend. It takes time to remain a friend. And it takes time to pray for your friends.

So, precious friend, choose wisely. *Be* the best friend you can be to everyone...but *choose* wisely who your best friends will be. And how will you recognize those friends?

A friend will
strengthen you with her prayers,
bless you with her love, and
encourage you with her heart.[19]

Are you this kind of friend to others, a *loyal* friend?

Things to Do Today to Develop a Heart That Is Loyal

♡ As you review the ten guidelines for loyal friendships, did you find an area where you are especially strong as a friend? What was it?

- ♡ As you review the ten guidelines for loyal friendships, did you find an area (or two!) where you need improvement in the friendship department? What was it, and what do you plan to do about it?

- ♡ What will you do to be a better encourager to each of your friends tomorrow? This week?

Would You Like to Know More? Check It Out

✓ Read 1 Corinthians 13:4-8. List the marks of loyal love found in these few verses. As you think about the level of your love for your friends, how would you rate yourself, and why? Go a step further and write out what you plan to do to get a better grade. (And don't forget to ask God for His help!)

✓ What do these scenarios teach us about friendships? Read Psalm 41:9; Psalm 55:12-14; Matthew 26:50; Acts 15:36-41. As you read, note what people were involved and any details mentioned. What conclusions can you draw about friends and friendships?

✓ Paul had a passion for prayer and for praying for his friends. Read the content of these prayers: Philippians 1:9-11; Colossians 1:9-12; Ephesians 3:14-19. Do you need to beef up your prayers for your friends? (Or do you perhaps need to beef up your prayer life, period?) What changes and improvements will you make to become a better friend, a woman after God's own heart who prays for her friends?

12

A Heart That Grows

And Jesus grew in wisdom and stature, and in favor with God and men.

LUKE 2:52

It may be hard for you to believe, but I used to sit exactly where you're sitting right now—sitting for hours on end in classrooms at school and in my room at home at night for even more hours of homework. In fact, I can say that I probably spent *more* hours at school and at school work than you do. Why? Because both my parents were schoolteachers—which meant that every day of my life I went to the school where my mother taught or to the school where my father taught! I got to school early (and sat in their empty classrooms studying), and I stayed at school late (sitting in their empty classrooms doing homework). *Then* I got to go home...and put in even more time on my homework!

Yes, my parents definitely put a premium on education. So much so that they worked long and hard—even teaching nights and summers—to put all four of their children through college. For this I am most thankful!

But I have to admit that I wondered almost daily all through junior high and high school and even college, *Why?!* Why was all this school work so important? I could understand why it was important for my three brothers. But me? I mean, wasn't I supposed to grow up, meet a great guy, get married, and have a family?

Why Grow? Why Learn? Why Go to School?

What I've just expressed above is pretty much how my thoughts went all the way through my 16-plus years of schooling, right up until I graduated from the University of Oklahoma. And sure enough, I did meet a great guy (Jim), get married, and have a family. And believe me, *that's* when I really had my eyes opened to the value of my education! (And please realize that when I say *education* I'm not talking about college. No, I'm talking about *all* schooling—the kind of education you are getting right now by going to school—whether on a campus or at home, and as you faithfully do your homework assignments.)

Well, dear heart, I can only tell you today that I wish my parents were still here to hear me tell them one more time, "Thank you for my education!" I can't tell you how many times in the passing decades I've spoken these words to them.

I say this because these many years later—after being a wife and homemaker for 38 years and after raising two daughters—I know that the things I learned in school and the skills, habits, and character qualities I obtained because of the work and grind of school equipped me for my roles as wife, mother, and homemaker. I was able to learn how to fulfill these God-assigned roles because I already knew from my time spent being a student how to learn, to grow, to read, to organize, to schedule, to study, and to manage projects. I had learned how to acquire knowledge. And I had learned how to complete and finish work assignments.

Therefore, over the years and through the seasons of my life, I've been able to tackle daily problems and learn new skills. The know-how achieved through my years of going to school has also enabled me to minister, whether taking on the challenge of teaching a Sunday school class of little ones or doing research and creating a curriculum for a large women's Bible study, as well as teaching the study. And I am still learning new things, as God has given me a fresh and different (and stretching!) ministry of writing books for Christian women.

I truly love and enjoy everything I do and everything I've done. For instance, I love being a homemaker. Homemaking is an art, and as a homemaker I have the privilege of expressing and developing all my talents in my little place called home. I get to build...beautify...organize...create...fuss...express myself. I get to read and study and grow and master nutrition, finances, horticulture, design, and wardrobe. And I love being a mother. I loved teaching and training my children and giving their precious lives a bent toward God. And now I love passing on the truth about Jesus to yet another generation, to my grandchildren.

But, my dear young woman after God's own heart, here's the point I'm trying to make—to do all this, or to do whatever God is asking of you (and me), means that you've got to be a woman who is continuing to grow. You've got to be dedicated, organized, and a woman of purpose.

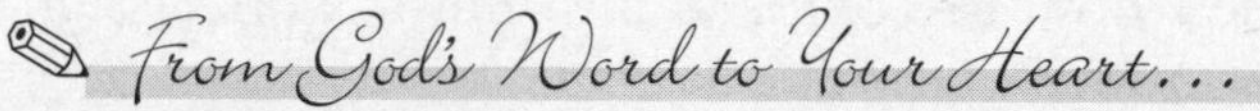

The Bible is filled with examples of God's servants who had to learn before they could lead. Moses, Daniel, Jesus, Paul—all had years of training and schooling. Even the women of the early church were taught by those older than they were (Titus 2:3-5). As you read these scriptures, what comes to your mind regarding the importance of all education and learning and your daily schoolwork?

> *Let the wise listen and add to their learning, and let the discerning get guidance* (Proverbs 1:5).

> *For the LORD gives wisdom, and from his mouth come knowledge and understanding* (Proverbs 2:6).

> *And Jesus grew in wisdom and stature, and in favor with God and men* (Luke 2:52).

Whatever you do, work at it with all your heart, as working for the Lord, not for men (Colossians 3:23).

But grow in the grace and knowledge of our Lord and Savior Jesus Christ (2 Peter 3:18).

Yes, But How?

Are you catching on? Catching a glimpse of God's plan for you to learn and grow? Catching a vision of why, as you prepare for a lifetime of serving God and others, your school work is an important part of your life?

That's my prayer for you. And here are some actions you can take that will hopefully motivate you even further to develop a heart that grows.

1. *Accept*—You need to accept that God is calling you to follow the normal course of events in your life. And that normal course includes your schooling. In God's economy, everything is "done in a fitting and orderly way" (1 Corinthians 14:40). You cannot skip over any part of life that is unpleasant, that isn't fun. Just think about Jesus. We've already noted in our book that Jesus—God in flesh(!)—lived at home

and was subject to His parents' authority. But He also "grew in wisdom and stature, and in favor with God and men" (Luke 2:52). Nothing and no normal phase was omitted from Jesus' life.

Just as God the Father had a plan for Jesus' life, He has a plan for yours, too. And the Father's plan includes the normal process of developing mentally by going to school and maturing through the knowledge and experience gained in the process. You gain the treasure of education when you accept that your schooling is God's will for your life.

2. *Embrace*—You also need to embrace God's plan for academic growth. Yes, you prepare spiritually for the future, but you also prepare academically for your future.

   Here's the way it is—you have your whole life in front of you. You don't know yet what God has planned for you, but you prepare for a life of serving Him and others. You don't know whether you're preparing to serve God by working on the homefront as a wife, mother, and homemaker, by working on the mission field, or by working at a job. Any one of these "professions" will be demanding and require years of focused preparation. So I urge you to embrace this aspect of your life, this aspect of preparing by schooling. Accept it with great excitement, anticipation, and prayer!

3. *Excel*—God wants you to excel at everything you do. In His Word He tells us, "Whatever you do, work at it with all your heart, as working for the Lord, not for men" (Colossians 3:23). And that "work" for you as a young person includes your school work. Therefore you should "work at it with all your heart," heartily and hard! Why? So you can develop habits and skills of excellence for managing your life today and for all of your future. The disciplines acquired by excellence will give you the greatest education of all—a life of wisdom. Wisdom—not academic excellence or good grades or a bushel of knowledge, but wisdom—is your goal as a Christian. As Solomon, the wisest person in Old Testament times, wrote, "Wisdom is supreme; therefore get wisdom" (Proverbs 4:7).

And here's another benefit of doing the best work you can—it gives you credibility with your peers. I'm not talking about being popular. Being a strong Christian with moral convictions is difficult on the school campus and makes you stand out as different. No, popularity is not to be your goal. But if you are "the best" at your schoolwork, people will be interested in knowing more about you and your life. They may still think you're "weird," but they will respect you and your standards for excellence and your accomplishments, which then may open the door for you to share about your faith in Christ.

4. *Examine*—You must develop discernment in order to examine what is being taught in your classrooms. And your ability to discern truth from ungodly teaching will be in direct proportion to the wisdom you have gained from your study of the Bible, through prayer, and through wise counsel (Proverbs 1:5). So if you attend a public school, there will be times when a teacher will teach something you as a Christian don't believe. (I'm sure this has already happened to you!) And even if you attend a Christian school, there may be times when a teacher will teach something different from what your church or parents or pastor teaches. What can you do at such times? Here's a preliminary checklist of do's and don'ts:

    - Do ask for clarification.
    - Do ask your parents' advice.
    - Do follow your parents' advice.
    - Do ask your pastor, if your parents aren't able to help.
    - Do pray about the situation and for wisdom.
    - Don't overreact and cause a scene.
    - Don't confront the teacher in the classroom.
    - Don't show disrespect for the teacher's position of authority.

Combining all the *do's* and *don'ts,* do make sure you respond with Christian love and with respect for your teacher.

5. *Exemplify*—You need to exemplify Christ and uphold the standard He sets in the Bible for your conduct on your school campus. For instance, do you dress like everyone else at school? If someone were to look down the crowded halls of your school, would you blend in with the crowd? If someone new arrived on your campus and followed you around for a few days, would they say that you adhered to different beliefs and values than most of the other kids in the school? If you are modeling Jesus Christ at your school, then there will be a noticeable difference between you and the other students. Your days and years spent at school are the training ground for living the Christian life. You must decide who you are living to please—your friends?...or your friend Jesus?

   And one more thought before we close this most important chapter—if you are having a hard time living for Christ at school, then you will have a hard time living for Christ in the world. How you model Christlikeness at school today is how you will more than likely model Christ in the future when you are an adult. I've said this before, but I simply must say it again—what you will be tomorrow, you are becoming today. So live for Christ today and, my friend, you will live for Christ tomorrow.

Heart Response

I hope you enjoyed this chapter. I know I did. It was my opportunity and delight to have a heart-to-heart time with you. As I said, I love being a woman after God's own heart—every aspect of it! And I so desire for you to love it, too!

To me, being a woman is like being a flower. As the seasons of life pass from one to the next, God presents new roles for us to take on, new things for us to learn, and new challenges for us to conquer. As these challenges arrive, we call upon God's great grace and tackle them full-on. We put God's wisdom and our education to use. We tap into all the strong character traits and solid learning skills gained through our hours and days and years spent in school. And we draw upon God and His Holy Spirit to strengthen us and help us walk along life's way. And then, through this process of growth, the flower of our life develops, blossoms, blooms, and flourishes as we serve God in each and every place where He plants us. The days pass. The decades pass. The flower grows. And then one day we meet our Lord face to face. And it is then, dear one, that we present ourselves to Him, in full bloom.

Being a Christian woman is a wonderful life! So make sure yours is a heart that is growing so you can enjoy the journey!

Things to Do Today to Develop a Heart That Grows

- Look at your schedule for this past week and estimate the number of hours you spent in these three categories: time goofing off, time with friends, and time on homework. What does your schedule reveal? Are there any changes called for?

- How would you evaluate your Christian presence on your school campus? Are you a "secret agent" for Christ? Or are you a "special agent" for Christ? Please explain your answer. Then ask a Christian friend at your school to pray for your witness to be loud and bold, and to hold you accountable. (P.S., you might want to do the same for her!)

♡ Where does the thermometer of your heart's commitment register on the "attitude scale" when it comes to school and your schoolwork? How will you turn up the heat of your heart in this most important area of life?

Would You Like to Know More? Check It Out

✓ Read Daniel 1:1-7 and 17-20. Describe the process of learning for the teen Daniel and his three friends. How does their experience motivate you in your own schooling?

✓ Read Luke 2:41-49. What do Jesus' younger years teach you about your own developmental process?

✓ Gamaliel was one of the most prominent teachers of his day. Read Acts 5:34. Who was Gamaliel's famous student, according to Acts 22:3? Again, what example is being set for you?

✓ Read Titus 2:3-5. Besides the teaching you receive in the school classroom, what further training should you have for the future, according to verses 4 and 5? Who is helping you to grow in some of these areas? Or who *could* help you if you asked?

13

A Heart That Serves

Always give yourselves fully to the work of the Lord, because...your labor in the Lord is not in vain.

1 CORINTHIANS 15:58

Everyone has a hero or two. And an amazing thing about heroes is that most of them have hearts that serve. Joan of Arc loved God, served God, and fought valiantly as she served others. Do you know her story?

Joan of Arc was a French peasant who lived in the thirteenth century. When France was occupied by the English, she convinced the king to put her at the head of 10,000 troops. She rallied the French forces to liberate France and has been since dubbed "The Maid of Orleans," heroine of France. Joan of Arc couldn't read or write, but she cared deeply and she prayed passionately. And here's the shocker—Joan of Arc was 19 when she died. She was a teenager! To this day this teenage woman is considered to be a national heroine of France. As she prepared for death, Joan of Arc prayed, "I shall only last a year; use me as You can." Hers was a heart committed to serving others to the very end.

Well, my young friend, God wants you and me to have hearts that serve, too. He has given us everything we need for living our lives in a godly way (2 Peter 1:3), He has blessed us with every spiritual blessing (Ephesians 1:3), and He has gifted us spiritually to serve others in the church (1 Corinthians 12:7). It's like this—God has given us everything we will ever need in life, and He expects us to, in turn, reach out and share what we have with others, to help better the lives of others.

We've talked about our roles with family, friends, and those who do not know our Jesus. But now it's time to talk about our responsibilities to other Christians. So let's see how it is that God wants us to serve one another in the church.

Learn to Reach Out

Again and again Jesus tells us to give—to give to everyone (Luke 6:30), and to give without expecting to get anything back (verse 35), to give in the generous way God, who is kind to the ungrateful and wicked, gives (verse 35), and to care for others by giving (verse 38). So how can you and I go about giving in this way? How can we learn to let our hearts overflow with care for others? How can we begin to reach out and serve others? Here are a few ideas:

- *Be there*—When it comes to reaching out to others in ministry, remember that you must first be there. In order to serve others in the church, you must be there. So make your attendance at church and at your youth activities a high priority.

And here's another benefit to being there—your very presence is a source of comfort and help to others. You may not always know exactly what to say or do, but you can be there. So if someone is suffering, you can at least go up to her and speak to her, stand beside her, talk to her, and put your arm around her shoulder. But first you must be there!

- *Be a giver*—The Bible says "do not withhold good from those who deserve it, when it is in your power to act" (Proverbs 3:27). So open your heart and give. Give the smile, the greeting, the interested question, the touch, and the hug. These are small things that mean a lot to others.

- *Be bold*—By this I mean that when God puts someone in your path who is suffering or hurting, don't think, "I've got to go find someone to help her. I've got to go find Pastor." No, you be bold. First reach out to that person, find out what the need is, and *then* go find Pastor or someone else to help if you need to. Maybe all the person needs is a shoulder to cry on or someone to pray with her. That someone can be you!

- *Be generous*—And by this I mean not only with money and things, but with praise, encouragement, thanks, a greeting, kindness, good deeds, and notes of appreciation. You and I can *choose* to give these tiny blessings that cost us so little and mean so much to others, or we can choose *not* to give them. So when someone shares something difficult from her life in your Bible study group, tell her that you appreciated what she had to say...and that you appreciate her. Thank your Bible study leader for the lesson and for her hard work. Go another step and tell her what meant the most to you from the lesson, what you learned. Tell those who organized your church group outing or camp or who opened their homes to your group that you are thankful for their hard work.

Learn to Look Out

Do you know the story in the Bible of the shepherd who had 100 sheep and discovered that one was missing (Luke 15:1-7)? Well, what amazes me is that the shepherd dropped everything and went looking for that one sheep. And what amazes me even more is that that's the way God cares for you and me. And here's something else that's amazing—God expects you and me to care for others in this same way! So here are a few tips on learning to look out.

- *Develop a "bountiful eye"*—The Bible says that "he who has a bountiful eye will be blessed" (Proverbs 22:9 KJV). I think of a bountiful eye as being like the eyes of the Lord, which "run" and "range throughout the earth to strengthen those whose hearts are fully committed to him" (2 Chronicles 16:9). So here's what I do. Whenever I go out in public, I intentionally look for wounded sheep.

And believe me, they are everywhere! I've found women crying in the restroom at church, sitting on a planter on the patio weeping, even standing behind the prayer room door at church sobbing their eyes out. When you find someone in need...then what?

- *Be direct*—I've had to learn (yes, *learn!)* to be direct and to reach out to hurting people. It's not always easy, but it's the right thing to do.

One night at church I was sitting beside a stranger, a visitor to our church. Well, this woman bawled through the entire evening. I could hardly wait for my pastor to say "amen" so I could turn to her and say, "Is there *anything* I can do for you? Do you want to talk? Can I pray with you? Can I get you something?" Well, my friend, hers was a spiritual need. She needed the Savior...and that was the night she became a Christian! God was working in her heart and He used me in a small way to help her. Praise Him!

Go to Give

I'm so happy to share with you some words that have changed my life. They are from missionary and martyr Jim Elliot, who once said,

> Wherever you are, be all there.
> Live to the hilt every situation
> you believe to be the
> will of God.[20]

I try to keep these words in mind wherever I am and whatever I'm doing (like writing this book right now while the sun is shining and the gorgeous weather outdoors is trying to woo me away from my computer!). But I especially try to keep these words in mind whenever I attend any church or ministry event. I go expecting God to use me. And, of course, I want to encourage you to do the same. How?

- *Be all there*—Before I go to any event, I pray that I will go to give. I pray to reach out, to look out, to be direct, to withhold nothing. Then, as I go, I put all other thoughts on hold. While I'm at Bible study, I don't think about what I'm going to do when I get home. And during my pastor's message I don't plan my week and worry about my to-do list. Plus, I don't want to be concerned about what happened before I got there or what will happen after the event. I want to be all there!

- *Live to the hilt!*—Not only do I want to be all there, but I want to also live each moment to the hilt! My philosophy is that as long as I'm there, as long as I'm giving an evening or a morning to be at a church event or at the worship service, I want to give totally. I want to reach out to as many sheep as I can, to minister to as many people as I can and in as many ways as I can. And, dear one, I (of course again!) want that for you, too, so that *you* can be used by God to touch the lives of others, and so that the lives of others can be bettered by your great heart that serves!

- *Divide and conquer*—This is a hard one...but I want you to agree with your closest girlfriends *not* to sit together, walk together, share together, or visit while you're at church. Instead I want you and your group to divide and conquer. Here's what will happen if you do this. You came to give, right? So how can you give to others if you are constantly with your best friends? You can talk to them any time at school or on the phone or over at your house or theirs. But what about the stranger, the first-time visitor who's all alone at church and doesn't know anyone? And what about those who are hurting, who are lonely, who had a rough time at home before they came to church (or maybe who have a rough time at home *all the time!)?* Your closest friends have open access to you and your time. They have plenty of one-on-one time with you in private. So why should they have your *public* time too? You can talk and get together later. So make a pact to divide and conquer. If you find you are gravitating toward each other, say, "Come on! Let's go touch some sheep!"

Give in Prayer

Hmmm. Here we are again—back to prayer. We began our book with prayer, and over and over again we keep returning to it. But by now you and I both realize that that's what a woman after God's own heart is all about. She is a pray-er! So pray, dear one! Pray for others. Pray for your pastor and those who work at the church. Pray for your youth leader. If he or she is married, pray for the spouse and family. Pray for your church's missionaries. Pray for others to come to Christ. Prayer is a ministry, a ministry that makes a huge difference in people's lives. So do whatever it takes to develop your prayer life. How? As we learned earlier...

- *Determine a time*—make sure you have a time (*your* time) for prayer.
- *Determine a place*—make sure you have a place (*your* place) for prayer.
- *Determine a plan*—make sure you have a plan for organizing your ministry of prayer (a notebook, a list, a journal). And while you're at it, set up a plan for exactly what days you want to pray for which people. Some people (like your family and friends) you'll want to pray for every day. And you'll want to choose a specific day of the week to pray for others (like your pastors and missionaries and teachers at school). Put all this information in your master plan for prayer.

Dear sister after God's own heart, there's one more thing I want to share as you and I dream of developing hearts that serve. As we look out and reach out and give and serve, as we let God use us in these small ways, something wonderful happens—you and I are blessed beyond what we can imagine. As we take these small but sometimes difficult steps and serve others, we grow a character that desires to look out, reach out, give, and serve even more. And that, my friend, is the character of a hero! A hero has a heart that serves others.

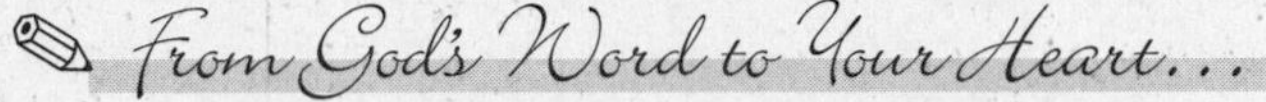

I know I've shared a lot of scriptures as we've made our way through this chapter, but now I want you to look at some more. Whisper a prayer to God to use His Word in your heart to transform it into a heart that loves His people and serves them selflessly and compassionately. As you read, ask your heart, "How can I become a better servant to the people of God?"

> *Whoever wants to become great among you must be your servant, and whoever wants to be first must be your slave—just as the Son of Man did not come to be served, but to serve, and to give his life as a ransom for many* (Matthew 20:26-28).

> *Always give yourselves fully to the work of the Lord, because you know that your labor in the Lord is not in vain* (1 Corinthians 15:58).

> *Serve one another in love* (Galatians 5:13).

> *Serve wholeheartedly, as if you were serving the Lord, not men* (Ephesians 6:7).

> *And pray in the Spirit on all occasions with all kinds of prayers and requests. With this in mind, be alert and always keep on praying for all the saints* (Ephesians 6:18).

Heart Response

We began this chapter talking about heroes. What makes a person a hero? A person doesn't become a hero because he or she decides to. No, a hero is born when some incident occurs, and he or she answers the call with a heroic act. A hero is just an ordinary person who, on one day, with one act, does the extraordinary. Or a hero could be someone just like you—a young person who serves others faithfully.

When I think of someone who had a heart that cared and served, I can't help but think of one particular woman in the Old Testament. You can read her story for yourself (see 2 Kings 4:8-10), but for now, let me give you the condensed version. This nameless woman, who is referred to as "the Shunammite" in the Bible, saw that the prophet Elisha had no place to stay when he came to her town on his preaching tours. So this dear woman asked her husband if they could build a small room on their roof for the prophet to stay in when he came to town.

So what did the Shunammite do that was so great? So heroic? She did what you and I *could* do and *should* do—She *looked out* and saw a need, she *reached out* and extended a helping hand, and she *gave out* of a heart of love for another person.

Dear young sister, God has given us an example in this woman and her actions (and her heart). We, too, should be looking out and reaching out and extending a helping hand to those around us. The Shunammite woman will never be found on any list of heroes. But we can be sure that every time God's weary prophet Elisha entered that little room on the top of her house, the Shunammite was a hero in his eyes.

You can be a hero, too. How? By following the advice of the apostle Paul, who said, "as we have opportunity, let us do good to all people, especially to those who belong to the family of believers" (Galatians 6:10). Begin with goodness. And then stand back as God grows in you a heart that serves. The instructions are simple (read them below). However, the follow-through will take a lifetime!

> Do all the good you can,
> by all the means you can,
> in all the ways you can,
> in all the places you can,
> at all the times you can,
> to all the people you can,
> as long as ever you can.[21]

Things to Do Today to Develop a Heart That Serves

- As you are finishing this chapter, what church event is next on your calendar? How can you put the principles you've just learned about developing a heart that serves into action?

- Review again the principles from this chapter about serving others. Then list three things you can definitely do to serve those in your church. Now, who can you call for some accountability as you pray to follow through on your good intentions?

- Just for today...do all the good you can, by all the means you can, in all the ways you can, in all the places you can, at all the times you can, to all the people you can.

Would You Like to Know More? Check It Out

✓ Read now the story of the Shunammite woman in 2 Kings 4:8-10. What principles for serving others did she live out? How does she set a good example for you in your service to others?

✓ For a look at another hero, read about Dorcas in Acts 9:36-41. What principles for serving others did she live out? How does she set a good example for you in your service to others?

✓ The Bible teaches that every Christian has been given *spiritual gifts* "for the common good" of those in the church (1 Corinthians 12:7). According to 1 Peter 4:9-11, what are some of these spiritual gifts that you can use in your church? How can you be faithful to serve other believers "for the common good"?

✓ Jesus, of course, is God's ultimate example of a heart that serves. Prayerfully read Philippians 2:3-8. How did Jesus serve others (verses 5-8)? And what does the apostle Paul say you should do to develop a heart that serves (verses 3-4)?

14

A Heart Marked by Purity

An unmarried woman or virgin is concerned about the Lord's affairs: Her aim is to be devoted to the Lord in both body and spirit.

1 CORINTHIANS 7:34

As I interact with women of all ages and listen to their hearts, answer their letters, and hold their hands as they sob and share their problems and regrets, believe me, this whole area of purity ranks right at the top. It's a big issue for every woman.

Before we dive into this all-important area of your life, I hope and pray you realize that all that's gone before this chapter in this book is foundational to this issue of purity of body, soul, and spirit. Your love for God and your family, coupled with your obedience to God and to your parents, is meant to make you whole and surround you with loving relationships that build lasting godly character in you. What an advantage you possess if these basic elements of purity are present in your life!

I know that whole books have been written on the subjects of purity, dating, and premarital relationships. And depending on your age and your situation, you may want to read some of them. But for my purpose of presenting an overview of the priority areas of your life as a young Christian woman, I want to give you a brief, to-the-point summary or checklist. And as you read, keep this in mind—God has given you His Word, your church, and your parents to walk you through (and walk *with* you through!) the teen years of your life. And He has also given you the power of the Holy Spirit to enable you to stay pure, to resist the flesh, and to fortify you with His self-control (Galatians 5:22-23).

A Few Words About Purity

Like all the areas of your life, God expects you to oversee and manage your purity. God has entrusted you with this most precious possession—your purity. And purity must be maintained on all levels. For instance...

- Your physical purity is something very special and should be preserved at all cost.
- Your mental purity is where it all starts. What you think greatly determines how you behave.
- Your spiritual purity deals with your heart. The heart of a woman after God's own heart is a pure heart, a heart that desires to be pure.

God makes it very clear in the Bible that He wants His women to be pure. In fact, in Titus 2:3-5, God specifically instructs the older women in the church and in the faith to teach and train the younger women "to be...pure" (verse 5). It amazes me that there are only six topics listed that these older saints are to teach to their younger sisters in the Lord, and *purity* is one of them. That, my friend, most definitely ranks purity high on God's list for you and me!

So a woman after God's own heart—no matter what her age, whether a preteen, a teen, a collegian, a career woman, a young wife and mom, a middle-aged woman, or senior saint—pays close attention to purity. Indeed, God calls *all* Christians to be pure and to keep themselves pure.

The word "pure" (Titus 2:5) is translated in different versions of the Bible as "chaste" and "pure-minded." And if you look up the word "pure" in your dictionary, you'll discover that it means to be without stain, to be free from pollution, to be clean, and to be innocent and guiltless.

✎ *From God's Word to Your Heart...*

Let's pause a minute and take these scriptures to heart. As we head into this rubber-meets-the-road topic, pray as you read the following verses. Pray that God would sear them into the tender flesh of your heart (Proverbs 3:3). Pray that God's Holy Spirit and God's Holy Word would impress upon you the changes you must make regarding your own purity and your view of the importance of your purity. Pray about the instruction each scripture sends to your heart about your purity.

Keep yourself pure (1 Timothy 5:22).

Finally, brothers, whatever is...pure...think about such things (Philippians 4:8).

Flee the evil desires of youth, and pursue righteousness, faith, love and peace, along with those who call on the Lord out of a pure heart (2 Timothy 2:22).

To the pure, all things are pure (Titus 1:15).

A Word About Dating

I'm sure you're aware that a raging battle is going on in Christian circles about the whole area of dating—do you or don't you date? Should you or shouldn't you date? If yes, at what age? And do you call it *dating* or *courting?* And if you do go on a date, do you go as a couple or in a group? On and on the discussions go.

At the time our two daughters were growing up, every family was pretty much on its own to decide its own standards and guidelines. There were few, if any, books written on the subject of dating. Everyone—both the teenagers and their parents—was left to themselves to fumble their way through the teen years. With much prayer and consultation with older, wiser parents, my husband, Jim, as the head of our household, laid out these three standards for our girls.

- There would be no dates or even discussions of dates until our girls were 16.

- After 16 there would still be no dates, but Katherine and Courtney could go to special events, such as the annual high school banquet, with a boy and a few other couples *if* that boy asked Jim first.

- After graduation from high school the girls could go out with a guy *if* he called Jim (even long distance) to ask for permission. This applied even if it was only to get a Coke.

I don't know how this sounds to you (I can only imagine!), but these three standards protected our daughters from dealing with unnecessary and premature emotions, from peer pressure, and from the wrong kind of young men. (And, by the way, our daughters have continued to thank us for these guidelines ever since!)

That's the way it was in our family with our teenage daughters. Now, what will it be for you? Why not set a high standard? Why not…

- *Choose* not to date all the way through high school. There's a 99 percent chance that any boy you date before you reach marriageable age will *not* be your future mate! (Think about that!) So what's the point of dating? Be aware that dating is an emotional roller coaster that can leave you sick after each ride.

- *Choose* to concentrate on group activities, preferably church activities. Interact with the young men there.

- *Choose* to make sure your family is involved and gets to know any boy friends well.

- *Choose* to remain morally pure no matter what. You must make this choice before you begin dating and before each date you go on, whatever your age.

I can almost hear you wondering, "But what if I'm already dating?" Well, my dear friend, read on! And especially note what I say about being around the right kind of friends, whether male or female. You want to make sure you are dating a young man who desires to follow God's heart—and that means a young man who is an active Christian, a young man whose love for God keeps him committed to God's command for purity in his life...and yours, too! Christ must have authority in his life just as Christ has authority in your life. And his heart, like yours, must be set on obeying God's plan for your purity and his.

Now, let's learn more about the marks of a young man after God's own heart!

A Word About Boys

It's a given that you will be around boys. But, I repeat(!), by all means, make sure the boys you are around are vibrant active Christians! Surround yourself with the kind of friends—male or female—who pull you along in your spiritual growth and pull you up toward godliness. Starting now, use the Bible's highest standards for a Christian man as your guideline for guys. These standards are found in 1 Timothy 3 and Titus 1, but in a nutshell they call for a man of God to be blameless in character and godly in conduct. This standard is high. That's because it's *God's* standard, not man's standard. Dear one, God desires the best from *you*, and you should desire the best in a young man. Don't settle for anyone less than the best—a man after God's own heart!

A Word About Your Dress

I want to share two things in this area of dress. First, I want you to know what the Bible says about your dress (and it says it in one word!)—it's to be *modest* (1 Timothy 2:9).

But second, I want you to hear what a young man has to say about your dress. His name is Jason Perry of the Christian music group Plus One. Jim and I were on a panel with Jason that answered questions about dating—questions asked by representatives of a large Christian bookselling chain. In his book *You Are Not Your Own*, Jason has this to say about your dress:

> When I see girls dressed [in] a suggestive way, I not only turn my head away, but I pray for them. Obviously, there's a deeper issue—they are looking for affirmation in the wrong ways. My question is, Is that how you want guys to see you—as a sex object? Or would you rather have a guy know you and care for you because of your character, not just your outward beauty?
>
> I love seeing girls who dress in a way that is not disrespectful to themselves. Girls, God tells us to be holy and pure with our bodies. Even though our culture tells you it's OK to wear clothing that is sexy or almost nonexistent, I want to challenge you to walk a different road. There are plenty of ways to be hip and trendy and to look great without being seductive or flirtatious.[22]

Now, my friend, let's both agree "to walk a different road" when it comes to our dress. Let's be holy and pure and modest in our dress.

A Word About Your Mind

Where do impure thoughts and interests come from? Well, it's obvious they come from the flesh (Galatians 5:19)! But where else? They come from the world, from what we see on TV and in movies, from what we read in magazines and in books, and from what we hear from others. Such information is then planted in our minds.

Beloved, God calls you and me as His women to obliterate impure thoughts from our minds. What does He say to think on instead of sensuous and worldly thoughts? "Whatever is *pure*...think about such things" (Philippians 4:8)! God also tells us that our impure thoughts reveal an impure heart—"Out of the *heart* come evil thoughts...adultery, sexual immorality" (Matthew 15:19). Did you catch it? Our thoughts are a matter of the *heart!* So do a quick heart check—what do you think about? And what do you think about others? Is it pure? Then heed God's advice:

> *How can a young man [or woman] keep his way pure? By living according to your word. I seek you with all my* heart; *do not let me stray from your commands. I have hidden your word in my* heart *that I might not sin against you* (Psalm 119:9-11).

A Word About Your Mouth

And here's another lesson about purity—God's Word says "Do not let any unwholesome talk come out of your mouths." What are we to talk about instead? That which "is helpful for building others up" (Ephesians 4:29). Whether we acknowledge it or not, what we allow ourselves to think will sooner or later be expressed by our mouths. Our thoughts lead to words. It's just as Jesus said, "Out of the overflow of the *heart* the mouth speaks" (Matthew 12:34). (Did you catch it again—our speech is also a matter of the heart!) To sum up what we are learning, I immediately think of these simple words of caution:

> Be careful, little eyes, what you see,
> Be careful, little ears, what you hear,
> Be careful, little mind, what you think,
> Be careful, little mouth, what you say,
> If you want to grow.

A Word About Your Parents

If being a teenager is difficult, then you've got to realize that being the *parent* of a teenager is difficult, too. But remember that no one knows you better, loves you more, or wants your best more than your parents. That's why I'll say it again—heed their guidelines when it comes to your relationships and their standards for your purity, and desire their approval of your friends of both sexes and your activities.

A Word About Your Standards

On this matter I have a very brief word for you—*set* your standards, and set them *high!* When my daughters were in grade school, Jim asked them to write down the kind of man they thought God wanted them to marry. Then, as the years passed, and cute, cool, popular guys began to flow through their lives, Jim would get out the lists the girls had written and ask, "Does this guy meet your standards?" I urge you to do the same thing. As I said, *set* your standards, and set them *high!* (And while you're at it, set standards for yourself, for the kind of godly woman this godly man would want for a wife!)

A Word About Your Body

Your physical purity is important to God. Why? Because...

- Your body is a temple—"Do you not know that your body is a temple of the Holy Spirit, who is in you?" (1 Corinthians 6:19).

- Your body is not your own—"You are not your own" (1 Corinthians 6:19).

- Your body is bought with a price—"You were bought at a price" (1 Corinthians 6:20). And what was that price? "The precious blood of Christ" (1 Peter 1:19).

- Your body is to honor and glorify God—"Honor God with your body" (1 Corinthians 6:20). Therefore, "it is God's will that you should be sanctified; that you should avoid sexual immorality; that each of you should learn to control his own body in a way that is holy and honorable, not in passionate lust" (1 Thessalonians 4:3-5).

A Word About Your Friends

Don't forget to choose your friends wisely! They will make all the difference in the world in your purity. God's Word says you are to "pursue righteousness, faith, love and peace, along with those who call on the Lord out of a pure heart" (2 Timothy 2:22). Remember...no friends is better than the wrong friends!

A Word About the World

The Bible urges you and me as His cherished women, "Do not conform any longer to the pattern of this world" (Romans 12:2)! It's soooo easy for us to be conformed to the standards and morals of our society. Therefore...

- You must be "transformed by the renewing of your mind" (Romans 12:2).
- You must not "love the world or anything in the world" (1 John 2:15).
- You must "flee the evil desires of youth" (2 Timothy 2:22).
- You must not pattern our lives after those "who do not know God" (1 Thessalonians 4:5).
- You must remember that you are *in* the world, but not *of* the world (John 17:14,16).

A Word About Your Future

God has a plan for your life, even for your life right now as a young single woman. What is it?

> *An unmarried woman or virgin is concerned about the Lord's affairs: Her aim is to be devoted to the Lord in both body and spirit* (1 Corinthians 7:34).

God's plan for you is that you keep yourself pure in body and mind and that you serve Him. *God* is to be the consuming priority of your life. You are His child. Therefore you are to live for Him and according to His Word. You are to live the way *He* wants you to live. And not only are you to keep yourself pure in body and in mind for God *now* as a single, but you are also to keep yourself pure in body and in mind for a future husband, if marriage is God's will for your future.

A Word About Your Looks

We couldn't have a book for women and not say something about our looks, could we? However, it's interesting that the Bible contains very little about our outward appearance. Perhaps that's because the Bible is a spiritual book and focuses our attention on the "inner" man and woman (2 Corinthians 4:16).

But there are definite ways you and I can take care of our looks. And God does comment on the outward appearance of some of the women of the Bible. For instance...

- Sarah was called a beautiful woman by her husband Abraham (Genesis 12:11).
- Both Rebekah and Rachel were described as beautiful of form and face (Genesis 24:16 and 29:17).

- The exquisite Esther took care of her appearance, dressed with care, and "won the favor of everyone who saw her" (Esther 2:15).

- We don't know what the Proverbs 31 woman looked like, but we do know that her clothes were special—fine silk and purple (Proverbs 31:22).

It seems clear that beauty and the care of your appearance has a place in your daily life. Don't worry so much about what you look like. You look exactly as God meant you to look (Psalm 139:14). But you can make an effort in the care of your appearance. So fix up...a little! Make up... a little! Dress up...a little! Shape up...a little! Others will be most grateful.

But never forget these words from the Bible: "Charm is deceptive, and beauty is fleeting; but a woman who fears the LORD is to be praised" (Proverbs 31:30). Friend, it's what's inside that counts! So make sure what's inside is pure. And make sure what's on the outside (your clothes, your conduct) reflects that purity.

A Word About Forgiveness

Just a word of encouragement—everyone fails. The Bible says "*all* have sinned and fall short of the glory of God" (Romans 3:23). That *all* means you, and that *all* means me. *All!* But thanks be to God, He extends His forgiveness to us when we fail. Dear heart, you can enjoy God's forgiveness for past, present, or future sin. Just follow the two steps we discussed in chapter 5:

- Confess your sin (1 John 1:9).
- Forsake your sin (Proverbs 28:13).

These two steps represent our heartfelt response to our sinful actions. But aren't we thankful that God has done His part by sending His Son to die for our sins? Because of Jesus' death on our behalf, we have His forgiveness. "He is faithful and just and will forgive us our sins and purify us from all unrighteousness" (1 John 1:9).

Heart Response

As you can tell, your purity is highly important throughout every day and every phase of your life. It's at the core of what makes you a woman after God's own heart. It's an issue of heart and mind and character.

Now, let's give much prayer (and action!) to these few practical ways to ensure our own purity as we look upward to God and to His divine, dazzling, holy purity.

✓ **A**cknowledge God's standard.

✓ **A**ssume God's standard as your standard.

✓ **A**dmit any and all sin against God's standard.

✓ **A**void compromising situations.

✓ **A**void compromising people.

✓ **A**sk for accountability.

✓ **A**cknowledge the consequences impurity reaps.

✓ **A**spire to a life of obedience—a holy life has a voice!

Things to Do Today to Develop a Heart Marked by Purity

♡ Look up the words "pure" and "purity" in an English dictionary. Write out the definitions. Then put them into your own words.

- ♡ Just for one day, monitor your thoughts and conversations. What did you discover? Were they pure? Do you need to make any changes? What changes?

- ♡ As you think about the words we've been covering in this chapter regarding purity, can you pinpoint any areas of your life that would not pass a purity test? Go through the "steps for forgiveness" and then make radical changes!

- ♡ Pray the prayer on the next page as often as you need to in order to help you remain pure in body, soul, and spirit.

My Prayer for Purity

Lord...

I give You all the desires of my heart—
may You bring them into line with
Your perfect will.

I give You my mind—
may it be filled with thoughts that could be brought
into Your holy presence.

I give You my mouth—
may I speak only that which honors You,
encourages others, and reveals a pure heart.

I give You my body—
may I keep my body pure so that it is
a holy and honorable vessel, fit for Your use.

I give You my friendships with young men—
may I set my heart on purity.
May You have authority over all my passions.

I give myself afresh to You.
Take my life and let it be
ever, always, pure for Thee.

Would You Like to Know More? Check It Out

✓ Read (or better yet, memorize!) Psalm 119:9-11. What question is asked, and what answer(s) is given? What is God's message to your heart? And what will you do about it?

✓ During the next month read one chapter of the book of Proverbs each day, the chapter that corresponds to the date of the month. As you read, make two lists—a list of the character traits and actions of "the wise man or woman" and a list of the character traits and actions of "the foolish man or woman." Your goal is to take note of the kind of person you are and want to be, the kind of people you want for friends, the kind of friend you want to be, and the kind of man you would want to marry.

Part Three

The Practice of God's Priorities

15

A Heart That Belongs to God

Set your hearts on things above,
where Christ is seated at
the right hand of God.

COLOSSIANS 3:1

Congratulations! You made it! Thank you soooo much for hanging in there with me. I know we've covered a lot of ground. But my goal in writing this book was to look at the major areas of your life as a young woman and then see what God says about each one of them in His Word. Then you would have, as the cover of your book says, "a guide to friends, faith, family, and the future." Hopefully by now you have a better understanding of God's guidelines for each of these important areas of your life.

And now it's your turn. It's your turn to make these truths real in your own life. I know you want to. So please, I beg you, don't hold back. Follow the three steps—my three final words to you—that follow. They are meant to help you set your heart on things above, where Christ is seated at the right hand of God (Colossians 3:1).

Final Word #1: Kick It Up!

When I say "Kick It Up!" I'm referring to the catch-phrase used by Chef Emeril on his televised cooking program on The Food Channel. This chef has a *very* dynamic personality (and that's putting it mildly!). And when he's preparing food, he teaches his audience that there is food...and then there is *food!* He instructs those who cook that they can fix food that is okay...or they can fix food that knocks the socks off of those who eat it, food that is outstanding, above par, off the scale, in another category. How can one accomplish this? Chef Emeril says it's simple—just "kick it up a notch!" Just add the spices that kick up the flavor. Go over the edge with seasonings that make each dish memorable, the best it can be.

Well, my faithful reading friend, as we end our time together in this book about being a young woman after God's own heart, that's what I want for you (and me, too). When it comes to developing a heart that belongs to God, I want you to "kick it up a notch" and be forever kicking it up a notch. I want you to "*love* the Lord your God with *all* your heart and with *all* your soul and with *all* your strength and with *all* your mind" just like Jesus said to do in Luke 10:27. I want you to love *Him* more than you love anyone else or anything else in your life, including yourself.

I'm going to ask you to dream about your future in a minute, but do you want to know what my dream for you is? I dream (and hope and pray) that you will sell-out to Christ—now, not later. That you will step over any and all lines to follow Christ—now, not later. That you will passionately and wholeheartedly embrace His plan for your life and that you will live that plan "to the hilt"! That you will be consumed with living for God and serving the Lord—now, not later.

Oh, precious one, don't tolerate any holding patterns in your life or your spiritual growth. Don't put your heart on hold. Don't wait for something to happen, to change, to pass, or to improve. You don't have a day…or even a minute!…to lose. I just finished reading again a book written by a woman I heard speak at my church some years ago. It's a book that details the death of her lovely teenage daughter Kathi. And the title of the book? *18…No Time to Waste*. Dear one, Kathi was 18 when she and two other teenagers were killed in a car wreck.[23] So my plea to you is, don't wait on anything—sell out *now*. Kick it up a notch *now*. Do whatever you have to do to be a woman whose heart belongs to God *now*. Truly, there is no time to waste.

Final Word #2: Look Up!

A woman with a heart that belongs to God makes sure that her relationship with God is growing each day by looking to God through His Word and by praying. This is the upward look, dear heart. As you look to God for His wisdom, guidance, and strength each day by looking into His Word, and as you look to Him about the course of your life through prayer, you look up. You look full into His wonderful heart.

That's what the Word of God is, you know—it's His heart. And reading God's Word is how you can hear His heart. David put it this way in one of his psalms: "The plans of the LORD stand firm forever, the purposes of his heart through all generations" (Psalm 33:11). Another translation refers to the Word of the Lord as "the counsel of the LORD" that stands forever and as "the thoughts of his heart" extended to all generations (KJV)—even yours. As your heart and soul looks up, you are marvelously transformed and conformed into the likeness of His dear Son (1 Corinthians 4:18 and Romans 8:29).

Now here's an assignment for you, shot straight from God's heart to yours—"set your hearts on things above, where Christ is seated at the right hand of God. Set your minds on things above, not on earthly things" (Colossians 3:1-2). So exactly how do we set our hearts on things above? How do we resist the pull of earthly things? Answer: We look up. We look into God's Word. And we pray.

In years past sailors guided their ships with the aid of the stars. As they looked up, they could get their bearings and chart their path by studying the positioning of the stars. But when it was cloudy and the stars were hidden from sight, these seafarers became hopelessly lost because they had no point of reference. It's the same way for you and me. When we look up into the face of God by prayerfully reading and studying His Word, we have a point of reference to guide the ship of our life. Otherwise, we can become hopelessly lost.

I'm sure you've heard Christians give testimonies saying things like...

I wandered off the path…

I became like the prodigal son…

I fell away from the Lord…

I got sidetracked in sin…

I lost my first love…

I strayed from the truth…

I made some wrong decisions…

I went off the deep end…

I got in with the wrong crowd…

Do you ever wonder, *What happened?* How does someone wander off the path? How does a prodigal become a prodigal? How do we become sidetracked? How does one lose his or her first love, stray from the truth, begin making wrong decisions and mistakes? What leads up to going off the deep end, leaving the flock of God, choosing a lifestyle of wallowing in the mire, and eating the husks meant for pigs, like the prodigal did?

We both know what happened, don't we? Somehow, at some time, for some reason, God's Word took a secondary place to other pursuits. The lesser choices were made regarding how time was spent, until time was not taken each day to develop a passion for knowing God's plan and for following after His heart.

So look up! Prayerfully read your Bible each and every day. This one act will reveal the direction you are headed in, will point you in the direction you must go, and will help you to make the needed corrections along the way.

Beloved, at the heart of a woman seeking to live out God's plan for her life is a passion for God's Word. And when you and I fail to purposefully and willfully develop this passion, we begin to spend our precious time and days on lesser pursuits...which can lead to wandering off the path of God's purpose for our lives and out of His will. Therefore do whatever it takes to develop a passion for God's Word and the disciplines that will fuel in your heart an intense passion for the Bible.

Final Word #3: Dream On!

Motivation is key when it comes to nurturing a heart of devotion, and dreaming helps motivate us. As a wake-up call to the seriousness of daily life and to find fresh urgency about your walk with the Lord, I would like to ask you as we end our time together to dream, to *dream of being a woman after God's heart!* So to get your dreaming muscles into motion, here are a few exercises. Send up a heartfelt prayer to God and then let the answers put wings on your dreams.

- ♡ *Describe the woman you want to be spiritually in one year.* Do you realize that within one year you could attack a weak area in your Christian life and gain the victory? You could read through the entire Bible. You could be discipled by an older woman—or disciple a younger sister in Christ yourself (Titus 2:3-5). You could attend a Bible study for a dozen months. You could read 12 quality Christian books. And, of course, you could finish another year of school. But what *kind* of year?

♡ *Describe the woman you want to be spiritually in ten years.* Jot down your age right here right now. Just write it in the margin. Then add ten years to that figure and write that number down, too. Are you shocked? I mean, you are looking at a number that represents one year of your life multiplied ten times! Not to mention the multitude of new stages and phases that you'll pass through and enter between now and then. I admit, it's staggering!

> Imagine now what those intervening ten years might hold, and you'll see that you will need God for the events of those years! You will need God to help you overcome areas of sin and grow spiritually. You will need Him in order to be His kind of daughter and sister. You will need Him to help you remain pure. You will need Him when you become a wife (if that's His will). And perhaps a mom (again, if that's His will). You will need Him should you continue being single (once again, if that's His will). You will need God to help you successfully serve others. You will need God if you enter college, Christian service, or the work force. And, dear one, you will need God should you die, if, like Kathi, that is God's plan for you. After all, yours is not only a heart but a *life* that belongs to God!

Do you believe you can be this woman? With God's grace and in His strength you can! That's His role in your life.

But there is also a place for your effort. As Scripture says, "[*You*] guard your heart, for it is the wellspring of life" (Proverbs 4:23). *You* determine some elements of the heart. *You* decide what you will or will not do, whether you will or will not grow. *You* also decide the rate at which you will grow—the hit-and-miss rate, the measles rate (a sudden rash here and there), the five-minutes-a-day rate, or the 30-minutes-a-day rate. *You* decide if you want to be a mushroom—which appears for a night and shrivels away at the first hint of wind or heat—or an oak tree, which lasts and lasts and lasts, becoming stronger and mightier with each passing year. So my question to you is, How far...and how fast...do you want to move toward becoming the woman of your dreams, a woman after God's own heart?

Heart Response

Well, my precious young traveling companion, here we are—two women with hearts after God, dreaming of "more love to Thee, O Christ, more love to Thee!" Here we stand, after looking to God's Word to find out what His heart's desire is for our hearts. Oh, what joy is ours when we submit ourselves to God and allow Him to grow in us hearts that truly belong to Him.

The future is yours, my cherished sister. My prayer for you (and me!) is that beginning today you will live each day as a woman after God's own heart. Then, precious one, every day will be beautiful in Him and for Him...until your days lived for Him are strung together to become a beautiful lifetime of living as a woman after God's own heart! And, oh, what a life that will be!

Quiet Times Calendar

Jan.	Feb.	Mar.	Apr.	May	June
1	1	1	1	1	1
2	2	2	2	2	2
3	3	3	3	3	3
4	4	4	4	4	4
5	5	5	5	5	5
6	6	6	6	6	6
7	7	7	7	7	7
8	8	8	8	8	8
9	9	9	9	9	9
10	10	10	10	10	10
11	11	11	11	11	11
12	12	12	12	12	12
13	13	13	13	13	13
14	14	14	14	14	14
15	15	15	15	15	15
16	16	16	16	16	16
17	17	17	17	17	17
18	18	18	18	18	18
19	19	19	19	19	19
20	20	20	20	20	20
21	21	21	21	21	21
22	22	22	22	22	22
23	23	23	23	23	23
24	24	24	24	24	24
25	25	25	25	25	25
26	26	26	26	26	26
27	27	27	27	27	27
28	28	28	28	28	28
29		29	29	29	29
30		30	30	30	30
31		31		31	

DATE BEGUN ____________________

July	Aug.	Sept.	Oct.	Nov.	Dec.
1	1	1	1	1	1
2	2	2	2	2	2
3	3	3	3	3	3
4	4	4	4	4	4
5	5	5	5	5	5
6	6	6	6	6	6
7	7	7	7	7	7
8	8	8	8	8	8
9	9	9	9	9	9
10	10	10	10	10	10
11	11	11	11	11	11
12	12	12	12	12	12
13	13	13	13	13	13
14	14	14	14	14	14
15	15	15	15	15	15
16	16	16	16	16	16
17	17	17	17	17	17
18	18	18	18	18	18
19	19	19	19	19	19
20	20	20	20	20	20
21	21	21	21	21	21
22	22	22	22	22	22
23	23	23	23	23	23
24	24	24	24	24	24
25	25	25	25	25	25
26	26	26	26	26	26
27	27	27	27	27	27
28	28	28	28	28	28
29	29	29	29	29	29
30	30	30	30	30	30
31	31		31		31

Notes

1. Carole Mayhall, *From the Heart of a Woman* (Colorado Springs: NavPress, 1976), pp. 10-11.
2. Slightly adapted from Ray and Anne Ortlund, *The Best Half of Life* (Glendale, CA: Regal Books, 1976), pp. 24-25.
3. Ray and Anne Ortlund, *The Best Half of Life,* p. 79.
4. Jim Downing, *Meditation, The Bible Tells You How* (Colorado Springs: NavPress, 1976), pp. 15-16.
5. Robert D. Foster, *The Navigator* (Colorado Springs: NavPress, 1983), pp. 110-11.
6. Corrie ten Boom, *Don't Wrestle, Just Nestle* (Old Tappan: NJ: Fleming H. Revell Company, 1978), p. 79.
7. Oswald Chambers, *Christian Disciplines* (Grand Rapids, MI: Discovery House Publishers, 1995), p. 117.
8. Curtis Vaughan, ed., *The Old Testament Books of Poetry from 26 Translations* (Grand Rapids, MI: Zondervan Bible Publishers, 1973), pp. 478-79.
9. Curtis Vaughan, ed., *The Old Testament Books of Poetry,* p. 277.
10. Edith Schaeffer, *What Is a Family?* (Old Tappan, NJ: Fleming H. Revell Company, 1975).
11. *God's Words of Life for Teens* (Grand Rapids, MI: The Zondervan Corporation/Inspirio, 2000), p. 71.
12. *Life Application Bible* (Wheaton, IL: Tyndale House Publishers, Inc. and Youth for Christ/USA, 1988), p. 128.
13. Eleanor L. Doan, ed., *The Speaker's Sourcebook* (Grand Rapids, MI: Zondervan Publishing House, 1977), p. 176.
14. Annie Chapman, *10 Things I Want My Daughter to Know* (Eugene, OR: Harvest House Publishers, 2002), pp. 15-16.
15. *Life Application Bible,* p. 121.
16. Roy B. Zuck, *The Speaker's Quote Book* (Grand Rapids, MI: Kregel Publications, 1997), p. 174.
17. R. Kent Hughes, *Disciplines of a Godly Man* (Wheaton, IL: Crossway Books, 1991), pp. 62-63.
18. Roy B Zuck, *The Speaker's Quote Book,* p. 159.
19. Alice Gray, Steve Stephens, John Van Diest, *Lists to Live By: The Third Collection,* (Sisters, OR: Multnomah Publishers, 2001), p. 51.
20. Elisabeth Elliot, *Through Gates of Splendor* (Old Tappan, NJ: Fleming H. Revell Company, 1957).
21. Eleanor L. Doan, ed., *The Speaker's Sourcebook,* p. 114.
22. Jason Perry, *You Are Not Your Own* (Nashville: Broadman & Holman Publishers, 2002), p. 109.
23. Margaret Johnson, *18...No Time to Waste* (Grand Rapids, MI: Zondervan Publishing House, 1971).

A Young Woman's Call to Prayer

Elizabeth George

HARVEST HOUSE PUBLISHERS
EUGENE, OREGON

Harvest House Publishers has made every effort to trace the ownership of all quotes. In the event of a question arising from the use of a quote, we regret any error made and will be pleased to make the necessary correction in future editions of this book.

Italicized text in Scripture quotations indicate author emphasis.

Acknowledgment

As always, thank you to my dear husband, Jim George, M.Div., Th.M., for your able assistance, guidance, suggestions, and loving encouragement on this project.

A YOUNG WOMAN'S WALK WITH GOD

Published by Harvest House Publishers
Eugene, Oregon 97402
www.harvesthousepublishers.com

Library of Congress Cataloging-in-Publication Data

George, Elizabeth, 1944-
A young woman's walk with God / Elizabeth George.
p. cm.
Includes bibliographical references (p.).
ISBN-13: 978-0-7369-1653-0 (pbk.)
ISBN-10: 0-7369-1653-9
1. Teenage girls—Religious life. 2. Christian teenagers—Religious life. I. Title.
BV4551.3.G47 2006
248.8'33—dc22 2005029083

Printed in the United States of America

Contents

An Invitation to...

Become a Young Woman of Prayer

Talking to God about the issues of your life is important...and prayer is the key! But if you're like most women—old or young!—you can use a little help with your prayer-life. That's why I've written this practical book—to help you make your desire to pray regularly a reality.

The journey to a dynamic and authentic prayer-life is an exciting adventure! First, you'll find out what God says about prayer in the Bible. It's awesome! You'll also enjoy stories from the hearts and lives of Bible characters. These people learned to pray...loved to pray...and witnessed the mighty effects of prayer and its impact on their relationship with God. Along with insights from my own prayer journey, I share inspiring examples of others who have answered God's call to prayer. You'll discover tips for revolutionizing your own personal prayer-life, including...

> ...*12 practical ways to become a woman of prayer*—You'll discover what to do...and what not to do. And you'll understand why prayer can be so difficult to do!

... *"My Checklists for Prayer"*—Each chapter gives three immediate prayer-steps you can take—today!—to make your dream of becoming a woman of prayer come true.

... *"Would You Like to Know More?"*—If you want to "put the icing on the cake" of prayer, you can grow even more by interacting with a few additional scriptures and questions. They are tailor-made just for you!

... *"Things I Don't Want to Forget"*—Every chapter has exciting life-changing suggestions for your everyday life...if you don't forget them! So to help you remember what speaks most to your heart, I've added a special page at the end of each chapter for you to journal or record your thoughts and "take-away truths." Your written personal insights will become a testimony of your spiritual growth, a cherished keepsake you can refer to in the days, months, and even years ahead.

... *"My Prayer Calendar"*—I've also put a reproducible prayer calendar at the back of this book. It will help you see how you're becoming a woman of prayer. Be sure you make a photocopy because you'll want to use it year after year...and share it with your friends!

Dear praying friend, as you grow in prayer, and as prayer becomes more and more a part of your life, you'll find God becoming your closest friend. And you'll find He can help you with *everything* that's important in your life right now and always—your family, your friends, your school, and your dreams for the future.

So journey on! Read and study this book alone, or go through it with a friend, a mentor, or in a group. Whichever way you choose, you'll be blessed. Why? Because prayer is the "highest activity of which the human spirit is capable."[1] Through prayer you...

—worship God...and express your love for Him,

—bring your needs before God...and see how He answers, and

—talk one-on-one with the God of the universe...about your life.

My precious new friend, I am praying for you right now as you answer God's call...to pray!

In His great and amazing love,
Your friend and sister in Christ,

Elizabeth George

Making Your Desire to Pray a Reality

1

Beginning Your Journey into Prayer

Prayer.

Just say the word and I begin to yearn and squirm at the same time. As a woman after God's own heart, I *yearn* to pray. My soul longs for it. My spirit craves communion with my heavenly Father. My heart sings with the words of King David found in the Old Testament:

> As the deer pants for streams of water, so my soul pants for you, O God....My soul thirsts for you; my body longs for you" (Psalm 42:1; 63:1).

And yet I also *squirm* at the thought of prayer. Why? Because even though prayer is a blessing, approaching our holy, holy, holy God is also an awesome thing. Then there is the search for time to get alone with God to talk with Him.

> "We're not talking to a brick wall when we pray—we're talking to Someone who really listens."[1]

What a battle! I know that I need to pray...and I want to pray! And yet the work and the discipline praying calls for is quite real! Do you, my dear new friend, share these same mixed feelings? Then let's decide to answer God's call to us to be women of prayer...no matter what! Let's embark on a journey together to learn more about prayer. Let's seek to live our lives "on bended knee."

Hearing God's Call to Prayer

On any journey, a first step must always be taken. What will your first step be? I remember my first step into seriously learning how to pray. It was on Mother's Day, May 8, 1983. My daughter Katherine (age 13) gave me the gift of a tiny wordless book. It was purple...and I still have it because it's a real keepsake to me. It's special, first of all, because my daughter gave it to me! (That really touches a mother's heart! Trust me on this one.)

Anyway, Katherine had the idea for the gift and arranged with Jim (my husband and Kath's dad) to do extra work chores to earn the money to purchase it for me. Then the two of them went off together to shop for just the right present for Mom. The little treasure was then inscribed by Katherine on the bookplate in her careful handwriting, lovingly gift wrapped, and proudly given to me on that Sunday morning so many years ago.

Oh, believe me, I screamed! I squealed! I did everything but turn cartwheels to express my thanks to my sweet daughter. But then I faced a problem—what to do with a wordless book. For several months I let the small book lie on the coffee table so my dear Katherine would know how much I truly appreciated it. Then one day, not knowing exactly what to do with it, I moved it into the bookcase...and it was gone forever....

...until September 12, four months later. That day was my tenth birthday in the Lord. As I sat alone before God, I looked back over my first ten years as God's child. Of course, that led to a time of thanking Him for His mercy, His grace, His care, His guidance, His wisdom, my salvation through Christ....

On and on my prayers of appreciation to God gushed. Then after dabbing my eyes with a tissue, I turned my thoughts forward and I prayed, "Lord, as I start a new decade with You, is there anything missing from my Christian life that I should focus on for the next ten years?"

Oh, dear friend, I can only report to you that before I put the question mark on the question, I knew in my heart what the answer was! It was *prayer*! And suddenly I knew I had "heard" God's call to prayer in my heart. And just as suddenly, I knew what to do with that tiny purple wordless book. I ran to the bookcase, pulled it out, opened it up, and wrote on the very first page:

> I dedicate and purpose to spend the next ten years in the Lord, Lord willing, developing a meaningful prayer life.

Making a Commitment

Why did I pick ten years for my commitment to develop a meaningful prayer life? Probably because it was my tenth birthday in Christ. And now 20 years have passed. And I want to tell to you right now—I am *still* learning how to pray! You know, you and I don't just wake up one day at the point where we can mark "learn to pray" off our to-do list! No, no one prays enough. And no one prays as passionately as she would like to pray or should pray. And no one prays for as many people as need to be prayed for.

"Lord, teach us to pray" (Luke 11:1).

And so we must continue on our journey into prayer until we "get it," until we can even say that we've *begun* to know even a little bit about prayer. And until that happens, a lot of Christians pray what I call "Christopher Robin" prayers. He's the little boy who struggled with his evening "Vespers."[2] Little Christopher became so distracted by anything and everything that he couldn't remember who or what to pray for. So he ended up praying "God bless ________" prayers, filling in the blank with the names of his family and friends.

Boy oh boy, can I ever relate to Christopher Robin's "prayer" experience! And maybe you can, too! That's exactly how I prayed...that is, before my commitment to answer God's call to pray. Yes, that's how I had prayed. And, like Christopher Robin, my mind wandered. I didn't know who to pray for...or how to pray for them. So my prayers basically consisted of lame efforts, until they finally wound down to a muttered "God bless me and my family today."

But, praise God, I can say that some progress has been made! I believe that my prayers and my prayer-life have improved. But I want to quickly say, "No, I have not yet arrived." Being a woman of prayer is still a daily challenge and constant struggle for me. And I imagine it will be that way until I see my Savior face-to-face.

In the chapters to come, we'll go deeper into what it means to answer God's call to prayer. But for now (and at the end of each chapter), I want you to pause and consider some practical steps you can take *right now.* They will help you to grow a heart for prayer and grow in your heart-relationship with God. I left some space for you to write your answers.

My Checklist for Prayer

✓ *Pray now!*—It's one thing to read about prayer. And oh, how we love to talk about prayer! And oh, how we dream about being women of prayer! But it's quite another thing to actually pray. So *Step 1* is this: Put your book down, grab a kitchen timer, and go somewhere where you can shut the door or be alone. Then pray for five minutes. Use these five golden minutes to pour out your heart's desire to your heavenly Father. Tell Him how much you love Him. And tell Him how much you long to answer His call upon your life to become—and be!—a woman of prayer. Then share here a little about what happened.

✓ *Get organized*—Round up some kind of notebook. It can be anything—a spiral pad, a three-ring binder, even a little wordless book. Whatever it is, do what you can to make your notebook personal and fun. Make it something you want to use. For instance, is your favorite color purple? Then make your prayer notebook a purple one! (And don't forget to include a pen with purple ink!) And don't worry about your choice being permanent. Also don't get hung up on needing to make the "right" choice. Just choose something—anything!—that will help you and inspire you to take your first steps down the path of your journey into prayer.

I just looked in my own little purple wordless book, and based on dates, I used it for ten weeks. Ten weeks is a l-o-n-g time, which means that little book was enough to launch my commitment to learn to pray. That also means using my book for ten weeks was long enough to show me I needed a different kind of notebook.

This will probably happen to you too, as you begin your prayer efforts. But be excited when it does! Praise God you are growing in your prayer skills…and look forward to creating a fresh, new, made-by-you prayer notebook.

Describe your current notebook or journal. What do you like about it? Do you need to make any improvements?

✓ *Look ahead*—Look over…and pray over…the next week on your calendar. What is the pattern of your life, your daily routine? What are your school and work commitments? What kind of time do you need for family and friends? Then mark on each day for the next week the exact time you will schedule as your prayer time. It can be the same time each day, or it can be customized to fit the demands and flow of each individual day.

Next mark your prayer appointments in ink on your calendar. Then, of course, be sure you keep them…just like you keep your dates with your friends! As one of my prayer principles says, "There is no right or wrong way to pray…except not to pray!"

For a place to record your prayer progress, I've provided a "My Prayer Calendar" in the back of this book. Just shade in the squares for the days you do pray, and leave those blank when you don't pray. And then, my dear praying friend, one picture is worth a thousand words! All you have to do is glance at the "My Prayer Calendar"…and the tale of your times in prayer will be told! Now, what tale will your efforts in prayer tell?

What do you dream will be true of your "Prayer Calendar"? And what can you do today to make your dream a reality?

✎ Answering God's Call to You

Prayer is truly the queen of all the habits we could desire as women of faith. As we leave this chapter about "Beginning Steps in Prayer," I want you to take this thought with you.

> He who has learned how to pray
> has learned the greatest secret
> of a holy and a happy life.[3]

I'm sure you caught the word "learned." But I hope and pray you also caught the reward, too. All of your learning and efforts in prayer will help lead you to "a holy and a happy life"! And the beautiful miracle is that a holy and a happy life can be yours each day...one day at a time...as you answer God's call to pray. So let the outpourings of your heart begin now—*today*! The opportunity and privilege of talking to God through prayer is yours...*if* that is the desire of your heart and *if* you act on that desire.

Now, what will your beginning steps be?

Would You Like to Know More? Check It Out!

We'll look at these topics later in our book, but for now, what do these verses from the Bible tell you about prayer and your prayer-life?

Matthew 6:6—

Matthew 7:7-8—

Luke 18:1—

Romans 12:12—

Ephesians 6:18—

Philippians 4:6-7—

Colossians 4:2—

1 Thessalonians 5:17—

1 Peter 3:12—

My Commitment to Prayer

What commitment to prayer will you make? Write it here. (And remember, it doesn't have to be long. Just a few sincere words can change a life…and a heart!)

(Signed)

(Date)

My List of Things I Don't Want to Forget...
...from This Chapter

2

What Keeps Me from Praying?

Why is it that so many of the things we as responsible women—young or old—must tend to in life are hard to do? And if they're not hard to do, they are at least hard to get started on? Take, for instance, getting out of bed in the morning. For me, this is one of those hard-to-do things (and I'm sure you agree!). Then begins a day-long list of people to see and places to go.

On and on the list of a busy gal's "musts" and "have-to's" goes—a list of important things that are necessary and that others depend on us to do.

But "The Most Vital and Important Thing" that we as God's women "must" get around to and "have to" include in our every day is *prayer*. No matter how difficult our personal and school work is, it is even harder to do the *spiritual* work of prayer! If we aren't careful, we can spend all day—and all night—doing less-important tasks—anything!—to put off the most-difficult-yet-most-rewarding "task" of all—praying.

There's not a doubt in our minds that prayer is critical to every part of our lives. So why is it so hard for us to pray?

After thinking through the Scriptures and looking at my own heart and life, I've discovered some reasons—and excuses—for not praying.

1. *Worldliness*—We live "in the world" (John 17:11), and the world affects us more than we think. It daily bombards us with "everything in the world—the cravings of sinful man, the lust of his eyes and the boasting of what he has and does," all of which "comes not from the Father but from the world" (1 John 2:16). Not one voice in the world is telling us to take care of spiritual things. And prayer is a *spiritual* exercise.

   So watch out for the world! Resist the world by watching in prayer (Matthew 26:41). As the hymn writer expressed it, "Turn your eyes upon Jesus…and the things of earth will grow strangely dim in the light of His glory and grace."[1]

2. *Busyness*—Another reason we don't pray is because we just don't take the time to pray. And usually the culprit is busyness. Don't get me wrong! The Bible says a strong work ethic is a mark of strong character.

   But the Bible also shows us in the story of two sisters named Martha and Mary that a priority order must be set between our *spiritual* duties and our *daily* duties. (You can read about them in Luke 10:38-42.) In a nutshell, Martha was a very busy woman who did a lot of good things…but carried them to such an extreme that she "lost it" on the glorious day when Jesus came to visit. She literally fell apart when her sister stopped her kitchen work to go sit at the feet of Jesus, God-in-flesh!

Both sisters loved Jesus, and both gladly served Him. But Mary knew when to stop with the busyness and do the best thing, the *one thing* that's most important—spend time with God. And, dear sister, you and I must do the same.

> "A woman who is too busy to pray is simply too busy!"

3. *Foolishness*—Whenever we become consumed with what is foolish and trivial, we will fail to pray. It's a given! And then what happens? We begin to lose our ability to know the difference between good and evil (Hebrews 5:14), between what is wise and foolish, between the essential and meaningless. And then what happens? We lose sight of *the* primary thing in life—our relationship with God! We foolishly spend our very limited and priceless time and energy on the "wrong" and inferior things. We fail to "seek first his kingdom and his righteousness" so all the other things we need in life can be given to us (Matthew 6:33).

   But, praise God, the opposite is true when we pray! God gives us wisdom—*His* wisdom! *He* helps us direct our energy, efforts, and time toward what truly matters in the big picture of life—living life as God means for it to be lived. He helps us remember that secondary things in life—comfort, security, money, fashion—come "not from the Father but from the world" and will most definitely "pass away" (1 John 2:16-17).

So pray, dear one! Commit your life to what *really* counts. Focus your life on the eternal, not the earthly! That's what the wise woman does—and it's done through prayer.

"He is no fool who gives what he cannot keep to gain what he cannot lose." —Jim Elliot

4. *Distance*—You can talk all day long with people you know really well, but you probably have difficulty talking even five minutes with a stranger. And the same thing happens in our communication with God. When you and I don't have a close enough relationship with God, we find it hard to talk to Him. So the solution is obvious—we must begin talking to God through prayer. We must "come near to God" (James 4:8).

   If for *any* reason you are putting off talking to God through prayer, make a step—*now!*—to reconnect. It's urgent! Don't put it off! God hasn't changed, disappeared, or withdrawn His love for you or stopped listening to you. No, if there's a problem, it is always with you and me. So, close the gap. Draw close to God. Simply take a step in prayer! He's waiting for you.

5. *Ignorance*—We don't really understand God's goodness or His desire and ability to provide for us "immeasurably more than all we ask or imagine"

(Ephesians 3:20) and to "meet all our needs" (Philippians 4:19). Therefore, we don't ask or pray. Yet the truth is that God wants to grant our requests, to give us the desires of our hearts, and to bless us. It's His nature. God is good, my friend! And God is a giving God (James 1:5). But God also wants us to ask.

- ❀ *Call to Me* and I will answer you and tell you great and unsearchable things you do not know (Jeremiah 33:3).
- ❀ *Ask* and it will be given to you…for everyone who asks receives (Matthew 7:7-8).

Dear one, answer God's call to pray and start asking! Ask boldly and passionately for the salvation of your family and friends (James 5:16). Ask earnestly for God's will as you make decisions (Acts 9:6). Ask for your daily needs at home, at school, at your job, and with your friends (Matthew 6:11). Cultivate the childlike faith of the little boy who, ready for bed, came in to announce to his family in the living room, "I'm going to say my prayers now. Anybody want anything?"

6. *Sinfulness*—We don't pray because we know we have sinned against our holy God. Adam and Eve hid themselves from God after they sinned (Genesis 3:8). And King David ceased praying and "kept silent" after he sinned (Psalm 32:3).

So what is the solution to our sinfulness? King David says, "Confess [your] transgressions to the LORD" (Psalm 32:5). James says, "Confess your sins" (James 5:16). John says also to "confess our sins" (1 John 1:9). And Jesus says to pray to God, asking Him to "forgive us" the wrongs we have done (Matthew 6:12). And then what happens? The floodgates of communion with God are again opened. As David put it, he was once again "clean...whiter than snow." And he experienced fresh and renewed joy (see Psalm 51:7-12).

So, as women who are called to prayer, we must not deny our sin, blame others for it, hide it, or excuse it. Instead, do as David did. He declared to God in his brokenness, "Against you, you only, have I sinned and done what is evil in your sight" (Psalm 51:4).

Oh, please! Don't forfeit your ability and your opportunity to pray for yourself, your family and friends, and those in need because of being too proud or stubborn to deal with sin! Too much is at stake—and at risk—to hold on to secret or "favorite" sins. Keep short accounts with God. Deal with any sin as it comes up—on the spot!—at the exact minute that you slip up and fail!

Remember, "the prayer of a *righteous* [woman] is powerful and effective" (James 5:16). In other words, the prayer of a godly woman—the one who seeks to walk in obedience, who confesses and forsakes sin (Proverbs 28:13)—brings powerful results.

7. *Faithlessness*—We don't really believe in the power of prayer. We don't think prayer makes any difference…therefore we don't pray. And yet our Lord taught that when you and I ask according to His will, "if you believe, you will receive whatever you ask for in prayer" (Matthew 21:22). If you are running low in faith, do as Jesus' disciples did. Ask God to "increase" your faith (Luke 17:5)!

8. *Pridefulness*—Prayer reflects our dependence on God. When wc fail to pray, we are saying that we don't have any needs…or worse, we are saying, "God, I'll take care of it myself, thank You!" However, God calls out, "If my people who are called by my name, will humble themselves and pray and seek my face and turn from their wicked ways, then will I hear from heaven" (2 Chronicles 7:14).

   So let's be quick to humble ourselves—to bow both heart and knee—and pray to God. Let's pray as David did: "Search me, O God…see if there is any offensive way in me" (Psalm 139:23-24). Let's enjoy the blessings that come from a humble heart.

> "The LORD is close to the brokenhearted" (Psalm 34:18).

9. *Inexperience*—We don't pray because…we don't pray! And because we don't pray, we don't know how to pray…so we don't pray! It's a vicious cycle. Yet prayer, like any skill, becomes easier when repeated. The more we pray, the more we know

how to pray. And the more we know how to pray, the more we pray. It's as simple as that.

And in case you're feeling like you are the only person who ever lived who's had difficulty praying, I want to quickly tell you that you're not! Even those closest to Jesus—His disciples—had the same problem. They watched Jesus pray. They heard Jesus pray. They even heard Jesus pray for them! Finally they went to the Master Pray-er Himself and asked, "Lord, teach us to pray" (Luke 11:1).

Pray this same prayer for yourself, dear younger sister. Pray, "Lord, teach *me* to pray!" But also take the first step and start praying...and keep praying, even when you don't feel like it, even when you think it doesn't make any difference, even if you don't know what you are doing or fear you are doing it badly. Pray! Break the cycle!

> "It is sheer nonsense to imagine we can learn the high art of communing with the Lord without setting aside time for it."[2]

10. *Laziness*—We admit that the nine obstacles to a powerful prayer life that we've discussed so far are prayer killers. But even if we overcome these nine reasons for not praying, this tenth one—laziness—will make or break us in the Prayer Department!

    We've both been there and done that when it comes to laziness, right? I know I had to break some bad habits that were robbing me of the time I needed to become a woman of prayer. Two simple acts helped me move forward in beating laziness...and they still work. Take them yourself!

First is my principle of "Head for bed." As soon as dinner is over I start getting ready for bed. I finish my work (for you that's homework), wash my face and brush my teeth, check my schedule for the next day and begin a "to-do" list for tomorrow, and then get into my pj's. Then I set out my prayer notebook and Bible in the place where I will (Lord willing!) have my devotions the next morning. You see, I'm on a mission—to get to bed as early as possible...so I can get up in the morning, as early as possible, and meet with God.

Second is my principle of "Something is better than nothing." I had to stop looking for the "sweet hour of prayer" and try for something more realistic. I started with "a sweet five minutes of prayer." Then, in time, as I began to taste the fruits of time spent in prayer, I graduated, little by little, to greater lengths of time spent on bended knee.

My Checklist for Prayer

✓ *Check your heart*—Check your daily input. And check your environment. What...or who...is influencing you? And is it influencing you positively for the things of God?

I know that as a young Christian I had to turn my back on some of the most popular women's magazines. The more I read my Bible and prayed, the more I realized those magazines were feeding me a steady diet of worldliness. Sure there was some practical help there. But overall, the messages were the exact opposite of the messages God's Word was sending to my heart.

Now, how can you "turn your eyes upon Jesus" so that the things of this world will grow steadily more dim? Identify three things you can do to turn your back on the world and your heart toward spiritual things—toward God.

✓ *Check your relationship with God*—Ask yourself, "Am I praying regularly?" If your answer is *yes,* praise God...and continue on in your faithfulness. However, if your answer is *no,* ask "Why? What happened?" Then run through the list of reasons on the next page and circle the culprit that is robbing you of tending to your relationship and friendship with God. Identify the Number One excuse you are allowing to keep you from prayer.

neglect	bitterness
laziness	putting it off
sin	other interests
pride	other reasons

I'm sure you know the next step: Stop right now, bow your head and your heart before God, admit your failure to pray...and then pray, even if just for five minutes. Or, put another way, what excuses have you been using for neglecting to pray? Remember, God is waiting for you! What would you like to talk over and settle with Him now?

✓ *Check your desire*—In almost every TV or radio interview I take part in concerning prayer, I'm usually asked to share one step a woman can take right away to begin making prayer a reality in her life. And my answer is always the same—"She must desire it!" Dear one, all said and done, we must desire to pray, desire to be women of prayer, desire to answer God's call to pray.

You see, you and I can know we need to pray, and we can learn the skills involved in praying. Yet, if we never desire to pray, our knowledge and skills mean nothing. Praying will never become a habit or a discipline if the one main ingredient—desire!—is missing. How do you rate your Desire Quotient?

None at all?	So-so?
Getting there?	Red hot?

How could you increase the level of your desire to pray? What do you think would help?

✎ Answering God's Call to You

We've spent a great deal of time, space, and effort looking at the reasons you and I don't pray. So now we wonder, *How does a woman after God's own heart (that's you!) answer God's high calling to pray?* Believe it or not, it's not as difficult as you think. Once you begin to tend to your heart and to the issues that keep you from praying...

Prayer is so simple;
It is like quietly opening a door
And slipping into the very presence of God,
There is the stillness
To listen to His voice;
Perhaps to petition,
Or only to listen:
It matters not.
Just to be there
In His presence
Is prayer.[3]

Now, won't you slip into the very presence of God? He's waiting for you to talk with Him about your life.

Would You Like to Know More? Check It Out!

Read 1 John 2:15-17. How does the world tempt us? What will ultimately happen to the things of the world?

How did Jesus say to handle the temptations the world throws at you (Matthew 26:41)?

Read Luke 10:38-42. What do you see these two sisters doing that was good? What problem did Martha have? What did Jesus say to her? What did Jesus say about Mary? How can you make the same choice Mary made?

Read Psalm 32:1-5. What happens when you don't confess your sin to God? What happens when you do? What does 1 John 1:9 say happens when you do?

Read Luke 11:1-4. What was the scene in verse 1? How did Jesus answer His disciples? What do you like most about "The Lord's Prayer"? What can you add to your prayers from Jesus' model prayer?

My List of Things I Don't Want to Forget…
…from This Chapter

Praying from the Heart

3

When You Are in Trouble or in Need...Pray!

What is prayer? Referring to prayer as "the pathway to the heart of God," my friend and author Terry Glaspey writes,

> To ask the question, "What is prayer?"...probes not only the mysteries of what it means to be a human being, but even inquires into the mystery of God Himself.... Because it is a topic too deep for the human intellect, it requires that we look to God as our teacher.[1]

And this, my young praying friend, is exactly what you and I must do right now! We must look to God's Word—the Bible—for *God's* definition of prayer. At the same time we must not forget that prayer is a part of "the mystery of God Himself." That means we will never completely understand it.

Think of prayer as being like a gem with many facets carved into it, each one being beautiful and brilliant, making the gem truly magnificent. In this chapter we'll examine two of prayer's exciting facets, two slightly different kinds of prayer.

In Times of Trouble...Pray!

First of all, when you are in trouble you are to pray. And by "trouble" I don't mean when you've done something wrong. (We'll deal with that later.) No, this is the kind of prayer for those times when you have a big problem and desperately need God's intervention.

That's when we ask God for help. As Philippians 4:6 tells us, "Do not be anxious about anything, but in everything, by prayer and petition, with thanksgiving, present your requests to God." Clearly we are to cry "*Help!*" when we are troubled by someone, something...or anything! We are to go to *God* and pray to *Him* for help with our needs...like the young woman Esther did.

Queen Esther faced trouble—Queen Esther's story is told in the book of the Bible called Esther. And when the beautiful Esther faced trouble, she went to God and talked things over with Him. Here's what happened...

In order to save the lives of God's people, Queen Esther had to risk her life by approaching her husband, the king. However, coming uninvited into the presence of the king was punishable by death...and Esther hadn't been called for. Therefore, Esther fasted for three days and nights before she acted. Then, and only then, did Esther humbly draw near to the only person who could possibly help her and her people (the Jews). The Scriptures report that Esther went to the king to beg for mercy and plead with him for her people."

And the end of the story? God went to work in the shadows of the night and set in motion a fantastic series of events that led to the salvation of His people!

King Hezekiah faced trouble—Hezekiah, king of Judah, also prayed to God in a time of great trouble. Briefly, Sennacherib, ruler of Assyria, sent a letter to King Hezekiah threatening him and putting down "the living God."

What did the king do? Hezekiah took the letter, "spread it out before the LORD," and asked for God's help. He pleaded, "O LORD our God, deliver us from his hand" (2 Kings 19:19).

And the end of the story? The answer to Hezekiah's prayers to God for help? God Himself said, "*I* will defend this city and save it" (verse 34).

And we can't stop there! Oh, no! The next verse reports, "That night the angel of the LORD went out and put to death a hundred and eighty-five thousand men in the Assyrian camp. When the people got up the next morning—there were all the dead bodies!" (verse 35).

Now, *that's* an answer to prayer!

Jesus spoke of trouble—Jesus also tells us to pray in times of trouble. He "told His disciples a parable...that they should always pray and not give up" (Luke 18:1). Praying instead of giving up means looking to God in times of trouble. This kind of praying keeps us from caving in.

And what causes a cave-in? Weakness on one side and pressure on another. When the going gets rough, we are not to faint, lose heart, give in, give up, and cave in. Instead we are to pray to God, trust God, and move forward.

"He who kneels most stands best."
—D.L. MOODY

Dear heart, in times of trouble...pray! You can always pray in helplessness, when you can't do anything else. So put your prayer-weapon to good use in your times of trouble.

I once read a story about a young boy who was saved from drowning by his brother and carried home unconscious by his group of friends. The grateful father wanted to know exactly who had done what so he could properly thank each child. So he said to John...

"Well, John, what did you do?" He replied, "Oh, I jumped into the water and pulled him out!"

"And James and Thomas, what did you do?" questioned the dad.

"Oh, we carried Danny home!"

"And Mary, what did you do?" came the next inquiry.

And poor little Mary, who was only three years old, burst into tears and said, "Daddy, I couldn't do anything at all, so I just prayed and prayed!"

Then her father gently said, "Mary, you deserve the most praise of all, for you did all you could, and God answered your prayers through John and James and Thomas."

My friend, in times of trouble...when you can't do anything at all...just pray and pray! Turn to God in prayer during the tough times, when you don't know where else to go or what else to do.

In Times of Need...Pray!

I'm sure you're like me—you have an extremely l-o-n-g list of things you need to talk over with God—issues, school problems, people problems, parent problems, boy- or girlfriend problems, loneliness problems. As you and I well know, we encounter trouble daily. Plus we get hurt by others. And we can become overwhelmed by the stresses and pains of life. Add to this list our doubts and worries about ourselves and our lives, and it's easy to see our tremendous need for prayer!

So what can we do? This next facet in God's jewel of prayer gives us instruction regarding the personal needs of our hearts and lives as God's women: In times of need... pray!

Think again about Philippians 4:6. Here God tells us that "in everything, by prayer and petition, with thanksgiving, present your requests to God." We are told to "pray in the Spirit on all occasions with all kinds of prayers and requests" (Ephesians 6:18). In other words, there is something you can—and should!—do about the pressing needs in your life, your family, your friendships, your schooling, your job, and your everyday life: You are to pray to God about your *specific* needs—to talk over the *specific* needs in your life with Him, with the God of the universe! For instance,

- Jesus told His followers to pray for their enemies, for those who hurt them (Matthew 5:44).
- Jesus also taught His disciples to pray regarding their need for food each day (Matthew 6:11).
- Paul asked others to pray for him to have opportunities to share the gospel of Jesus Christ (Colossians 4:3).
- Paul prayed for the Philippian believers, for his friend Timothy, and for the salvation of his countrymen (Philippians 1:1-4; 1 Timothy 2:1-6).
- Jesus prayed about His death (Matthew 26:36-46).

Our Savior and these saints of old prayed for specific needs, desires, problems, and requests. And we are to do the same. We must lift up the daily details and the personal needs in our lives to God through specific prayer requests. What kind of needs?

Health and energy—This is first on my list! God has given us hefty job assignments as Christian women. Our to-do lists are long…and so are our days! Therefore, we need to pray for energy and endurance, for focus and staying power so we can continue moving toward the goal of getting our work done, whether that's our housework, homework, or work on a job.

Attitude—Place this one near the top of your prayer list! Pray for a joyful spirit, patience with any obstacles…or people-problems…that come up during your day. And pray for self-control so emotions don't spill out and hurt someone else (Galatians 5:22-23).

Faithfulness—Pray, too, to keep your eyes—and heart!—fixed on the end of the day so that you will continue pressing and reaching to its very end. Pray to finish fully on your projects. When you would dearly love to be doing something else but you need to go to practice, finish your school work, help your mom with the housework, help your dad with yard work, or help out with your younger brother or sister, pray to be "trustworthy in everything" (1 Timothy 3:11).

Work—My "work" is probably different than yours. (It's more like your homework—I have to turn in my writing on due dates!) But if you have a job babysitting or working part-time somewhere, then your prayers should include your workplace, your workmates, and your faithfulness on the job. Pray to work willingly and eagerly with your heart and hands "as to the Lord" (Proverbs 31:13 and Colossians 3:23).

Wisdom—And every woman, whatever her age, needs God's wisdom with decision-making! So we must ask for it: "If any of you lacks wisdom, he should ask God...and it will be given to him" (James 1:5).

Relationships—All women—whether younger or older—have relationships with parents and family members that need to be prayed over. There are also friendships and a desire for companionship (both male and female!) that need to be talked over with God. We must pray, as Romans 12:18 says, to "live at peace with everyone."

"Prayer perfumes every relationship."

Well, I'm sure you realize that on and on...and longer and longer...the list of our prayer needs grows! And the balm to our hurting hearts and consuming needs is to answer God's call to prayer and *pray*! So give your stressful concerns—each and every one of them—to your all-wise, all-powerful, and all-gracious God. Only by praying always in the Spirit will we keep in the eye of the storm. Only then...and there...will we know "the peace of God, which transcends all understanding" (Philippians 4:7).

Now, let the prayers begin! Don't get bogged down under a load of heavy concerns about your daily life. Pray instead! "In *everything,* by prayer and petition...present your requests to God." Let your prayers ascend! Send your heart-cries to God every day as you pray minute-by-minute, step-by-step, and word-by-word.

My Checklist for Prayer

✓ *Look for trouble*—Does this sound strange? We must always remember that trouble is part of the Christian life. It's something we must accept as a fact of life. It helped me tremendously to underline the little word "whenever" in James 1:2: "Consider it pure joy, my brothers, whenever you face trials of many kinds." As he wrote about trials in life, James did not say *if*...but he said *whenever*. The apostle Peter also wrote of the fact of trials and troubles. He urged us, "Dear friends, do not be surprised at the painful trial you are suffering, as though something strange were happening to you" (1 Peter 4:12).

You and I, dear one, must face life with our eyes wide open! We must accept the fact of trouble. Then we must devise a plan for handling trouble and for dealing with it—God's way. For instance, what will you think when trouble arrives? What scriptures will you use to stay strong in the Lord as you walk through your own painful trials? And what, when, and how will you pray about the troubles of life—past, present, and future? Be prepared for trouble.

Wisdom always has a plan, so create your plan of action for facing trouble. What will it be?

✓ *Look to God in prayer daily*—Your needs arrive daily...and so do challenges and difficulties. Don't make the mistake of thinking you can meet trouble head-on, take it in stride, and enjoy victory *without* your all-powerful heavenly Father's help! Be wise and ask for help daily. It's His day, and you are His child. And "with God we will gain the victory" (Psalm 60:12).

"Much prayer, much power."[2]

"Be strong and take heart, all you who hope in the LORD" (Psalm 31:24). You need guidance for today, and God promises to "instruct you and teach you in the way you should go" and to "watch over you" (Psalm 32:8). You need wisdom for today, and it's yours...if you will "trust in the LORD with all your heart and lean not on your own understanding" (Proverbs 3:5). You need patience for today, and patience is His specialty, one of His fruit of the Spirit (Galatians 5:22).

And the list goes on...as does God's provision for your needs! What are your special needs today? Which of the verses just mentioned encourage you, and why? Now, pray!

✓ *Look for highlights*—Trouble is a fact of life, but so are God's rich, abundant blessings! So remember to look for...and thank God for...His blessings. What kind of blessings or highlights? One highlight arrives with the sunlight each new day—"Because of the LORD's great love we are not consumed, for his compassions never fail. They are new every morning; great is your faithfulness" (Lamentations 3:22-23). Here's another—"Weeping may remain for a night, but rejoicing comes in the morning" (Psalm 30:5). So..."praise the LORD, O my soul; all my inmost being, praise his holy name...and forget not all his benefits" (Psalm 103:1-2).

What benefits has God brought your way this week? Today? Name them right here and now. That way they will be recorded and not forgotten. Then thank Him...profusely!

✎ Answering God's Call to You

Are you grasping the importance of a deep-rooted prayer-life? When you are in the habit of praying, you are more likely to pray when trouble arises. And when you are in the habit of praying, you are more likely to think of asking for God's help *first* instead of later...or last, when all else fails.

So I pray God's message to your heart is crystal clear. When you're in trouble...pray! When you're helpless... pray! When you've done all you can do but you're still in need of help...pray! When you encounter an only-God-can-meet-it need...pray! When you have a specific need... pray! Prayer is God's avenue for you. He calls you to pray whenever something—anything!—is important to you. So in times of trouble and need...pray!

Now, what change must you make to be more consistent at regular prayer? What could you do that would make all the difference in the world in your prayer-life? Think of that one thing. What difference would it make? And when can you get started? Put it on your personal prayer list, enlist the aid of another person to help you with accountability, and then go to work on kicking your efforts at prayer up a notch!

Would You Like to Know More? Check It Out!

Read Esther 4:8-17. Note several ways Esther approached her troubles.

Read 2 Kings 19:14-19. Note several ways King Hezekiah approached his troubles.

What lessons do you want to remember from Queen Esther and King Hezekiah?

List your top five specific "needs," whether issues, attitudes, problems, or relationships.

How do the following verses encourage, comfort, or instruct you about your needs and how to deal with them?

Matthew 6:11—

Romans 12:18—

Philippians 4:6-7—

Philippians 4:19—

James 1:5—

My List of Things I Don't Want to Forget...
...from This Chapter

4

When You Are Dissappointed or Hurting ...Pray!

I'm sure you know how it feels to be disappointed or hurt by another person. Friends and family are part of life—and both can bring us extreme joy...and sometimes extreme sorrow and pain. Like me, you've probably had some friendships that started out great, but in time something was missing or went wrong. Maybe the other person got a new best friend...or a new girlfriend. Maybe your friends said something about you that wasn't true...or that hurt you. Maybe they turned against you. Maybe they walked away from your special friendship...and joined a clique. Maybe they let you down when you were really counting on their help. And in the end you were left wondering, "What happened?"

Whatever it was, we've both been there and done that when it comes to being let down or wounded by friends and family. And when it's over, we feel confused and discouraged. So what are we to do when such frustrating and heartbreaking things happen in our relationships? What are we to do with our broken hearts? And how are we to go on afterward?

As always, God comes to our rescue. He has all of the answers for us...and prayer is one of them!

Forgive and Pray for Others

Oh, is it ever hard to forgive people who have disappointed us or failed us as friends! And if we aren't careful, we can carry a grudge toward them and allow bitterness or resentment to take root in our hearts (Hebrews 12:15). Or we can follow another natural tendency and no longer have anything to do with them. But God's Word has wisdom for us here. We are to be "*forgiving* each other, just as in Christ God forgave [us]" (Ephesians 4:32; Colossians 3:13). Jesus, too, models the right way—*His* way!—of dealing with those who disappoint us. He says we are to *pray* for them (Luke 6:28).

And so we *forgive*...and we *pray*.

Three godly men in the Bible show us God's better—no, make that best!—way to handle our pain when people—even friends and family—let us down.

When people disappoint you, look to Samuel—Samuel spent his life teaching God's law and standards to God's people. But, sadly, the day came when they rejected Samuel and his message to them. That's when God told Samuel to speak to the people about their sin. What sin had they committed? They wanted a king to lead them instead of trusting God to lead them through His prophets—prophets like Samuel!

When Samuel confronted the masses with their sin, they were ashamed and begged him to pray for them. And what was Samuel's response to their request that he pray for them, the very people who had rejected him and disobeyed God? Did he snub them? Leave them to fend for themselves? No, Samuel *forgave* God's people…and *prayed* for them. He said, "Far be it from me that I should sin against the LORD by failing to pray for you" (1 Samuel 12:23).

When family disappoints you, look to Moses—Moses prayed for his brother, Aaron, after Aaron disappointed him and God. While Moses was away, Aaron, the high priest of God and Moses' co-leader, was in charge of God's people. And he clearly disobeyed the commands of God by making a golden calf for God's people to worship (Exodus 32:8; Deuteronomy 9:12-20), and God was on the warpath!

And how mad was God at Aaron? The Bible reports that the Lord was very angry with Aaron and would have destroyed him (Deuteronomy 9:19). Aaron had had it. He was done for. It was over! There seemed to be no hope for Aaron's life. Yet Moses *forgave* his brother and *prayed* and asked God to spare the life of his sinning brother.

When friends disappoint you, look to Job—Job is described in the Bible as "blameless and upright," as one who "feared God and shunned evil" (Job 1:1). Yet Job was verbally attacked by his friends at the very same time he was enduring the loss of basically all that he had—family, health, and wealth.

How did Job handle his friends' criticism? How did he respond to their lack of understanding and their failure to help in his time of need? Job was patient. Job was humble.

And, finally, it was God Himself who stepped in and put an end to Job's friends' wrong accusations and guesses about why Job was suffering.

Yet Job, after receiving much criticism from these close companions, prayed for his friends. In fact, God sent the sinning trio of friends *to* Job, saying, "Go to my servant Job. ...My servant Job will pray for you, and I will accept his prayer and not deal with you according to your folly" (Job 42:8). And the righteous Job *forgave* his friends and *prayed* for them.

Watch Your Heart!

Samuel forgave God's people...and prayed for them. Moses forgave his brother...and prayed for him. And Job forgave his critical friends...and prayed for them. And that's what you and I need to do. How is this possible? It is possible when you watch over your heart. As Psalm 66:18 explains regarding prayer, "If I had cherished sin in my heart, the Lord would not have listened." And, as Proverbs 28:9 states, "If anyone turns a deaf ear to the law, even his prayers are detestable."

> "We must forgive others so we can pray for them."

If we fail to forgive others, we are failing to obey God. That means our hearts are no longer pure, and our prayers become repulsive to God. Then we are unable to pray for others...due to our sin of failing to forgive. It's a vicious cycle—one you don't want to get into! So here's what we need to do: We must forgive others...so that our hearts are right before *God*...so that we can pray for those who sin, who fail, and who disappoint us (James 5:16).

So be careful, dear heart! Jesus says, "Love your enemies" (Matthew 5:44). When it comes to praying for others in a hurtful situation, there can be no personal accounting system of wrongs committed.

> "Love does not keep account of evil. Love keeps no score of wrongs."
> —1 Corinthians 13:5[1]

What should we do? Forgive others and pray to God for them—even those who disappoint and hurt us. Our heart attitude—even toward our enemies—should be like that of Samuel: "Pray for you? Yes, to my latest breath! God forbid that I should sin against the Lord in ceasing to pray for you."[2]

Offer a Helping Hand

Are you familiar with the fable that tells of a man who is crying for help while he is drowning in a river? Meanwhile, on the bridge that spans the water, another man is casually leaning over the rail looking at the struggling man. According to the story, the observer is telling the dying man what he *ought* to have done and letting him know what he *should* do if he ever gets into that situation again. Instead of reaching in with a helping hand and saving the dying man's life, he talks on and on. Clearly the perishing man didn't need a lecture. He needed help! He needed someone to save his life!

And that's what you and I have to do when it comes to praying for those who have fallen and failed. We must help them! We must set aside our disappointment, stop with the lectures, put aside judgment, and go to work helping and praying for others. Sure, correction and instruction may come later. Talking about the incident and trying to rebuild our relationships may come later. But when a person has failed and is in trouble, be sure to pray…*and* offer a helping hand!

> LORD, make me a channel of Thy peace
> That where there is hatred, I may
> bring love,
> That where there is wrong, I may bring
> the spirit of forgiveness,
> That where there is discord, I may
> bring harmony.
>
> —St Frances of Assisi

Help for Your Hurting Heart

Are you ready for more help for your hurting heart? Yet another facet in the treasured gem of prayer is the opportunity to fight your battles in prayer instead of against a person. When you have been harmed by someone, when your heart hurts because of betrayal or unfairness or evil, you can become a prayer-warrior.

Meet someone whose heart was hurt—Meet David, a warrior and a king—*and* a prayer-warrior! In Psalm 55, David poured out his torn and bleeding heart in a prayer and cried out to God against his enemies. David had been betrayed—by both family and friends—and he went to battle through prayer.

The background of this psalm is absolutely heartbreaking. Jerusalem, "the city of David," was taken over from David by Absalom, David's own son. To make things worse, Ahithophel, David's best friend, turned away from David to follow Absalom. The people of the city also turned against David and threw him out.

Are you someone who's been hurt?—As I'm sitting here writing at my desk, I am thinking of you, my dear younger sister. I'm wondering, *Are you someone who's been hurt?* Not one day goes by that I don't receive letters and emails from women—young and old...and everything in between—who have been hurt by others. I know firsthand that people hurt people. I also know that God's people hurt God's people. And I'm aware that family members hurt family members.

So what are we, as God's women, to do when our hearts hurt and when we've been hurt by loved ones, friends, family, by those we looked up to and respected, by those we trusted? The answer, of course, is...*pray!* And David shows us how.

Lessons on Praying from a Hurting Heart

Lesson #1—Cast your burden on the Lord. David knew *where* to turn and *what* to do. He knew to "cast [his] cares on the LORD" (Psalm 55:22).

> Listen to my prayer, O God, do not ignore my plea; hear me and answer me....My heart is in anguish within me; the terrors of death assail me (verses 1-2,4).

"God is the very One who says to us—roll your anxieties over on Me, for I have you in My heart!"[3]

Like David, you and I have an almighty and all-loving Father to help us carry our loads.

Lesson #2—Resist the temptation to run away. David's natural desire was to leave the scene, to flee from the problem and the pain. Who wouldn't think, "No way am I going to stay here and take this. I'm out of here! I don't need this"? So David wished for wings!

> Oh, that I had the wings of a dove! I would fly away and be at rest—I would flee far away, and stay in the desert; I would hurry to my place of shelter (verses 6-8).

Beloved, when you find yourself surrounded by "enemies" or suffering because of the failure of your friends, you will most certainly wish for the wings of a dove that you might fly away and be at rest! But you must stay and fight your battle by placing your prayers into battle array. And you must pray, pray, pray!

And be assured, dear praying heart, that if "a way out" becomes necessary, if the heat of battle becomes more than you can bear, "God is faithful." He promises that *He* will provide an escape route (1 Corinthians 10:13). *He* will deliver you. *He* will come to your aid. *He* will rescue you. *He* will see to it! You can depend on *Him*. As David declared, "I call to God, and the LORD saves me....He hears my voice" (Psalm 55:16-17)!

Lesson #3—Believe that God will sustain you. David's confidence in God is powerful. He pounds out his prayers, never letting up, repeatedly hammering out the truths that God will take care of him: "The LORD saves me....He hears my voice....God...will hear [my enemies] and afflict them. ...He will never let the righteous fall" (Psalm 55:16-22). Finally, after such praying and after counting on God's promises, David shouted out his final assurance—"I trust in you" (verse 23)! His prayers have at last gotten through to his own soul. At last, David stops thinking about the enemy and turns his full focus—and trust—upon the Lord God Almighty who hears His people's pleas and saves them.

Oh, dear reading friend, when all seems hopeless, put your God-given faith to work and trust in the Lord. Believe that no matter what burden you bear, He will sustain you in it today...and all the days of your life!

My Checklist for Prayer

✓ *Check your heart*—A forgiving heart is a heart that can pray for others. And if you think you can't forgive someone, consider these truths about *your* heart: "For all have sinned and fall short of the glory of God"; "if you think you are standing firm, be careful that you don't fall"; "if we claim to be without sin, we deceive ourselves and the truth is not in us."[4]

Is there anyone you are failing to forgive? What example did Jesus set for us when He prayed on the cross, "Father, forgive them, for they do not know what they are doing" (Luke 23:34)? How can you follow His example?

✓ *Check your relationships*—Christ calls you to love others—even your enemies. His instructions concerning those who have wronged you come from Luke 6:27-28:

> *love*...your enemies,
> *do good*...to those who hate you,
> *bless*...those who curse you,
> *pray*...for those who mistreat you.

What good can you do for someone who has harmed you or let you down? Are you speaking kind words to and about those who have slandered or verbally attacked you? What commitment can you make to pray for those who have hurt or disappointed you? Look to God for His help. Then do what He leads you to do to love your enemies.

✓ *Check your prayer-life*—When your heart hurts, that's exactly when you must seek God on bended knee. Pray! Don't allow yourself to rant, rave, dissolve into a puddle, fall apart, or collapse. Instead of giving up, pray (Luke 18:1)! And while you are praying, cast your cares and burdens upon the Lord (Psalm 55:22).

With God's help and with much prayer, go on with life…silently, cheerfully, in the power and grace of the Holy Spirit (Galatians 5:22-23). Go on, knowing that God is still on His throne. He is still in control, He is still sovereign, He is still all-powerful, and He is still able…and He always will be! And He will deal with those who harm His children (Psalm 37:7-9). He promises it!

What was your reaction the last time you were disappointed or hurt by someone? The next time someone lets you down or is cruel to you, what better response (by God's grace!) would you like to give? How can prayer help?

✎ Answering God's Call to You

What happens when you turn to God and answer His call to prayer during your times of distress and pain? God sweetens what is bitter (Exodus 15:23-25). He makes the one who is sad become glad (Psalm 30:11). And He turns something bad into something good (Romans 8:28). Oh, please, don't wish your hard times away! Some of your most meaningful times with God will come when you talk to Him about your hurting heart. So fly away in prayer… and rest in Him!

Now, what is troubling you, my precious reading friend? I'm praying here at my desk for you as you face your challenges. I'm praying that in your times of trouble you never forget to pray to your almighty, all-powerful, miracle-working, mountain-moving God! Don't just stand there! Don't cave in! Don't worry! And don't suffer! "Is any one among you in trouble? He should *pray*" (James 5:13).

What a Friend We Have in Jesus

What a Friend we have in Jesus,
All our sins and griefs to bear!
What a privilege to carry
Ev'rything to God in prayer!
O what peace we often forfeit,
O what needless pain we bear,
All because we do not carry
Ev'rything to God in prayer!

Have we trials and temptations?
Is there trouble anywhere?
We should never be discouraged—
Take it to the Lord in prayer.
Can we find a friend so faithful
Who will all our sorrows share?
Jesus knows our ev'ry weakness—
Take it to the Lord in prayer.

Are we weak and heavy laden,
Cumbered with a load of care?
Precious Savior, still our refuge—
Take it to the Lord in prayer.
Do thy friends despise, forsake thee?
Take it to the Lord in prayer;
In His arms He'll take and shield thee—
Thou wilt find a solace there.[5]

Would You Like to Know More? Check It Out!

What do these verses say you should do when someone disappoints or hurts you?

Ephesians 4:32—

Colossians 3:13—

Luke 6:27-28—

1 Corinthians 13:5—

What should your attitude be when others fail?

Proverbs 24:17-18—

1 Corinthians 10:12—

Galatians 6:1-2—

What do these verses teach you about suffering?

John 16:33—

2 Timothy 2:12—

James 1:2—

1 Peter 1:6—

What does God say to do when you are suffering?

Psalm 55:22—

1 Peter 5:7—

My List of Things I Don't Want to Forget...
...from This Chapter

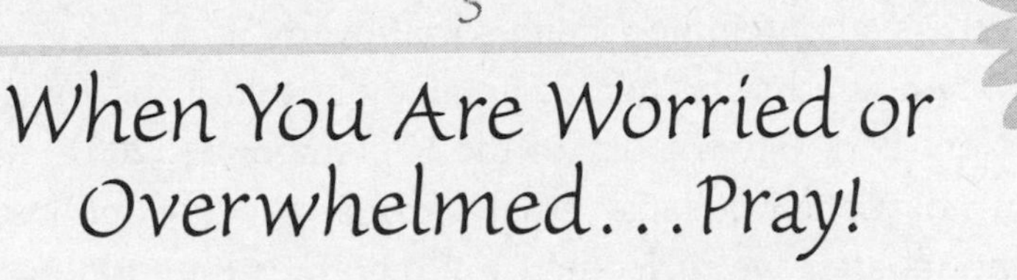

5

When You Are Worried or Overwhelmed...Pray!

Would you like to meet a first-class worrier? Well, check that off your goal list. You have...and it's me! In fact, I should write a book entitled *Confessions of a Worrywart*. But until then, believe me, I've seen the inside of a doctor's office more than a few times. You name it—a bleeding ulcer, colitis, and eczema up to my elbows—I've been there. And I know I'm not alone. Women of all ages love to worry... about anything and everything!

What do we worry about most?

About our relationships with our parents, brothers and sisters, friends and acquaintances. And we can't stop there! Oh no, we've also got to worry about relationships with our enemies—about knowing what to do and how to handle these problems!

Then there are other items on "The Great List of Things to Worry About." These include worrying about what others think of us, what we look like—if we are too fat or too thin, if we are pretty enough. And don't leave out worrying about health, safety, finances for schooling, boyfriends, dating, the future...nicely topped off with worrying about our schoolwork, exams, and grades, about getting up in front of others, about an upcoming social event.

And here's another big area! My husband and I were in New York City the day of the September 11, 2001, World Trade Center collapse. That terrorist attack came just six hours after we welcomed my daughter Katherine's little baby Matthew into this world...in the very hospital that became the burn unit for the victims of the disaster that day. Many New Yorkers continue to worry about another terrorist attack...as do most of us.

And we worry about war.

On and on the list of worries goes. And yet...

God Commands Us, "Do Not Worry!"

Did you know that over 300 times in the New Testament God commands us to not worry or be anxious? Just one of these times is Philippians 4:6-7:

> Do not be anxious about anything, but in everything by prayer and petition, with thanksgiving, present your requests to God. And the peace of God, which transcends all understanding, will guard your hearts and minds in Christ Jesus.

Beloved, these are the verses that finally knocked some sense into me about my worrying habit and its devastating effects. They spoke so clearly to my fretting heart that I wrote the verses out on a card and memorized them. I reviewed these scriptures and recited them over and over. I never went anywhere without my memory card. I carried

God's command with me—physically on the card and spiritually in my heart—and took it apart word-by-word.

And sure enough, just like God's active and powerful Word always does, it began to change my heart and mind (Hebrews 4:12)! I went from worrying to worshiping. Instead of fretting, I began to trust the God of the promise. Here's what I discovered.

"Trust in the LORD with all your heart" (Proverbs 3:5).

The command—"Do not be anxious about anything." God's Word clearly instructs us to take care of our responsibilities and relationships and daily life. But beyond that, we are not to worry…about anything…ever…period! In the book of Philippians, where this medicine for worriers is found, we meet some people who had a lot of causes for worry.

First of all, the Philippians themselves had *people* problems—they had enemies who stood against them in their battle for the faith of the gospel (Philippians 1:27-28). As a result, they had potential *emotional* problems—their joy in the Lord was at risk (3:1). And they had potential *spiritual* problems—their strength for the battle was in danger (4:1).

Then there was Paul, the man who is writing this advice to the Philippians. Talk about problems! Paul was in prison…waiting to see if he would live or die! On top of his stressful situation, Paul also suffered from some kind of physical or personal "thorn in the flesh" (2 Corinthians 12:7). Writing from his own problem-ridden life, Paul shared this command with his friends in Philippi…and with you and me:

Do not be anxious about anything.

These six words make it plain that, for the Christian, all worry is forbidden by God. And that's that!

The scope of the command—"Do not be anxious *about anything*." Take your pen in hand and circle the words "about anything" in the six words above. The New King James version translates the first part of Philippians 4:6: "Be anxious for nothing." And what is "nothing"? I once heard a Bible teacher say, "*Nothing* is a zero with the rim kicked off!" And that's God's message to our hearts. When it comes to worrying, we are to be anxious "for nothing." There aren't many other words beyond *nothing* and *anything* to use to describe the scope of God's command!

Are you wondering, *Yes, I get it...but how do I not worry?* Well, take heart! God has the answer to all your problems...

The solution—Prayer! "Present your requests to God." Yes, life is difficult, full of problems and filled with stress. And yes, worry is a natural tendency. And, praise God, yes, there is something we can do to keep from worrying! And yes, we *can* obey God's command to "not be anxious about anything." God's solution is this: When you are worried...pray! Pray *from* your heart and *with all* your heart! Pray, pray, pray!

And like the colors in the arch of a rainbow across the sky, God gives us several brilliant ways to win over worry. Instead of worrying about *any*thing, He says, "in *every*thing...present your requests to God." How?

- By prayer—Prayer is worship, but it's also where all true worship begins...and all worry ends!
- By petition—Do you have a need, a concern? Then pray! Boldly go before God's throne of grace in your times of need...and with your needs (Hebrews 4:16). Don't fail to shoot your prayers heavenward and ask the all-powerful, almighty God of the universe. He can solve all your problems! You see, we can either ask and not worry... or we can worry because we don't ask. It's one or the other—and the choice is ours.
- With thanksgiving—A thankful heart that focuses on God's sovereign power over everything and on His purposes in everything cannot be a worrying heart. Neither can a heart of trust, a heart that is at rest. So give God thanks now. Thank Him profusely!
- By requests—"Present your requests to God" with utmost trust. Keep nothing back, great or small. Withhold nothing—none of your concerns—from God. He wants your *every* concern! So present them to Him. Leave them in the lap of the Almighty.

The result—And then what happens? "The peace of God" comes to our rescue. It "will guard [our] hearts and [our] minds in Christ Jesus." In other words, as a tribal missionary so beautifully and simply translated this truth, "Jesus will make your heart sit down."

And once your heart sits down, peace keeps watch over it. Like a soldier, God's peace guards your heart—and mind!—against fear, worry, stress, and fretting. And the result? The battle against worry is won.

But there's another life situation that is far beyond worry, and that is when you are overwhelmed. I'm sure you've been shaken to the core at some time in your life by a serious, earth-shattering, almost overwhelming crisis. A time when you felt crushed. A time when you believed you could not go on...or weren't sure how to go on. Unfortunately, pain and sorrow, loss and tragedy, confusion and frustration touch every life. It's just as Jesus warned us, "In this world you will have trouble" (John 16:33). It's terrible, isn't it?

If terrible trials are a fact of life, what can we do when we go through such experiences? Answer: We can go straight to God because He has a set of instructions for making life work when it seems like it will never work again. God has given us two—yes, two!—glorious resources for dealing with a crushing situation.

First, when we are overwhelmed, we have the Bible, God's guidebook for handling all of life and its every problem (2 Peter 1:3).

And second...

God Helps Us to Pray

Through the act of prayer you and I can seek the heart and mind of God *in* our difficult situations. That's because God gives us help for answering His call to prayer. He gives us this assurance for our difficult times:

> In the same way, the Spirit helps us in our weakness. We do not know what we ought to pray for, but the Spirit himself intercedes for us with groans that words cannot express....The Spirit intercedes for the saints in accordance with God's will (Romans 8:26-27).

Here we discover that God Himself gives us help and hope in our impossible situations. The Holy Spirit literally comes to our rescue as He "happens" upon us in our trouble. He lends us His helping hand by praying and pleading to God on our behalf, with "groans" and sighs that baffle words. It is supernatural, so we cannot understand it. But in simple language, the Holy Spirit groans and sighs *for* us in prayer.

What good news! When you don't know what to pray for, how to pray, or what words to use, the Holy Spirit does! And He takes over and expresses our requests to God *for* us. The Spirit takes over for us and appeals to the only person who can help us—God Himself.

Thank God that you are not left alone to cope with your problems! That's the way it is for you (and me, too) when you are in overwhelming pain and sorrow. The Holy Spirit intercedes. Sometimes you are suffering personally from physical or emotional distress. At other times you pray for hurting parents or for a wounded brother or sister. You also reach toward God when there's been a loss, a tragedy, a trauma, an attack, an accident. You know you should pray. You want to pray. You try to pray. You search for the words to tell God all about your broken heart...but find none.

But take heart! When your heart is so sorrowful and bewildered that you don't even know how to pray or what to say to God, again, the Holy Spirit takes over for you.

A word for you—Again I say to you, "Thank God!" Thank Him that He knows your weaknesses, that He knows your heart, that He knows your suffering, that He knows your desire, and that He knows your need to pray. He also knows when you cannot pray, so *He*—through His Holy Spirit—comes to your rescue and prays for you!

Now, what exactly can—and should—you do when you run up against an overwhelming adversity?

My Checklist for Prayer

✓ *Don't*...miss a day of prayer—If you play hit-and-miss with your daily prayer time, you will most certainly discover that your worry level is higher on the days when you don't pray. Prayer is God's surefire solution for eliminating worry. *If* you pray, *then* you won't be anxious. *If* you pray, *then* you will experience peace of mind. And the opposite is true, too. If you *don't* pray, you will be anxious. If you *don't* pray, you will not experience peace of mind.

So...be faithful to pray. Talk with God about your life...instead of worrying about it. What are the issues that tempt you to worry? Write them in a special place—in your journal or notebook. Be sure you are recording your faithfulness in prayer on your "My Prayer Calendar" (see pages 196-97). Also record any changes in your level of concern in these areas as you pray about them.

✓ *Do*...determine a "worry day"—I can't resist passing on this fun—and funny!—practical solution for those times you think you just *have* to worry about *something*!

A man who was unable to put his troubles aside completely came up with his own solution. He decided that the best thing to do would be to set apart a single day, Wednesday, to do all his worrying. When something came up that disturbed him during the week, he wrote it down and put it in his "Wednesday Worry Box."

When the time came to review his high-anxiety problems, he found to his great surprise that most of them had already been settled. There was no longer any need for worry! He discovered that most worry is unnecessary and a waste of precious energy.[2]

I know you are praying—that was part of the first check-mark activity. But if you can't resist a good round of worrying, what day will you pick as your "worry day"? Just be sure you *wait* until that day to worry! Also be sure and to record what happened to your concern during the week.

✓ *Do...*your best—Sometimes your heart cries out, "It hurts so much! It's so bad, I don't think I can pray!" What are you to do when this happens? First, remember such feelings are okay! They are normal. They are *common* (1 Corinthians 10:13). This happens to everyone. Then begin to pray. That's your part. God's part is to "join in and help" you pray.[3] He will perfect your fumbling attempts to do the right thing—to pray even when your heart hurts so badly that you are not sure what to pray or how to pray.

What is your agonizing prayer concern? And what can you do to begin to pray? Can you at least kneel down? Can you try to pray in the ways you normally do? Adore and worship God now for who He is and for what He has done for you and His people. Go ahead and thank Him for His goodness. Also acknowledge any known sin. And pray for others. Then record what happened.

✎ Answering God's Call to You

How encouraging it is to know that, as a believer, you are not left on your own to cope with life's problems. Even when you don't know the right words to pray, the Holy Spirit does...and He prays with you and for you.

My prayer for you at this moment is that you will let the prayers of your heart flow. When you are in pain...pray! When you are speechless...pray! When you are heartsick...pray! When you are suffering, beaten up, or beaten down by life...pray! When you are troubled or perplexed...pray! When you are overwhelmed...pray! Your heavenly Father knows what you need before you ask (Matthew 6:32)...so don't be afraid to bring up anything and everything. God wants to hear from you. Use any fumbling words or wails you can muster up out of your hurting heart. Just be sure you pray...and leave the rest to God.

Would You Like to Know More? Check It Out!

God's solution to your tendency to worry is simple: Pray! Copy Philippians 4:6-7 here. Then write out what the following verses teach you about prayer.

1 Peter 5:7—

Hebrews 4:16—

How do you think praying faithfully about your problems helps to counteract worry?

Read Romans 8:26-34 in your Bible. In what ways does the Holy Spirit help believers according to…

…verse 26?

…verse 27?

What do you learn about God in verse 31?

What do you learn about Jesus Christ in verse 34?

How should these truths help you when you are worried or overwhelmed?

My List of Things I Don't Want to Forget…
…from This Chapter

Finding God's Will Through Prayer

6

When You Must Make a Decision...Pray for Faith and Wisdom!

I'm sure you've had a few wake-up calls in your life. (And I don't mean from your alarm clock!) Well, believe me, that happened to me one morning when a woman called to invite me to speak at her church. As she talked, my fingers drummed the table and my mind anxiously wondered, *When is she going to pause long enough for me to blurt out, "Sure! I'll come! When do you want me? I can come right now!"*

When this gracious lady was done, I breathlessly assured her I would be delighted to come to her event and went on with my day.

At about eight o'clock that night, the phone rang again. It was another sweet woman asking me to come speak at her church. As she described the event, I was shaking my head from side to side and already answering her in my mind, *No way! No how! No ma'am!* No, I didn't say these words, but they were in my heart.

The next day during my prayer time, I sat before the Lord and wondered, *Why my split responses? Each caller was a godly woman. Each invitation had to do with spiritual ministry. And each event was a wonderful opportunity for ministry. What had happened?*

As I thought and prayed, I realized that I wasn't making *spiritual* decisions. No, I was making *physical* decisions! And suddenly it all made sense. If I felt good, the answer was *yes!* And if I didn't feel good or was tired, well, the answer was *No way! No how! No ma'am!*

No Decision Made without Prayer!

Once God pointed out my problem, His Word—and example after example of Bible heroes—came rushing in to show me the right way to make decisions.

- King Solomon prayed for wisdom...and rose up from prayer to become the wisest man who ever lived (1 Kings 3:5-12).
- Nehemiah spent time praying "before the God of heaven" after hearing bad news...and rose up knowing what action to take (Nehemiah 1:4-11).
- Queen Esther fasted three days and nights to prepare to follow God's will in a life-threatening situation (Esther 4:16)...and rose up to boldly make her request to the king.
- King David was a man who prayed...and became a man after God's own heart who fulfilled God's will (Acts 13:22).
- The Lord Jesus sought His Father's direction through prayer and rose up...declaring, "Let us go

> somewhere else—to the nearby villages—so I can preach there also. That is why I have come" (Mark 1:35-39).

Right there and then, dear friend, I made a new prayer commitment: "From now on, *No decision made without prayer!*" To seal my commitment, I turned to a blank page in my prayer notebook and wrote across the top, "Decisions to Make." This prayer principle of *No decision made without prayer* has guided my life and helped me find God's will from that day on. And it can guide yours, too.

> "Out of the will of God there is no such thing as success; in the will of God there cannot be any failure."[1]

How does passing your decision-making process through the fire of prayer help? Read on!

You Are Called to a Life of Faith

What's a busy woman to do about all of the opportunities, invitations, and decisions that come her way? And how can she know which things are God's will for her and which are not? Here's a principle from God's Word that will help guide you into a life marked by strong, powerful, confident faith. It's a guideline for making decisions and handling the doubtful things or "gray areas" of daily life:

> But the man who has doubts is condemned if he eats, because his eating is not from faith; and everything that does not come from faith is sin (Romans 14:23).

This verse has to do with violating your conscience. In general, it tells you how to know when to move ahead in full faith...and when to hold back because faith, confidence, and a clear conscience are missing. The apostle Paul is saying that if we doubt something in our hearts, or we are not sure if an action is right or wrong, then we should not do it—whatever "it" is. Doing it would be sin for us because it would cause guilt and violate our consciences. (And just a note: In the case of the Romans Paul is writing to, "it" was eating food that was forbidden in the Old Testament.)

Exactly how does this principle of doubtful things and gray areas apply to your decision-making? How does it help you live a life of faith and confidence?

1. *You are called to act in confidence*—You (and all Christians) should be sure and confident that you are doing the right thing in your actions and decisions. This kind of confidence adds unbelievable power to your life. Instead of waffling and wavering and wondering, you can act decisively and without worry.

   However, as you well know, whenever you do something that you are not sure is right or wrong, doubt sets in and takes over, weakening your confidence and bringing on guilt.

> "Living without faith is like driving in the fog."

2. *You are called to pray for confidence*—Your goal is to live and act with the belief that what you are doing is right. Therefore, you must pray. With this goal and purpose in mind, I personally try not to

make a move or commit myself to *anything* until after prayer, which includes listening for God's response. That may take a day...or months. But what we are looking for is clear direction, a clear conscience, and the absence of doubt and guilt.

3. *You are called to peace of mind*—When you pray—and *wait* for God's answer and direction!—you will at last sense His clear direction. How will you know? Doubts will vanish, and your confidence in God's guidance will soar. When this happens to me after I've prayed (for however long it takes), I can commit and say *yes*...or refuse and say *no*...and move forward in God-confidence. But when the faith and peace of mind isn't there, this principle from Romans 14 regarding doubtful things comes to my rescue:

When in doubt, don't!
(or, put another way)
When in doubt, it's out!

You Are Called to a Life of Wisdom

Prayer is how we seek the *will of God*—Remember, *No decision made without prayer!* And guess what? Prayer is also how we seek the *wisdom of God*.

> If any of you lacks wisdom, he should *ask God...and it will be given to him* (James 1:5).

Do you want to discover God's will in your life? Then you must not fail to ask Him for His wisdom. And how will we recognize it?

Wisdom fears the Lord—"The fear of the LORD is the beginning of wisdom" (Proverbs 9:10). That means being careful about life and about rushing ahead of God's will...and perhaps missing it altogether. That means there is a deep respect for God and a worshipful "fear" of Him. Therefore, don't try to impress or please others. Instead seek to live out one passion in your life—that of pleasing God, of finding favor with Him, of walking in His will.

So pray! Talk things over with the Lord *before* you act, *before* you make a move, and *before* you say a word! Learn to say, "Let me pray about that and get back to you."

Wisdom applies God's Word to everyday life—Do you ever wonder if a day is all that important? Yet, if you think about it, all you really have for doing God's will is a day—today! Jesus Himself told us not to postpone, wait, think, and wonder about tomorrow. He said, "Do not worry about tomorrow, for tomorrow will worry about itself. Each day has enough trouble of its own" (Matthew 6:34).

In other words, handling today with all of its demands, quirks, and surprises will require all of your effort, all of your strength, all of your focus on God's wisdom. You will be called upon to walk and act with wisdom and according to God's will all day long...around every corner and in every encounter.

"Everything you do, every decision you make, every relationship you have, will be affected by your ability to apply wisdom to your experiences."[2]

So, how was your yesterday? And how is your today going? Be sure you pray yourself through your every day! Seek God's wisdom as the crises and curveballs of your day arrive as surely as the steady pounding of an ocean surf hits the shore.

Wisdom sees life from God's perspective—What is God's perspective? Here are a few observations from Proverbs.

The fool envies the wealthy.
The fool scorns his elders.
The fool does not ask advice.
The fool hates his neighbor.
The fool sleeps his life away.
The fool squanders his money.
The fool despises wisdom.
The fool speaks slander.
The fool lies.
The fool talks too much.
The fool argues and quarrels.

And there's more! But the real question is, Are *you* seeing and living life from God's perspective? Beloved, *prayer* makes the difference! *Prayer* sets the wise woman apart from the "fools" just described. Taking time to close your eyes in prayer helps open them to God's way of seeing things.

And be prepared—*God* sees life from a completely different angle (Isaiah 55:8-9). That's why wisdom is such a distinctive mark. It dramatically separates you from the masses and makes all the difference in the choices and decisions you make.

Wisdom follows the best course of action—You know, it's really easy to *know* the right thing to do. In fact, the Bible says wisdom is calling out in the streets, on the corners, in all the public places (Proverbs 1:20-21). Wisdom is everywhere! It's available…and it's free! But the final indicator of wisdom is to *do* the right thing.

That's why we must *pray* for a heart of wisdom. On our own it's easy to be a fool…and almost impossible to walk in godly wisdom. That's why we need God's help. Unfortunately, Solomon, the wisest man in the world, possessed wisdom and *knew* the right things to do and could tell it to others. But he failed to continue to *do* what he knew…and became a fool. So we need to decide to access God's wisdom and put it to use in our lives. Praying over our decisions gives our hearts that extra boost when it comes to taking the best course of action.

My Checklist for Prayer

✓ *Commit to pray*—The surest way to miss God's will and God's best is to not pray—to not even pause and ask Him. And the surest way to be sure you discover God's will is, of course, to pray. So learn to say, "Let me pray about that and get back to you." Practice it in front of your mirror if you have to!

> "Prayer is the first thing, the second thing, and the third thing necessary for a believer. Pray, then, my dear Christian, pray, pray, and pray."[3]

And now for some action! On the next page share what you did and when you did it. Make your own *No decision made without prayer* commitment. Write it out, put it in a special place, remember it, and rule your life by it. And don't forget to practice your motto for life: "Let me pray about that and get back to you." Keep track of how many times you say this when you are asked to do something this week, and write it here.

✓ *Set up to pray*—Purpose that from now on, *every* opportunity and *every* decision that must be made about *every*thing in your life will make its way onto your prayer page. Should you volunteer at work or school? Accept a date or go to a party? Get a part-time job? Attend college (and which college)? How should you spend your money…or your precious time and energy? Nothing is too small or too big to be prayed over. You are praying to know God's will for every detail of your life…and *that's* a big thing!

Make your own "Decisions to Make" prayer page. Then begin to fill it with the large or small decisions you must make. After all, it's *your* life! And that's important—vitally important!—not only to you, but to God!

Read again the prayer concerns above. What are yours? What decisions must you make? List both small and large issues that require your prayers now.

✓ *Pray faithfully*—Any and all decisions you must make are important. You can begin by using the scriptures shared on the page at the end of this chapter. The verses are like weapons for warfare. Be sure you pull them out of your arsenal and use them! Which one(s) do you like the best and why?

The best way to begin to build an arsenal for decision-making through prayer is to memorize three important verses. So write out each one on a card, carry them with you, and "write them on the tablet of your heart" (Proverbs 7:3)—memorize them! Which verse will you begin with? Write it here and let the memorizing and praying begin!

✎ Answering God's Call to You

As we leave this oh-so-brief overview of faith and wisdom, please acknowledge the role these two spiritual elements play in your decision-making process. They work mightily to help you find the will of God. I've referred to prayer many times in this book as being like a gem, a fantastic jewel with many flashing facets. And faith and wisdom are twin qualities in the glorious rock of prayer.

And, my dear praying friend, when you have answered God's call to prayer, when you have prayed, sought, and received God's faith, wisdom, and will, and when you have made your decision, praise Him! Praise God that you can ask Him through prayer for His faith and wisdom to guide your choices. Praise Him that you have done the praying, you have done the seeking, and you have made the best decision you can as you have sought His will.

Then proceed full-speed ahead with complete confidence that you are in the will of God. When yours is a seeking heart, He can guide and direct you as you go. Like a car that is tuned up and gassed up and turned on, He can steer you as you go. Then, all joy! Your life can bring Him the praise and honor and glory He so richly deserves!

Again, praise Him!

Putting God's Wisdom to Work in Your Life

What can you do about decision-making and the will of God? Follow this scriptural battle plan. These "weapons" work for every area of your life and lead you toward God's best.

First, ask God for help. Pray, "Lord, Your Word says in James 1:5, 'If any of you lacks wisdom, he should ask God...and it will be given to him.' So here I am, Lord! I need wisdom, and I'm asking You for it! Please reveal Your wisdom in this matter."

Next, pull James 4:17 out of your arsenal and pray, "And, Lord, Your Word says 'Anyone, then, who knows the good he ought to do and doesn't do it, sins.' Lord, I don't want to sin. I want to do the right thing, the good thing. So I've got to know what that is. Please show me the right thing so I can do it!"

Finally, reach for Proverbs 3:5 and 6 and pray, "And, Lord, Your Word says to 'trust in the LORD with all your heart and lean not on your own understanding; in all your ways acknowledge him, and he will make your paths straight.' I don't want to rely on my own heart, so I'm asking You right now, Lord, to guide my footsteps. What is the right thing to do here? What is the right decision? What is the path You want me to walk in? What is the *right way*?"

Six Scriptural Reasons to Pause and Pray

Revelation of God's will—"Trust in the LORD with all your heart and lean not on your own understanding; in all your ways acknowledge him, and he will make your paths straight" (Proverbs 3:5-6).

Clarity of God's will—"The way of the sluggard is blocked with thorns, but the path of the upright ['is made plain,' KJV]" (Proverbs 15:19).

Discernment of God's will—"All a man's ways seem innocent to him, but motives are weighed by the LORD" (Proverbs 16:2).

Insight into God's will—"All man's ways seem right to him, but the LORD weighs the heart" (Proverbs 21:2).

Blessing of God's will—"He who trusts in himself is a fool, but he who walks in wisdom is kept safe" (Proverbs 28:26).

Patience for God's will—"It is not good to have zeal without knowledge, nor to be hasty and miss the way" (Proverbs 19:2).

Would You Like to Know More? Check It Out!

Read Romans 14:5 and 23 and 1 John 3:21. What difference should prayer and careful thought make in your choices and your confidence?

Read Acts 4:23-31. After praying how did the early Christians act in faith and confidence?

Good decisions—God-based decisions!—require God's wisdom. What do these verses reveal about wisdom or what is wise?

Proverbs 9:10—

Matthew 6:33-34—

Proverbs 1:10-19—

Proverbs 1:20-23—

What do these verses say about *your* responsibility for walking in wisdom? List them here.

My List of Things I Don't Want to Forget...
...from This Chapter

7

When You Must Make a Decision...Pray for Understanding!

Yes, but...

Are these the two words you are thinking right about now? Are you wondering about God's will and how to find it? Are you feeling a bit uncertain about how everything adds up and fits together to indicate His will? Well, let's change your hesitation to three words—

Yes, but...how?

—and let me now share a few final *how's*. Let's look at the final step in the process I've been outlining for "Finding God's Will Through Prayer": *Pray for understanding*. When you pray for understanding, you will know more about God's will for you and the issues in your life.

Four Questions for Your Heart

It's hard to explain, but when we pray—when we do consult the Lord and wait upon Him for His direction—we *do* receive direction and confidence from God. Somehow He is able to impress His will upon our seeking hearts. And through Him we are able to understand what His will is.

So I have four questions that I ask my heart during prayer. I ask them in my effort to seek God's answers and guidance. While I'm praying about decisions that must be made, these four questions lead me right along the path of finding God's will. They help me to discover God's will for *me*, and they will work for you, too, as you seek His will for *you*. After all, God wants us to know His will. Why else would He ask or expect us to do it (Ephesians 6:6)? To begin your walk through these four questions, understand that honestly answering Questions 1 and 2 will surface your *motives*. Some of your motives will be pure and good, and others will be selfish and evil. After all, as Jeremiah pointed out, "The heart is deceitful above all things and beyond care. Who can understand it?" (Jeremiah 17:9)!

Then, as you continue on with your decision-making through prayer, you'll discover that Questions 3 and 4 will surface your *convictions*—what you know and believe the Word of God says about your decisions. Here's how this exercise has worked for me.

Question 1: Why would I do this?—One day I received a phone call from someone in my church asking me to teach a series of Bible classes. As I began praying, I asked *Why would I do this?* I could hardly believe that the first response that popped out of my heart was one of those sinful, wicked motives! My heart replied in answer to this question, *Oh, my name will be in the bulletin! Everyone will see my name in the bulletin as a great Bible teacher!*

I don't have to tell you that such a prideful response would *never* be a good reason to say *yes* to anything! No, the kinds of answers you and I are looking for as women after God's own heart include "because God would be glorified...because God's Word would be lifted up...because lives would be helped and changed...because the purpose of this Bible study is God-honoring."

You see the difference, right? In these heart-responses we are certainly getting closer to pure motives and solid reasons for saying *yes* than I was with the sickening response that my name would appear in the church bulletin!

So what did I do with such an answer? I wrote it down on the prayer page I created for this decision entitled "Teach Women's Bible Study." On the spot, I confessed to God how *wrong* such a thought/motive was! Then I drew a line through the answer and placed the page in the "Decisions to Make" section of my prayer notebook so I could look at it each day while I prayed about it...and record the progress being made toward making a decision—one hopefully based in God's wisdom!

And why did I write down such an awful answer on my prayer page? Because if it came out of my heart once, it would probably come out of it more than once! And I wanted a record of my conviction that teaching God's holy Word for such a *sinful* reason would be *wrong*. It would definitely *not* be God's will if based solely on such a reason.

Question 2: Why would I not do this?—Here's another instance, one when I was invited to speak at a v-e-r-y large women's event. On Day 1 of praying about this opportunity for ministry (labeled "Speak at Women's Event"), I first asked *Why would I do this?* and recorded my answers.

Then I asked *Why would I not do this?* And in rushed the answer, *Oh, I'm afraid! I've never done anything this large or in front of this many women before. I'm afraid!*

Well, both you and I know that fear is never a valid reason for refusing to do anything...if God is asking us to do it. Oh no! Our God has promised to supply *all* our needs (Philippians 4:19)—and that includes power in weakness and courage in the face of fear. Our God has promised that His grace will *always* be "sufficient" (2 Corinthians 12:9) when we need it to do His will. And "God did not [I repeat, *not!*] give us a spirit of timidity, but a spirit of power, of love and of self-discipline" (2 Timothy 1:7).

The "fear factor" is certainly one that should be acknowledged and dealt with and prayed about. But fear should never be a reason for saying *no*.

So I acknowledged it. I recorded my heart-response of fear...and then I drew a line through it. I can tell you that *every* day that I prayed over that invitation, my heart immediately muttered, "I'm afraid!" And *every* day I was able to look at that first answer with the line marked boldly through it and the scripture reference "2 Timothy 1:7!" written just as boldly next to it.

Now, what if my answer had been: *Ah, that'll be a lot of work...or take a lot of time...or I just don't feel like doing that?* Or, *I'd have to give up going to the mall...or sacrifice some time with my friends...to do that ministry*?

Well, you get the picture! Write it down, whatever your lame answer is, confess your laziness to the Lord, draw a line through it, and go on praying. You've just surfaced a weakness (maybe even a character flaw), one that you'll probably have to deal with again and again as you seek to *do* (note the energy that is required!) God's will, whatever doing it takes.

Now on to Questions 3 and 4, the ones that surface your *convictions,* what you know and believe to be right or wrong according to the Bible.

Question 3: Why should I do this?—When it was clear that my 93-year-old dad was dying from cancer, my Jim and I had a decision to make. We needed to know how much time I could—and should—give to help out and be present with him as he declined.

Practically, it was an easy decision for us. Our daughters were both married and the nest at home was empty. Also, I didn't have a job outside the home, so my time was my own to manage, and it was available so that I could help.

But most of all, the decision was made easier for us because both Jim and I believed this was one way we could follow the Bible's command to "honor your father and your mother" (Exodus 20:12 and Ephesians 6:2). As a couple we had a conviction about what the Bible said. Therefore, we believed I should do as much as I could to help.

My answers seemed to be lining up to something we could act on with confidence, with faith. Of course, we realized there would be a sacrifice of time, money (for airline tickets and long-distance phone calls), and companionship with one another. Yet we both believed helping my dad (who was 1,500 miles away) was the right thing to do. I had Jim's blessing, approval, and support. And my daughters certainly didn't need me at home.

So off I went to Oklahoma...on the six o'clock morning flight from Los Angeles to Tulsa every Monday morning, and back every Thursday evening when one of my brothers came to take over for the weekend. Little did we know when we prayed—and when God guided us into His will—that those commutes would go on for almost one entire year!

But, my dear young friend, *because* of the prayer process and *because* of praying to understand God's will in this decision, we were committed to do what it took and to see it through. And both Jim and I had perfect peace of mind and heart. To this day, we will tell you that we have no regrets. And here's another blessing! God's grace was sufficient for both of us during every minute of every day for that year.

"The will of God will never lead you where the grace of God cannot keep you."[1]

And I need to say very clearly: *Your* answers to *your* prayer concerns and *your* "decisions to make" will probably turn out completely differently than it would for someone else. You and others will be at different stages in life. Your home life will be different than that of your peers. Your parents may have strong opinions and encourage you in a direction that differs from that of your best friends. You may have a part-time job or school responsibilities (choral group, pep squad, school newspaper, sports team) that make it impossible to do some things that "everyone else" is able to do.

So what can you do? *Pray!* Pray and pray and pray for an understanding of what God's perfect will is *for you!* As you pray, He *will* lead you to find it! And, blessing upon blessings, it will be tailor-made...*just for you!*

Ask yourself, What would Jesus do, and what would Jesus have me do?

Question 4: Why should I not do this?—At one time I had an issue I prayed about long and hard. I agonized over trying to make some kind of decision. I turned to God's Word and read in the Book of Proverbs:

> The way of a fool seems right to him, but a wise man listens to advice (Proverbs 12:15).
>
> Listen to advice and accept instruction, and in the end you will be wise (Proverbs 19:20).

So I took the three pages of notes out of my prayer notebook where I had been recording my prayer progress each day on this particular item and gave them to my husband. As I handed them to Jim, I explained, "I just can't get any direction on this prayer request. Can you see if there is anything I'm missing?"

Well, dear Jim read through the decision that needed to be made then looked at my thoughts that I had written down. He knew I'd been praying about the situation. He went over the pros and cons, and then he gave me his advice. Since I respect Jim's opinion and I know he honors God, I accepted his take on the situation. And I made my decision!

And what about you? You don't have a husband you can turn to right now, but you do have mentors, teachers, and parents. So be a "wise" woman! Seek advice from people you trust and admire. And may I encourage you to especially pass your decisions by your mom and dad for their blessing and approval? They love you and will help you. I know it can be hard to consult your parents, but if you desire *God's* direction and blessing, *He* says to "obey your parents" and to "honor" them "that it may go well with you" (Ephesians 6:1-3). *Their* input will help guide you to *God's* will.

As I said, these are examples of how this four-question exercise has worked for me. And now I'm praying it will help *you* to better understand the will of God for *your* life...and your every decision. You will want to use these four questions for each and every decision you pray about, large or small.

Ask these questions about *every* prayer concern. Should you sign up for a Bible study? Volunteer for a ministry? Attend the Saturday youth conference at church? Apply to a certain college. Accept a date? Continue to go out with a certain guy? Purchase that CD? Go to that concert? Sign up for an after-school sport or extracurricular activity? Go out with your friends the night of your little brother or sister's birthday party?

On and on goes the list of issues and concerns that make up a woman's wonderful—and challenging!—life. And for every single one of them, you will definitely come closer to discovering God's will by first determining *No decision made without prayer!* and then by asking these four questions as you pray for understanding.

My Checklist for Prayer

✓ *Do it now!*—Stop making decisions you don't pray about! So far we've learned that a life of *faith*, a life of *wisdom*, and a life of *understanding* are all realized when we pray. So do it now! Make the decision that affirms *No decision made without prayer*. Begin putting every activity and possibility on trial through prayer.

Yes, *every* activity! There are plenty of activities that will compete for your time, attention, and energy. But which one or ones should you accept or attempt to accomplish? Put each one on trial. Pray over them. Ask God for His wisdom to choose your activities carefully and intelligently. And ask your parents or pastor, too. What glorious confidence you'll have in your heart as you walk—in God's will—into an activity or commitment *knowing* that it was chosen through and after much prayer!

Wow! Talk about becoming the woman after God's own heart that you've dreamed of becoming! Oh, dear one, prayer is the key! Prayer is the answer! Prayer is the way! When you answer God's call to pray, you become the woman He designed *you* to be—one who walks with Him in faith, wisdom, and understanding; one who walks confidently and graciously in His will.

Can you remember a decision you made without any help or guidance from God or others? Jot it down below. What happened? What would you do differently now, and why? Also name two or three people you will consult the next time you have to make an important decision.

✓ *Do it now!*—If you haven't already done it, create a "Decisions to Make" section in your prayer notebook or journal…*now!* (If you haven't yet created or purchased a notebook or journal, do it now, too.) Instead of reaping "the trouble in life" that quickly saying *yes* brings your way, *pray!*

"One-half the trouble in life can be traced to saying *yes* too quickly."[2]

And speaking of saying *yes* or *no,* what decision did the young man Daniel and his friends have to make in Daniel 1:1-20? What impresses you most about these bold guys many scholars believe were teenagers?

✓ *Do it now!*—If you haven't already, make a list of the current decisions you need to make. (I counted 14 on my list just this morning.) Create a page for each one and place them in your "Decisions to Make" section. Then prayerfully make your way through them.

And here's a quick fix along the way...just in case you are pressured for a quick answer, *Say no!* And say *no* often. In your life, as in art, less is more. You have prayed long and hard to know God's will. And finally, at last, it is evident what His will is. So, as you step into His good and perfect will, be prepared. You will now need to pray for God's help to say *no*...to yourself when you weaken or get tired, to your flesh when you want something other than God's will, to last-minute invitations to do something else, to the excuses you come up with as to why you don't think you can follow God's will.

Pray to God to help you make it through just this one day of walking in *His* plan and *His* will! And tomorrow plan to do the same. Realize, too, that if and when you are high-pressured into making a hurried decision, "the best answer is always *no*, because *no* is more easily changed to *yes* than *yes* is to *no*."[3]

Look again at Daniel and his friends, you know, the guys who said *no* to the king? What happened in Daniel 3:13-18? Again, what impresses you most about these men after God's own heart?

✎ Answering God's Call to You

Please pardon all of my exclamation marks and the *Do it now's*. But, beloved, this is getting most urgent! For two chapters we have addressed the importance of finding God's will. We admit we desire the benefits that walking in God's will reaps in life. But it is now definitely time to *do* something! It is time to move out in action. To make your commitment. To build your notebook or purchase a journal. To begin sweetly saying, "I'll have to pray about that. Let me get back to you"...instead of blurting out (like I did), "Sure I'll do it" or "No how! No way! No ma'am!"

Again, remember that God expects us to do His will. He also gives us everything we need to do it—

—His all-sufficient grace (2 Corinthians 12:9),

—His "I can do everything through [Christ]" strength (Philippians 4:13),

—His supply of "all your need" (Philippians 4:19), and

—His promise of "everything we need for life and godliness" (2 Peter 1:3).

Finally, when making decisions, pray...and do a heart check. The condition of your *heart* and your *heart's desire* is vital to understanding and doing God's will. Why? Because God gives this final key to understanding and doing His will—you are to be "doing the will of God *from your heart*" (Ephesians 6:6)!

Now, how's your heart?

Would You Like to Know More? Check It Out!

Read Proverbs 3:5-6, looking at each word. What is God's promise regarding His will in verse 6?

What is your part in discovering God's will according to

verse 5a—

verse 5b—

verse 6—

As you think about your part in discovering God's will, on which point(s) do you tend to fail? How do you think prayer will help?

Write down one decision you are trying or needing to make. Create a prayer page for it, and begin praying through the four questions below. (Make notes here if you'd like.) If you make a decision on it this week, note how you made your decision or why you made it.

Question 1: Why would I do this?
(Remember to confess any unbiblical motives.)

Question 2: Why would I not do this?
(Remember to rule out anything that goes against God's Word.)

Question 3: Why should I do this?
(Remember to look for reasons from God's Word.)

Question 4: Why should I not do this?
(Remember your goal is to obey and please God.)

My List of Things I Don't Want to Forget...
...from This Chapter

Discovering God's Formula for Effective Prayer

8

The Time—and Times—of Prayer

As a child growing up in a home where both parents were schoolteachers, great emphasis was put on learning. Not only were my three brothers and I to learn everything we could, but my parents continued expanding their knowledge. Even during the summer when school was out, one of my parents would go away for a few weeks to complete graduate-level courses toward yet another advanced educational degree.

Well, not for me! I determined. I foolishly thought when I graduated from high school, *No more school for me! I'm out of here!* But now I know better. I now know what you know and what my parents knew—All of life is about learning.

You and I are constantly learning how to do a variety of things, aren't we? We spend hours learning to use a computer, fix our hair, play the piano, or play a sport. On and on our learning opportunities go! And prayer is no different. Read what one man says about learning to pray...and the time it takes to do so:

> It is sheer nonsense for us to imagine that we can learn the high art of getting guidance through communion with the Lord without being willing to set aside time for it and learn to pray.[1]

So far in this book we've looked at God's Word and discovered some things about prayer, the meaning of prayer, and the blessings of prayer. But be prepared! Our focus is switching here. We're going to now learn more about the in's and out's of prayer, about "God's Formula for Effective Prayer"—a formula we can easily follow.

And we are pressing toward the finish line, toward the end of our book. So hang on tight! And hang in there! There will be a new flavor to these fun chapters. They are filled with motivating stories and practical tips to inspire your heart to pray. I like to think of this section as the "sparkle" that the facets in the gem of prayer produce.

The first component of God's formula is...

A Time for Personal Prayer

Do you ever wonder when to pray? If there is a good, better, or best time to pray? Well, looking at some of God's people at prayer shows us a few answers.

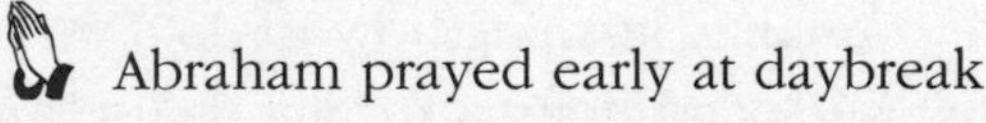

- Abraham prayed early at daybreak.
- Jacob wrestled in prayer all night long.
- Samuel, too, prayed all night.

- The psalmist advised that we pray evening, morning, at noon, day and night, at midnight, with the dawning of the morning, and in the night watches.
- Other saints prayed three times a day, even up to seven times a day!
- Jesus prayed in the morning, prayed through the night, prayed before eating, and prayed at midnight in the Garden of Gethsemane.
- Finally, we are to pray always (Ephesians 6:18) and without ceasing (1 Thessalonians 5:17).

It's easy to see that a common denominator for these faithful pray-ers was a definite time, or times, of prayer.

A Time for Emergency Prayer

In addition to a set time of prayer, "God's Formula for Effective Prayer" includes calling out to Him in a time of emergency. In fact, God pleads with us to "call to me." These words come from Jeremiah 33:3. The full instruction to God's prophet was, "Call to me and I will answer you and tell you great and unsearchable things you do not know." Many people refer to this verse as "God's phone number—JER333." And there are definitely those horrifying *times* of emergency or crisis when we will need to call God's number!

It is during these crisis times that we must do what I once heard described as 9-1-1 praying. Do you realize all that goes on when a 9-1-1 call is made? When you (or even a toddler!) dial those three numbers, you are almost instantly connected with the emergency dispatcher. And in front of that dispatcher is a readout that lists the telephone number you are calling from and the name of the person it is listed to, complete with an address. Also ready to respond are the paramedics and the police and fire departments.

Callers to the 9-1-1 line may not even know what's going on. They're just calling in a time of great need. They may not know what the problem is, or they may not be able to say what the problem is. They may not know where they are. They may be out of control and hysterical because something has happened to a loved one…or to them…or has been witnessed by them.

But the truth is, the dispatcher doesn't actually need the caller to say anything. All a person has to do is make the call…and help is on the way!

Reaching Out to God in Prayer

So it is with the times in our life when we are desperate and in pain. All we have to do is reach out to God in a 9-1-1 call. Just like God said to Jeremiah, "Call to me and *I will answer you.*"

Sure, sometimes we're hysterical. Sometimes we just don't know how to handle what is happening. Sometimes there aren't words to say about what is happening, or there isn't the energy to say anything. But God hears. He knows our trouble. And help is already on the way! He has already begun to bring the

"To flee unto God is the only stay which can support us in our afflictions." —John Calvin answer, the solution, the help, the grace needed when we call upon Him.

And this is what Hannah did when she had no child... and only God could help. Nehemiah called out to God when the city of Jerusalem, God's city, was lying in ruin and only God could change that. The church prayed a 9-1-1 prayer for Peter when he awaited death in prison. And Hezekiah cried out to the Lord when he encountered an illness unto death. Paul beseeched God over and over regarding his thorn in the flesh, something that would not go away, something that caused him great trouble. Moses raised his prayers in the midst of battle. And our Savior poured out His heart to His Father when preparing to meet death on a cross.

In these types and times of trouble—and emergency!—we must call out to the Lord in prayer.

Hearing God's Call to Prayer

"Call to me," saith the Lord. This is a clear command from the God of the universe to our hearts to call *to* and to call *on* Him! His desire for us to call out and pray to Him cannot be missed—"Call to me and I will answer you and tell you great and unsearchable things you do not know" (Jeremiah 33:3). Did you notice that in this call to prayer, you only have to do *one thing*—call upon God? Then He does *two things* for you—He promises to answer you *and* to tell you great and unsearchable things!

So turn your heart upward! In your distress and your concern for others, reach out to God in prayer. Call out to Him, the One who possesses all of the power that exists...as well as all of the comfort, mercy, and lovingkindness. Freely shoot your prayers heavenward. As many as you like! As many as you can! And as many as it takes!

And then stand back, faithful pray-er. For the God of the universe *will* answer you. And, as if that weren't enough, He will also *tell* you wonderful—incredible!—things you do not know.

Talking to God About Your Life

It's obvious, isn't it, that to answer God's call to prayer we must develop our own time for prayer? To make time to talk the important things in our life over with God, we must nail down a time that's best for us. And the exciting thing is, it can be *any* time! But it should also be a *set* time, a certain time, a specific time. That's the way it is with special appointments. For instance, there was a time when I chose early morning as my set time. At that time in my life, if I didn't pray early…I didn't pray! Then things changed (as they always do!), and I switched my time, choosing to pray first thing after everyone left the house in the morning.

So pick *your* time—the one that fits *your* lifestyle best—and then follow the three steps in the "My Checklist for Prayer." You'll be well on your way to becoming a woman of prayer!

My Checklist for Prayer

✓ *First, get organized*—Set a time for prayer. Plan it, schedule it, protect it, and keep it as if it were an appointment.

Perhaps you remember dating a special guy and how wonderful that was? Can you recall how you relished the thought of every time you were going to be able to see him? You had a "date"...and a date on the calendar! Why, you were so excited that you put in extra time in preparation to get yourself ready to meet him, taking great care to be at your best.

Well, the same should be true concerning you and a regular date with God to pray. This message came home loud and clear to me during one of my husband's annual two-week training camps for the Army Reserve. Something came up that meant I had to call him at exactly 5:45 A.M. So the night before, I set my alarm for 3:30 A.M. (!!!) to allow for the two-hour difference between our time zones...and some time to splash cold water on my face and drink a cup of coffee.

The night before I also wrote out a list of the questions I needed to ask Jim, knowing there wouldn't be much time to talk with him. I even laid out a pen and paper for writing down Jim's answers and advice.

The next day when the alarm went off, I tore out of bed, went through my waking-up drill, and sat...watching the clock, watching the clock, watching the clock. Finally, at last! at 3:44 (my time) I dialed the special phone number...and Jim picked up the phone and said, "Hello, Elizabeth."

Now, while I was sitting there with my heart racing in anticipation, sitting there waiting and going through all my preparations, I was also sitting there thinking, *Why can't I do this every morning to talk with God? Why can't I prepare to meet with the Lord in prayer the night before—get out a pad and pen, be organized about what I want to say to Him and need to ask of Him? Why can't I set the alarm, get right up and splash cold water on my face, have a cup of coffee or a glass of juice, sit and wait for that appointment with God, meet with Him right on schedule, and hear Him say (so to speak), "Hello, Elizabeth!"? Why can't I take the time and care to share my concerns with God in prayer and write down the answers He gives me?*

And the answer was crystal clear! I needed to *set* a time for prayer...so that I could *have* a time for prayer.

And the same is true for you. Get organized. What time is best for you? Pick a time and write your daily "date" with God right on your daily calendar. In fact, why don't you figure out when you can pray every day this week. Write it down here and follow through. I know you can do it, and you'll be amazed at the results!

✓ *Second, get ready*—Begin the night before and the morning of. It's true that...

— the prepared person succeeds and the unprepared one fails;

— 75 percent of victory and achievement is traced back to preparation—maybe even 80 percent!

Prepare by *thinking about your prayer time*... about how much you look forward to it, about how important prayer is to your spiritual growth, about how crucial it is that your loved ones be prayed for, about the sheer joy of being obedient in this commanded spiritual discipline, about the unbelievable privilege you have to commune with and worship God in this most intimate way.

Then continue your preparations by *thinking about your needs* during your prayer time. My needs for contacting my husband included a quarter-hour head-start (for clearing my head!), some nourishment, a pad and pen—all of which I also need for my daily prayer time.

Do your prayer needs include setting out your favorite pen and a prayer notebook or journal and making a cup of hot chocolate? What else? (Please answer on the next page.) I even read about one woman who feels like she needs to brush her teeth before she "talks" to God.

> "Before beginning, prepare carefully."
> —Cicero

Know what you need to do for making the most of your time of prayer.

Finally, prepare the night before by *getting to bed on time.* Schedule backward from your ideal prayer time to allow yourself the sleep time you need. Be ruthless as you beeline to bed. And don't forget to set the alarm! Then pray...to get up to pray!

Scheduling is everything when it comes to doing what you want to do. So what do you need to do in advance to get up and pray tomorrow morning? What time did you choose for prayer? And what time will you need to get to bed?

✓ *Third, get up*—And how is this accomplished? By getting up! I won't belabor the point, but I know people who sleep with their cell phones *and* telephones next to the bed. And believe me (and you know it, too), whenever either phone rings, they jump to answer! Their hearts are pounding, the adrenaline is flowing, and the blood is pumping...and they're up! (And it's just a telephone!)

"Mind over mattress!"

This must become your response to your alarm's sound. Treat it like it is God calling you to prayer. It's your Commander-in-Chief. It's the Ruler of your life. It's the Master bidding you to join Him in prayer. So...get up!

Now, review the list of "times" for prayer in this chapter under the subhead "A Time for Personal Prayer." How can you follow in the steps of these people who prayed? Again, what time have you chosen to be "your" time to answer God's call to prayer?

✎ Answering God's Call to You

My dear friend, although prayer is a sacred privilege, in some ways it is no different than any other activity you choose to undertake—you must first want to learn about prayer so you can enjoy praying. Won't you answer God's call to prayer by the simple act of choosing a time for prayer? Then be faithful. Keep your commitment. Show up at the appointed time...and revel in the joy of communing with Him.

> "He who has learned to pray has learned the greatest secret of a holy and a happy life."[2]

The Difference Prayer Makes

I got up early one morning
And rushed right into the day;
I had so much to accomplish
That I didn't take time to pray.

Problems just tumbled about me,
And heavier came each task;
"Why doesn't God help me?" I wondered.
He answered: "You didn't ask."

I wanted to see joy and beauty—
But the day toiled on, gray and bleak;
I wondered why God didn't show me,
He said, "But you didn't seek."

I tried to come into God's presence,
I used all my keys at the lock;
God gently and lovingly chided:
"My child, you didn't knock."

I woke up early this morning
And paused before entering the day;
I had so much to accomplish
That I had to take time to pray.[3]

Would You Like to Know More? Check It Out!

What do you learn about the time and times of prayer from these people?

Abraham in Genesis 19:27—

Nehemiah in Nehemiah 2:1-5—

David in Psalm 5:3—

Peter in Matthew 14:25-33—

Jesus in Mark 1:35—

Can you think of others? Who are they, and when did they pray?

Can you think of changes you need to make in your prayer-life?

Read Mark 14:32-42. What was Jesus' distressing situation here?

What words describe His agony?

How did He handle it?

What did He ask of Peter, James, and John?

How long was Jesus' time of prayer?

How many of these times of prayer did Jesus have?

What is your most distressing issue at this time, and what does Jesus' example teach you to do...or to do better?

Who do you know who is currently in a time of distress? How can you pray faithfully for him or her?

My List of Things I Don't Want to Forget... ...from This Chapter

9

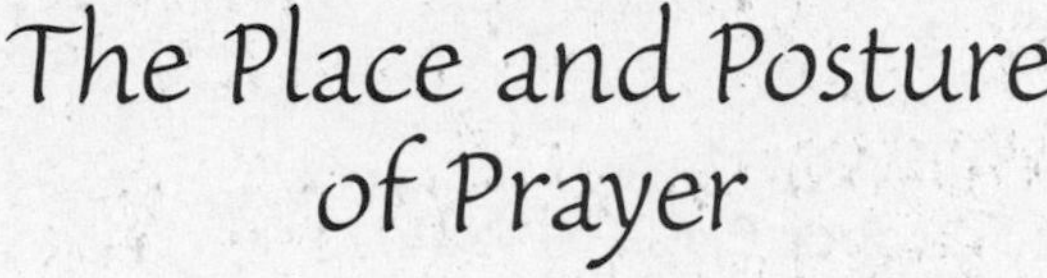

The Place and Posture of Prayer

I'm sure you've met people who impacted your life, making your time with them especially meaningful. Well, that's what happened to me one wonderful weekend in the beautiful state of Washington.

After a women's event, I stayed overnight in the home of the retreat coordinator so I could catch the first flight home the next morning. As Jennifer and I sat in her kitchen (where else!), she told me how she and her husband had purchased their home from her mother after her dad died and her mom moved to a smaller place.

Then Jennifer shared, "Elizabeth, we remodeled the whole house. But there was one thing in the house that I couldn't touch, and that's this kitchen counter." She went on to explain, "All my life, every morning when I came down from sleep, the first thing I saw was my mother, sitting right here at the end of this counter, praying. That's why I couldn't touch this counter. It was my mother's prayer place."

But the story goes on. The next morning when I came down the stairs that entered the kitchen, there was my hostess, sitting on a stool at the end of that kitchen counter with her Bible and notebook spread out, having her prayer time. You guessed it—Jennifer had made it her prayer place, too!

Is There a Proper Place to Pray?

We already know that we can pray to God at any time, day or night. God never sleeps, and He is always available to His people (Psalm 121:3). His ears are always open to us, and He hears our prayers (1 Peter 3:12). But let's take our desire to answer God's call to prayer and to discover His formula for effective prayer one step further and ask, *Is there a correct or proper place to pray?*

A quick look at both Old Testament and New Testament pray-ers shows us that we can approach God anywhere with our prayers. For example,

— King David prayed in a cave (Psalm 57).

— The Israelites prayed in the wilderness (1 Kings 8:33-34,47-49).

— Elijah prayed in an upper room in a house (1 Kings 17:20).

— Daniel prayed in his room (Daniel 2:19).

— Sailors prayed in their ship (Jonah 1:13-14).

— Peter prayed on a housetop (Acts 10:9).

— Lydia and a group of women prayed by the river side (Acts 16:13).

— Paul and Silas prayed in stocks in a prison (Acts 16:25).

— Paul and the disciples at Tyre prayed on the beach (Acts 21:5).

God's people are to pray *every*where (1 Timothy 2:8)...from *any* place...at *any* time. We can pray while we're doing homework, while we're in the shower, while we're driving a car or riding in an airplane, while we're down on our knees working on a project, or while we're at the kitchen counter...like my friend did.

A Journey to a Place of Prayer

I was just thinking through my own journey into prayer and the variety of my places of prayer. My first prayer place was a table with a nice big area for all my prayer "things." For years I did my praying there. Then, for some reason, I switched my place of prayer to the sofa. I covered the couch, the floor, the coffee table—every square inch!—with all my prayer stuff and prayed to my heart's content.

After we moved, my next place of prayer was my bed. I l-o-v-e my bed! And there was plenty of room on it for my Bible, prayer notebook, colored markers, and, of course, every girl's favorite—the Kleenex box! That was my favorite place to pray...then. But as time went on, I moved down to the cuddly chair in my little office. There I had a floor-to-ceiling bookcase where every kind of tool (such as Bible commentaries) I would ever need during prayer was available (that is...until an earthquake demolished my office!).

But I have to report that no matter where I settled in to pray, my notebook has been my Number One mainstay and prayer tool for the 20-plus years I've been on my personal prayer journey. I keep all sorts of prayer "lists" in it. For instance…

I have a page for my own "Personal list"—my dreams of serving God and my goals for life. Then I have a "Family list" and a "People list." We've already discussed the necessity of a "Decisions-to-Make list." I also keep a "Spiritual Growth list" that's filled with resolutions and the lists of "alwayses" and "nevers" that you and I both hope and pray will become true in our conduct! All the projects I'm working on are on my "Projects list," and ministry events are on my "Ministry list." I even have a "Crisis list" for all the crises that are going on in my or my extended family and friends' lives at any given time!

Your prayer place will be different than mine. And the tools you use to make your prayer-life more powerful and efficient—and exciting!—will differ from mine. But, oh, what a thrill it will be to see your prayer place and your prayer plan—and your prayer-life!—evolve into something that is organized. That indicates a serious pray-er, a woman who is making her desire to pray a reality.

The Places of Prayer for Others

Would you like to know how some others have prayed and where their places of prayer were? Let's peek in on a few!

Susannah Wesley, the mother of the famous brothers, John and Charles Wesley, would simply pull her apron up over her head, and that provided an instant place of prayer for her. Maybe as the mother of ten children that's the only place she could find to pray! Those children, though, came to recognize their mother's apron as a "Do Not Disturb—Woman at Prayer" sign! (What's your sign?)

John Wesley, the son of Susannah and the founder of Methodism, had a "prayer chamber" in his home. Jim and I actually got to tour Wesley's home and stood for some time in his private prayer chamber. It has been preserved exactly as it was when this great man of God knelt there before the Almighty. It's a little room off his bedroom. And there's nothing in it except a table with a candlestick and a Greek New Testament on it and a small stool—sort of a kneeling stool.

The guide told us that this little room, this "prayer room," was "the powerhouse of Methodism." It was Mr. Wesley's prayer place. (Do you have a place or a room or, more importantly, a habit of praying that others could point to as "the powerhouse" of your life?)

John Fletcher, eighteenth-century theologian, was said to have stained the walls of his chamber with the breath of his prayers lifted from his prayer place. (How do the walls of your prayer place measure up?)

Early African converts to Christianity were very earnest and regular in their personal devotions. Each man would go out through the bush to a private place to pray. Soon the routine of trekking through the grass marked out distinct paths as the grass became beaten down. One look and everyone could tell if someone was faithful in prayer because his path was obvious. But if anyone began to neglect his prayer time, it was also quite obvious. And, sure enough, soon one of the brothers-in-Christ would come and say, "Brother, the grass grows on your path." (How's the "path" to your prayer place? Is it well used?)

Ruth Graham, wife of Billy Graham, believes we should leave our Bibles out and open someplace in our room or house so that "whenever there is a lull in the storms of life, we can grab a cup of coffee and sit down for a time of pure refreshment and companionship."[1] (So…where can you squeeze in a soda and enjoy some rich companionship with "the God of peace"?)

The Place of Prayer for You

Do any of these examples inspire you to find a special place to pray? Jesus said, "Go into your room, close the door and pray to your Father, who is unseen" (Matthew 6:6). Some would call such a room their "prayer closet," a place where their prayer-life is nurtured. One writer—and pray-er—points out,

> Oh! You can pray anywhere…but you are not likely to unless you are off in some quiet place shut in with God….Enter into thine inner chamber, and shut thy door. That door is important. It shuts out, and it shuts in….God is here in this shut-in spot. One must get alone to find out that he is never alone.[2]

Do whatever it takes to have *your* place of prayer. Whether it's a literal closet or some other place, create *your* secret place where you meet with the Lord to pray.

Is There a Proper Posture for Prayer?

Many Christians believe that kneeling is the biblical posture for prayer. We think immediately of Jesus kneeling in the Garden of Gethsemane to pray (Luke 22:41). Or of the apostle Paul kneeling on the beach with the elders from Ephesus and with his disciples in Tyre (Acts 20:36; 21:5).

It's true that many of God's people throughout time have prayed on their knees. For instance, in the early days of our republic a stranger asked at Congress how he would distinguish George Washington from the rest of the people. He was told that he could easily recognize him. When Congress goes to prayer, Washington is the gentleman who always kneels.

Also it was said of hymn-writer Fanny Crosby that she never attempted to write music or lyrics without first kneeling to pray about the undertaking. That meant she spent a great deal of time on her knees because she wrote more than 8,000 hymns of faith!

Then there is James, the leader of the church in Jerusalem. He was known as "camel knees" by the early church. "When they came to coffin him, it was like coffining the knees of a camel rather than the knees of a man, so hard, so worn, so stiff were they from prayer, and so unlike any other dead man's knees they had ever coffined."[3] (How are *your* knees, dear pray-er?)

I have also saved these few lines from a poem that points to the usefulness of praying on your knees.

Traveling on My Knees

Last night I took a journey
to a land across the sea.
I did not go by boat or plane,
I traveled on my knees.[4]

Praying on your knees is a graphic picture of one who is humble of heart. But, as biblical as kneeling may be, the Bible shows us a variety of postures for prayer.

❀ The people of God *bowed their heads* in worship (Exodus 4:31).

❀ Moses and Aaron repeatedly *fell on their faces* to pray (Numbers 16:22 is one instance).

❀ Hannah *stood* at the doorway of the tabernacle, praying (1 Samuel 1:12-14).

❀ David *sat* before the Lord and prayed (2 Samuel 7:18).

❀ David also *fasted* and *lay on the ground* all night praying (2 Samuel 12:16).

❀ Solomon *knelt* with his *hands spread out* toward heaven and prayed (1 Kings 8:54).

❀ Elijah *bowed down* and *put his face between his knees* and prayed (1 Kings 18:42; James 5:18).

❀ Jonah prayed to the Lord *from the stomach of a fish* (Jonah 2:1). (Wc can only imagine what his posture was during his impassioned prayer on that wild ocean voyage!)

❀ Ezra *bowed down*, wept, and prayed (Ezra 10:1).

❀ The tax collector *hung his head* and *beat on his breast*, and in humility of heart *stood* afar off and prayed (Luke 18:13).

❀ Jesus poured out His prayers *on His face* in the Garden of Gethsemane (Matthew 26:39).

The Bible does not give any final instruction on the "right" posture of our praying. But one thing is certain from these examples—These people's postures during prayer indicated what was going on in their hearts! Some were worshiping as God's law prescribed. Some were torn in emotional agony. Some were suffering personally, and some were suffering for others. Some were sorry over sin. Some were in battle, either literal war or for the lives and souls of others. Some were asking for a miracle. Some were joyful or thankful. Whatever emotion their life situation evoked, it was expressed in the posture of the pray-ers.

"When You Pray…"

Jesus cautions us not to use prayer as a means of getting attention. Our voice and posture of prayer can actually distract others and interfere with *their* prayer and worship. Prayer can also so easily be done for the wrong reasons. So be sure and check your motives for the manner in which you pray. Jesus advises us...

> when you pray, do not be like the hypocrites, for they love to pray standing in the synagogues and on the street corners, to be *seen by men* (Matthew 6:5).

Jesus continues His instruction on prayer by giving a solution for making sure we don't use prayer as an avenue for "showing off":

> But when you pray, go into your room, close the door and pray to your Father, who is unseen. Then your Father, who sees what is done in secret, will reward you (verse 6).

Notice in both verses the issue is not "if" you pray, but "when you pray." Jesus assumes that you (and I!) are going to pray. His people are called to pray, commanded to pray, expected to pray, and instructed on how to pray. But the issue is always the heart—whether or not your heart is right before God.

And, dear one, if your only desire is to worship God and praise Him and petition Him and pour out your heart to Him, then there will never be a wrong posture for your prayers. Why, you could even pray standing on your head, as the following discussion illustrates!

The Prayer of Cyrus Brown

"The proper way for man to pray,"
said Deacon Lemuel Keyes,
"the only proper attitude
is down upon his knees."

"Nay, I should say, the way to pray,"
said Reverend Dr. Wise,
"is standing straight with outstretched arms,
with rapt and upturned eyes."

"Oh, no, no no!"
said Elder Snow.
"Such posture is too proud.
A man should pray with eyes fast closed
and head contritely bowed."

"It seems to me his hands should be
austerely clasped in front,
with both thumbs pointing to the ground,"
said Reverend Dr. Blunt.

"Last year I fell in Hodgkins' well,
head first," said Cyril Brown,
"with both my heels a stickin' up,
my head a pointin' down.

"And I done prayed right then and there,
the best prayer I ever said,
the prayin'est prayer I ever prayed,
a standin' on my head!"[5]

My Checklist for Prayer

✓ *Describe*...your place of prayer—Do you have one? Share about it below. If you are having trouble praying with all of the distractions of a bustling family, with a phone that won't stop ringing, maybe a prayer closet is what you need.

Or are you homeless when it comes to prayer? Or a vagabond...you pray here a little, there a little, everywhere a little-little? Answer honestly. If either is true, then...

✓ *Decide*...where your place will be—Experiment. Move around. Sooner or later you'll feel "at home" and enjoy success in your prayer efforts. Your heart will tell you when you're "home"!

So describe away! Also take time to list any "prayer-home improvements" you can make.

✓ *Dedicate...*yourself to private prayer—It's fun and exciting to pray with others, to pray for one another, and to praise God together. Such times of group prayer are a thrilling part of "body life"—*koinonia*—among Christians. But be sure you spend the majority of your time in prayer *out* of the public eye... "praying in secret." Why?

First, it will affirm your motives for prayer. You can commune earnestly and sincerely and passionately with God with no distractions. It's just you and Him behind that closed door. So pray, dear one, to your "audience of One"!

And second, a "secret" prayer life allows you to focus on the real and personal—and private!—issues of life that you need to talk over with God. When you're alone you can concentrate your full energy and efforts for a more meaningful and productive time of prayer.

Just for this next week, keep a record of the amount of time you spend praying in private. What does your record-keeping reveal?

Monday _____ Friday _____

Tuesday _____ Saturday _____

Wednesday _____ Sunday _____

Thursday _____

✎ Answering God's Call to You

Dear friend, God is calling you to a life of prayer. Prayer is one act of worship and service that you can do at any time and in any place. So lift your voice to God. Yes, prayer is a blessing—but praying is not easy! Your life, like mine, is filled with a multitude of activities that can crowd out your times for prayer. And there is also the battle against your flesh as you struggle with sin and spiritual laziness. And since prayer is a spiritual exercise, if you aren't careful you can find yourself fleeing from the presence of the Lord because of a divided, impure, and empty heart.

My dear sister-in-prayer, I hope you'll join me so that we may answer God's call to prayer together. Let us lift our voices to His throne of grace!

Would You Like to Know More? Check It Out!

Read Matthew 6:5-6.

What are Jesus' instructions regarding a place of prayer?

What is Jesus' message regarding your motives in your prayer times?

What does Jesus teach regarding your heavenly Father?

After reflecting on these teachings, how important is praying in private?

Review the list of people in the section in your book entitled "Is There a Proper Posture for Prayer?" What is the key message to your heart from these faithful pray-ers?

Read John 4:19-24. What is the most important element of true worship, of which prayer is a part?

My List of Things I Don't Want to Forget...
...from This Chapter

Developing the Habit of Prayer

10

How Can I Learn to Pray?

When we began our pilgrimage into prayer, you and I set our sights—and our hearts—on answering God's call to prayer. The deep desire of our hearts was to make prayer a reality in our lives. And to launch our journey together, we took a look in the mirror and asked, "What keeps me from praying?" And now we have come full circle. We've considered some reasons we don't pray more often...and hopefully done something about them. We've also looked at some of the distressing circumstances in life that move us to pray...and learned that we must talk them over with God, pray for wisdom, and leave our requests with Him.

And now that we are turning our hearts toward the end of our wonderful journey together, it's time to ask and answer the question, How can I learn to pray? Let's discover how to put our efforts at prayer into warp speed. Here we go!

1. *Use a prayer list or notebook*—How many times have you been guilty of telling people you would pray for them—and then not doing it? When you heard their request or their

problem, you were deeply moved and genuinely desired to pray for them…but then you forgot all about it!

With a place to write down your prayer concerns, you improve your prayer-life immediately. Learn to carry a small spiral pad with you or a 3" x 5" card. Then, whenever people ask you to pray for them or share that they are struggling with an issue, write it down. Later on, move it to your prayer notebook and, of course, pray faithfully!

(And P.S. If it's at all possible, pray with hurting people on the spot. Your instant, on-the-spot prayer can give them immediate relief and peace in their hurting hearts.)

And how about your own life—your own problems and concerns? A prayer list or notebook, although physically only paper and cardboard, is a marvelous spiritual aid to your prayer-life. It's a tool that…

- ❀ orders your prayers,
- ❀ helps you remember who and what to pray for,
- ❀ serves as a visual reminder of God's faithfulness and goodness as He answers your prayer requests, and
- ❀ creates a historical accounting of God's workings in your life and in other people.

2. *Schedule a prayer time each day*—When you or I don't schedule something, it usually doesn't get done. And the same is true with prayer. You can think about praying. You can talk about praying. You can worry about praying. You can wish to be praying. You can even pray to be

praying! But until you schedule the act of prayer, it probably won't happen regularly.

So pick an amount of time and a set time. I began my personal journey into prayer with five minutes a day! My overriding principle was *Something is better than nothing!* My five minutes became the bait that drew me into experiencing sweet, precious times of prayer—many of those times extending on and on. Forget the clock! Once I was started, I couldn't stop! Sure, there were those days when five minutes was all there was. But I began small...and, in time, witnessed mighty effects! And the same will be true for you when you schedule a prayer time each day.

3. *Spend time praying with others*—The habit of praying is born and nurtured in private. But praying with others matures and enhances your prayer-life. Do you know some sisters-in-Christ who share your heart for prayer? Maybe you can establish a prayer group with those young women who share your passion. You can meet at the church, in homes, at school, or even in a park! Just be sure you actually pray when you get together. Answer God's call to prayer together.

4. *Pray using Scripture*—God not only loves to hear His own Word, but there is power in His Word. Indeed, "the word of God is living and active. Sharper than any double-edged sword..." (Hebrews 4:12)! So make it a goal to incorporate scriptures into your prayers. You don't know which scriptures to use? Try this. Highlight your favorite prayer verses in your Bible with a marker. Then pray down through your Bible!

And here's another idea. Try inserting people's names into different verses. Do a trial run through Colossians 1:9-10. You'll love praying for your friends and family in this exciting—and easy—way!

5. *Borrow from the prayers of others*—Of course you'll want to pray your own prayers. But your praying shouldn't stop there. Expand! Grow! Read and pray through the written prayers of others. The powerful prayers of others can be used to bombard heaven like heavy artillery. They help us grow in our prayer skills and passion, and improve our "prayer language" by their eloquence. (To help you, I've included several titles of books of prayers in the back of this book.)

6. *Open and close each day with a time of prayer*—A favorite psalm of mine calls us to declare God's "lovingkindness *in the morning*" and His "faithfulness *every night*" (Psalm 92:2). Morning and evening prayers have been labeled "dawn and dusk bookends."

"Prayer is the key of the morning and the bolt of the night."[1]

Morning and evening. You can develop the habit of beginning and ending each day with prayer. First thing...and last thing! First word...and last word! They belong to God.

7. *Get inspired by the biographies of others who prayed*—Have you guessed yet that I have a passion for reading the biographies of people who prayed? I have a bookshelf full of books about the prayer-journeys God's people have

taken with Him down through the centuries. Each person I journey alongside becomes a friend, a teacher, a model, and a spiritual coach.

I encourage you to do the same thing. But try to take your reading a step further. *Journal* what you're learning! Copy out the most moving passages and quotes from these books. Yes, I mark in my books, but I can't always carry the books with me. However, I can carry my journal anywhere...and then sit back and read it over and over again.

(And here's another P.S.: I've included several of these book titles in the back of this book. Start with *Stepping Heavenward* because it's a diary that a young woman began on her fourteenth birthday and wrote in for 20-plus years.)

8. *Study the prayers of the Bible*—I've been sharing a lot of my "favorites" in this book—favorite quotes, stories, scriptures, books and authors, heroes of the faith, and prayer practices. But nothing is more powerful in the Prayer Department than the actual prayers recorded in the Bible.

For instance, the prayer of Mary, the mother of our Lord Jesus (Luke 1:46-55) is referred to as "Mary's Magnificat." Like the "Lord's Prayer" prayed by Jesus, you can learn a lot about prayer by reading this inspired worship prayer. Mary...

 verbalized her personal joy in the Lord's work in her life (verses 46-48),

 exalted the person of God and His work "from generation to generation" (verses 49-50),

- praised God for His dealings with mankind (verses 51-53), and
- pointed to God's mercy in fulfilling the covenant promise He made to "His servant Israel" (verses 54-55).

9. *Follow through with your resolve: No decision made without prayer*—Your first decision each day must be to pray. This choice will provide you with the time and opportunity to follow through. As you pray over your decisions, God will lead you to find and fulfill His will for your time, your day, and your life.

Amazingly, once time is spent making decisions in prayer, your time is better managed, spent, and saved as a result of walking in God's will. So never forget: *No decision made without prayer!*

10. *Feed your heart and mind with God's Word*—The Bible is the major stimulus for our prayer-life. Through it God speaks to us and fills our hearts and minds with spiritual truths. Prayer is a spiritual work, and no other book can inspire the spiritual work of prayer like the spiritual power of the Bible.

Think about it. Practically speaking, *nothing going in, equals nothing going out*. When we don't read God's Word and expose ourselves to its purity and power, we usually don't think about God and, therefore, we usually don't pray.

Also, *trivia going in, equals trivia going out*. When you hear a person talk trivia (about the latest TV talk show, movie news, gossip), you know what they are feeding on.

And the same goes for "trash"! *Trash going in, equals trash going out!*

But *God's Word going in, equals God's Word going out.* In the case of Mary and her "Magnificat," something was—and had been—going in...for years! And that something was God's law and the knowledge of His dealings with His people. Mary's heart and soul (and remember she, too, was a teenager!) were saturated with God's Word. How do we know this? Because it leaked out of her lips! Because her worship prayer contains about 15 references to Old Testament scriptures. Mary's heart and soul were filled-to-overflowing with God's holy Word. And overflow it did! Her praise and prayer came gushing forth as she "glorified" the God she loved and knew so well through His Word.

My Checklist for Prayer

✓ *Learn*...to leave things undone—Our Number One priority is God, and that includes time spent with Him. All things related to nurturing our relationship with Him—like prayer!—should be first on our "to-do" list. I had to learn that as soon as my husband was off to work and my girls were off to school, the first thing I had to do was pray. It was the only way I could ensure that the most important things—time in God's Word and prayer—got done first! *Then* came everything else in my day.

And it was a struggle! Devotional writer Oswald Chambers understood this well. He writes, We can hinder the time that should be spent with God by remembering we have other things to do. I haven't time. Of course you have not time! Take time! Strangle some other interest and make time to realize that the center of power in your life is the Lord Jesus Christ."[2]

Ask yourself the question, What do I do each day that I think is more important than spending time with God in prayer? The answer, of course, is *nothing!* And so we learn to leave lesser things undone...and pray!

> "Prayer does not fit us for the greater work; prayer *is* the greater work"![3]

I've said it before—we are extremely busy women! Make a list of the things that keep you from praying. Then read Luke 10:38-42. How will you begin to choose what is better—to choose "the thing" that "will not be taken away" from you?

✓ *Learn*...to switch disciplines—As I began to pray regularly, I had to learn to switch disciplines. I had to learn to take a discipline that was already a part of my life and add the new discipline of prayer *ahead of* it.

Let me explain. If you already have the discipline of reading or studying your Bible in place, that discipline is already a part of your life. It's a habit. So now, what you need to do is put prayer *ahead of* your other discipline. Put prayer *in front of* the discipline that's already in place. It takes some doing—and some discipline—but you can learn to leave other things undone until you take care of one of the most important things in your life—answering God's call to prayer.

List some of the things you do every day at the same time. Get up? Do homework? Go to a part-time job? Go to a practice? How can you fit prayer ahead of one of these "disciplines"?

✓ *Learn*...to combine disciplines—I recently met a woman, a "baby Christian," who told me when her time of prayer was. Sandy was going through physical therapy for an injury and had to ride an exercycle for 15 minutes a day at her therapist's treatment center. She said she decided to designate that 15 minutes as her prayer time! Here was a new Christian who had already gone to work on developing the habit of prayer...and had learned to combine her disciplines!

I personally combine walking each day with praying and memorizing Scripture...whether I walk outside or on a treadmill. What other discipline could you combine with prayer? And what do you need to do to prepare to use that time for prayer?

✎ Answering God's Call to You

Dear one, you (and I) are called to pray...period. You are to pray alone, to shut your door and pray to your Father in secret (Matthew 6:6). You are to pray with a handful of faithful others, like Daniel probably did with his three friends (Daniel 1:17-20) and like Paul and Silas did (Acts 16:25). And you are to pray along with others as a corporate body like the disciples of Christ did while gathered in an upper room (Acts 1:13-15). As we'll see in our final chapter, prayer is all-encompassing. It is to be such a vital part of your life that you are praying at all times, in all ways, for all people. (Oh, what joy!)

As we are bringing our thoughts to a close on this most important topic—that of developing the habit of prayer—

please, oh please, do these two things to improve your personal prayer-life:

- Do what you must to ensure that you pray daily, regularly, habitually.
- Do remember that prayer is not about you. It is about God, and about your relationship with God, and about your walk with God, and about your being a woman after God's own heart.

So pray, dear heart! Answer God's call to prayer. Do whatever it takes to make your desire to pray a reality. Do whatever you must to develop the habit of prayer.

> "Prayer crowns God with the honor and glory due to His name."[4]

Would You Like to Know More? Check It Out!

List the ten ways to improve your prayer-life and look up the corresponding Bible references. Then write out what you have done or plan to do about each one. Also share how you have been blessed or seen God work with each of these steps as you have begun answering God's call to prayer.

1.

2.

3.

4.

5.

6.

7.

8.

9.

10.

My List of Things I Don't Want to Forget...
...from This Chapter

11

When You Are Anywhere and at Any Time...Pray!

We did it! We made it to the end of our book about a woman's call to prayer and about our desire to answer God's call. As we look back together, I hope the following truths were communicated to your heart.

Biblical—First and foremost, my prayer throughout this book was to emphasize what is biblical. I wanted us to see a little of what the Bible teaches about prayer. I hope you now have a better understanding and more insights into prayer (although, as we learned, prayer "is beyond our limited human understanding" and "is a topic too deep for the human intellect"[1]).

Practical—I also prayed as I shared the practical elements concerning prayer. I am a nuts-and-bolts-type person. I love studying the Bible—it tells me *what* it is I am to do. But I also want to know *how* to put the *what* into practice...immediately. I have a desire to know how to do what it is I am learning in the Bible.

That's why I included the "My Checklist for Prayer" after each body of teaching. And that's also why I included the reproducible "My Prayer Calendar" at the back of this book. (Have you been using it all along the way? If so, I'm sure you can see progress as you've moved forward on your journey into prayer!)

Beneficial—Then I prayed that what I wrote would be beneficial. My constant prayer has been that your prayer-life will be enhanced, strengthened, sweetened, and bettered. For oh, what glory and honor such a life of prayer will bring to our God!

Mechanical—All the way through this book I trust the undercurrent of my prayers was evident as I sought to communicate that prayer is *not* to be mechanical. My greatest fear is that in my effort to share what the Bible teaches about prayer you may have been discouraged from realizing the simplicity of prayer. In no way do I want you to think that following a formula + jumping through a series of spiritual hoops = prayer!

Natural—Prayer is to be natural. True, prayer is hard work, a spiritual discipline. It must, like anything of value, be tended, cultivated, and cared for. But prayer should be natural. It should flow from your heart to God's. God has built into our hearts and souls a desire to pray, to communicate with Him, to talk to and seek fellowship with Him as our Father. Indeed, we have much to talk over with our God!

- When we are afraid, we talk it over with our Protector.
- When we are hurting, we talk it over with our Comforter.
- When we have been mistreated or wrongfully accused, we talk it over with our Advocate.
- When we have a need, we talk it over with our Provider.

Simple—As we close this volume about developing a more meaningful prayer-life, I want to leave you with this simple thought: You can—and are to—pray anywhere, at any time, and at all times! How's that for simplicity? God has made it possible for you to be successful in your desire to pray. You can...

...pray always (Ephesians 6:18), and

...pray without ceasing (1 Thessalonians 5:17).

You Can Pray Anywhere!

Do you realize that you and I can pray anywhere? Neither posture nor place is to limit our praying. It's amazing that we can be in a class at school, at a ball game, listening to a friend talk to us in person or on the phone, exercising, driving a car...well,

> "The man who does all his praying on his knees does not pray enough."[2]

you name it, and whatever it is we are doing, we can pray at the same time.

The very act of praying makes us more wise, sympathetic, discerning, godly, and spiritually alert. We don't miss a thing! In fact, everything we are doing is bettered by the act of prayer.

Even in sadness or when we are hurting or confused by something that is going on in our lives, we can continue to function in a noble way and a gracious manner because we are praying.

"Certain thoughts are prayers. There are moments when, whatever be the attitude of the body, the soul is on its knees."[3]

You Can Pray at Any Time!

How busy are you? I think I can guess. You're so busy you don't have time to think about how to answer this question, right? But you and I can thank God that because He is everywhere and because of the indwelling of the Holy Spirit in our lives, we can reach out and touch God at any time through our prayers.

Here's a look at another woman who was busy. Although her lifestyle probably differs from yours, her attitude—and practices—should apply to your life today.

"Forgive us for thinking that prayer is a waste of time, and help us to see that without prayer our work is a waste of time."[4]

How one woman prayed without ceasing—It seems that a number of ministers were assembled for the discussion of difficult questions; and, among others, it was asked how the command to "pray without ceasing" could be complied with. Various suppositions were stated; and at length, one of the number was appointed to write an essay upon it, to be read at the next meeting. This assignment being overheard by a servant, she exclaimed, "What! A whole month waiting to tell the meaning of that text? It is one of the easiest and best texts in the Bible."

"Well, well!" said an old minister. "Mary, what can you say about it? Let us know how you understand it. Can you pray all the time?"

"Oh, yes, sir!"

"What! When you have so many things to do?"

"Why, sir, the more I have to do, the more I can pray."

"Indeed! Well, Mary, do let us know how it is; for most people think otherwise."

"Well, sir," said the girl,

> "when I first open my eyes in the morning, I pray, 'Lord, open the eyes of my understanding;'
>
> and while I am dressing, I pray that I may be clothed with the robe of righteousness; and,
>
> when I have washed me, I ask for the washing of regeneration; and,
>
> as I begin to work, I pray that I may have strength equal to my day;
>
> when I begin to kindle up the fire, I pray that God's work may revive in my soul; and,

> as I sweep out the house, I pray that my heart may be cleansed from all its impurities; and,
>
> while preparing and partaking of breakfast, I desire to be fed with the hidden manna and the sincere milk of the Word; and,
>
> as I am busy with the little children, I look up to God as my Father, and pray for the spirit of adoption, that I may be his child: and so on all day.
>
> Every thing I do furnishes me with a thought for prayer."
>
> Needless to say, after Mary's little "exposition" on the theology of prayer, the essay was not considered necessary![5]

It's true that you and I can answer God's call to pray from anywhere and at any time. And it's true, as sweet Mary put it, that the more a busy woman has to do, the more she can pray! That is...if our hearts are turned upward! That is...if we are thinking about God!

From my own experience, I've noticed that the heart that prays *is* the heart that is turned upward. The heart that prays *is* the heart that is thinking about God, that is relating everything that happens every minute throughout the day to God. It is when I am in the habit of praying each day that, lo and behold, miracle of miracles, that habit leads to praying all the time...everywhere...for all things...for everything!

You Can Pray All the Time!

You can pray anywhere, and you can pray any time. But you also need to be praying *all* the time! Do you remember God's two commands shared earlier in this chapter?

> *Pray always* (Ephesians 6:18).
>
> *Pray without ceasing* (1 Thessalonians 5:17).

In other words, you are to be praying all the time...to make your every breath a prayer. As one of my pastors loved to say, prayer is "spiritual breathing." You take a breath in...and a prayer goes out!

I would have to say that during the months I've been immersed in researching and writing this book about prayer and the practice of prayer, the main impact on my life has been being conscious of praying always. Actually, prayer has become an unconscious act. It seems like, wherever I go, I am lifting up the people around me or the event I'm involved in to the Lord through prayer.

For instance, one morning while I was driving somewhere, there was a terrible accident on one of the freeways. The newscasters were talking so coldly as they reported that it was a fatal accident. It was kind of like, "Well, as soon as someone gets the bodies out of there, and the wreckage cleared away, traffic can flow smoothly again."

And you know, I just started praying about the soul of the person who had died. *Was that person a believer?* I also thought, *That person has family members somewhere!* and I began praying for the relatives. I started praying that God would receive glory and honor through a fatal traffic accident and a jammed freeway filled with frustrated people!

Dear praying heart, everywhere you go, if you think of a person, pray. If you see a person (a new student at school or church, a clerk, a neighbor, a homeless man or woman, a young mom pushing a stroller, a soldier being interviewed on the news), pray. If you know about something that's going on in a person's life, pray. If you have an "enemy," pray. Always be "praying always"...like these people did!

"Are you focusing on a person's faults, or are you lifting that person before the Father?"

Mary Slessor—I once read a diary entry in Mary Slessor's journal. She was a single, nineteenth-century Scottish missionary to Africa who wrote, "My life is one long daily, hourly record of answered prayer. For physical health, for mental overstrain, for guidance given marvelously, for errors and dangers averted, for enmity to the gospel subdued, for food provided at the exact hour needed, for everything that goes to make up life and my poor service to my Savior."[6]

One long daily, hourly prayer! Yes!

John Fletcher—It was the custom of John Fletcher of Madeley, England, never to meet a Christian without saying, "Friend, do I meet you praying?" This unusual salutation reminded the person that his life should be an unbroken expression of prayer and fellowship with God.[7]

An unbroken expression of prayer and fellowship with God! Yes!

Stonewall Jackson—Confederate General "Stonewall" Jackson is described as a man of prayer. He said, "I have so fixed the habit of prayer in my mind that I never raise a glass of water to my lips without asking God's blessing, never seal a letter without putting a word of prayer under that seal, never take a letter to the post without a brief sending of my thoughts heavenward."[8]

"I have so fixed the habit of prayer in my mind...." Yes!

The message is clear, isn't it? We are to take *every* opportunity, during *whatever* is happening, and through *every* event of daily life, to pray...*all* the time. And we can do it, no matter what is transpiring. May the following prayer become yours as you call upon the Lord continually!

Lord...
Awaken in us the realization
That we need to call on You continually....
Teach us to have hearts that pray.
Teach us to keep ourselves focused on You.
To set up an altar in our hearts,
Where our soul might call out to
You continually. Amen.[9]

My Checklist for Prayer

✓ *Pray*—The Bible tells you to pray faithfully, fervently, always, without ceasing, continually. Pray, too, when you are in trouble, when you are disappointed by others, when you are hurting, when you are worshiping, when you are worried, when you are overwhelmed, when you are in need, and when you must make a decision. Whatever is happening, you name it...you are to pray! Prayer and praying is the foremost action of a woman—old or young!—who is serious about God's call on her life.

The hardest part about "praying always" is to remember to pray always. What can you do to remember to "think pray" all day long? (Will it be a sticky note? A special bracelet or ring? A scripture you repeat throughout the day? Go ahead and think about it. What will it be?)

✓ *Praise*—I have not focused specifically on praise in this book because the subject of praise could be a book in itself. (Hmmm, I wonder...?) But praise is yet another way we worship God. So during your times of prayer, lift your praise to Him who is most worthy of it! Give praise to "the glory of His grace" (Ephesians 1:6). "Praise our God, all you His servants and those who fear Him, both small and great!" (Revelation 19:5). Let your praise flow outward and upward. It will change your outlook on life!

Read Mary's words of praise in Luke 1:46-55. And read Hannah's words of praise in 1 Samuel 2:1-10.

What praise phrases do you like best from these women's prayers of praise to God? List them, take them, use them, and make them your own!

✓ *Proceed*—How can you become a woman who answers God's call to prayer? How can you make your desire to pray a reality? How can you do a better job of talking to God about your life? In a word, *proceed...*full speed ahead! Proceed to do what you've learned about prayer in this book. Proceed in following God's formula for prayer. Proceed toward finding God's will through prayer. Proceed in developing the habit of prayer. And above all, proceed in your efforts to pray from your heart!

Now, what will your first step be from this day forward?

Would You Like to Know More? Check It Out!

Read Nehemiah 2:1-10.

What was Nehemiah doing (verse 1)?

What question did the king ask (verses 2-4)?

What did Nehemiah do right away (verse 4)?

What were the results (verses 5-10)?

Read again the example of the servant named Mary and her practice of prayer. Which of her prayer habits do you already practice? Which of her prayer habits could you start doing?

Read Ephesians 6:18. What commands are given regarding prayer?

How can you begin to order your life more around God and His desires so that you can make prayer your first response to every situation throughout your days?

My List of Things I Don't Want to Forget…
…from This Chapter

Answering God's Call to Prayer

A Dazzling Prayer-Life

Throughout this book I've referred to prayer as a jewel. All along the way, you and I have been examining and admiring the many splendid facets of the precious gem of our prayers. They combine to make the jewel something special indeed—something that blazes forth and lights up your life and the lives of those you pray for, live with, and encounter! And now I want to focus one final time on prayer as a gemstone and on answering God's call to prayer.

As you know, diamonds are said to be a girl's best friend. So let's use a diamond as our jewel of choice. In my lifetime, I've seen two of the world's largest, most famous diamonds, each time while traveling with my husband on one of his ministry trips. One was the Star of Africa, the largest cut diamond in existence. It is set in the British royal scepter, which Jim and I viewed in the Tower of London. This pear-shaped stone "weighs in" at 530.2 carats! The other was the Hope Diamond, the largest deep-blue diamond in the world, which we saw in the National Museum of Natural History at the Smithsonian Institute in Washington, D.C. (We almost didn't stay to see this one because the line was so long. But the wait was well worth it!)

But, my dear journeying friend, please realize that scientists believe brilliant, priceless diamonds like these were formed underground at depths greater than 93 miles and some as deep as 420 miles beneath the earth's surface. And so it is with an even greater jewel—your prayer-life. The holy habit of prayer is formed underground, hidden from sight, "alone with the Eternal."

Why does the formation of a diamond require such incredible recesses? Because crystallization requires pressures and temperatures that only occur at such tremendous depths. And, oh, is that ever true of your glistening prayer-life! The more pressure, the better. The more heat, the better. Such uncomfortable conditions can only make your life of prayer more dazzling. For it is the pressures of life that press us upon God, that move us to lean upon Him...and to seek His power and might in our weaknesses.

So purpose to answer God's call to you to pray. Purpose to hide away with Him in prayer...daily. Doing so will change you. It will change your relationships. And it will change your life. Diamonds are the hardest substance on the earth. And you, dear one, will resemble a diamond when you gather up the conditions and concerns of your life and "take them to the Lord in prayer." You will become, in a good sense, tough, solid, powerful, confident, full-of-faith.

So, dear one, don't cave in under pressure! Don't give in to life's troubles. Don't disintegrate into a puddle of tears and depression. Instead take Jesus' advice to heart. He said you "always ought to pray and not lose heart" (Luke 18:1). Answer His call to prayer! Make it your lifestyle!

A Prayer for Living Out God's Plan

1. *Pray over your priorities*—"Lord, what is Your will for me at this time in my life?"
2. *Plan through your priorities*—"Lord, what must I do today to accomplish Your will?"
3. *Prepare a schedule based on your priorities*—"Lord, when should I do the things that live out these priorities today?"
4. *Proceed to implement your priorities*—"Lord, thank You for giving me Your direction for my day."
5. *Purpose to check your progress*—"Lord, I only have a limited time left in my day. What important tasks do I need to focus on for the remainder of the day?"
6. *Prepare for tomorrow*—"Lord, how can I better live out Your plan for my life tomorrow?"
7. *Praise God at the end of the day*—"Lord, thank You for a meaningful day, for 'a day well spent,' for I have offered my life and this day to You as a 'living sacrifice.' "[1]

Suggested Books of Prayers

The Harper Collins Book of Prayers—A Treasury of Prayers Through the Ages, comp. Robert Van deWeyer. Edison, NJ: Castle Books, 1997.

The One Year® Book of Personal Prayer. Wheaton, IL: Tyndale House Publishers, Inc., 1991.

The Prayers of Susanna Wesley, edited and arranged by W.L. Doughty, Clarion Classics. Grand Rapids, MI: Zondervan Publishing House, 1984.

Elizabeth Prentiss. *Stepping Heavenward.* Amityville, NY: Calvary Press, 1993. The diary of a woman's life and prayers begun at age 14.

The Valley of Vision—A Collection of Puritan Prayers and Devotions, edited by Arthur Bennett. Carlisle, PA: The Banner of Truth Trust, 1999.

Notes

An Invitation to Become a Young Woman of Prayer

1. J.D. Douglas, *The New Bible Dictionary* (Grand Rapids, MI: Wm. B. Eerdmans Publishing Co., 1978), p. 1019.

Chapter 1—Beginning the Journey into Prayer

1. *God's Words of Life for Teens* (Grand Rapids, MI: Zondervan Corporation, 2000), p. 141.
2. A.A. Milne, "Vespers," from *When We Were Very Young* (New York: E.P. Dutton and Co. and Methuen Children's Books Ltd., date unknown).
3. William Law, source unknown.

Chapter 2—What Keeps Me from Praying

1. From the hymn "Turn Your Eyes upon Jesus" by Helen H. Lemmel.
2. Adapted from Paul S. Rees, as quoted in Albert M. Wells Jr., comp., *Inspiring Quotations: Comtemporary and Classified* (Nashville: Thomas Nelson Publishers, 1988), p. 160.
3. Eleanor Doan, *Speaker's Sourcebook* (Grand Rapids, MI: Zondervan Publishing Company, 1988), p. 197.

Chapter 3—When You Are in Trouble or in Need...Pray!

1. Terry W. Glaspey, *Pathway to the Heart of God* (Eugene, OR: Harvest House Publishers, 1998), p. 13.
2. *World Shapers—A Treasury of Quotes from Great Missionaries,* quoting Peter Deyneka, Founder of Slavic Gospel Association (Wheaton, IL: Harold Shaw Publishers, 1991), p. 49.

Chapter 4—When You Are Disappointed or Hurting...Pray!

1. Curtis Vaughn, *The New Testament from 26 Translations* (Grand Rapids, MI: Zondervan Publishing House, 1967), p. 771.
2. Herbert Lockyer, *All the Prayers of the Bible* (Grand Rapids, MI: Zondervan Publishing House, 1973), p. 64.
3. D.L. Moody, *Notes from My Bible and Thoughts from My Library,* quoting Cuyler (Grand Rapids, MI: Baker Book House, 1979), p. 93.
4. Romans 3:23; 1 Corinthians 10:12; 1 John 1:8.

5. Joseph Scriven, "What a Friend We Have in Jesus," 1855.

Chapter 5—When You Are Worried...Pray!

1. Fritz Rienecker, *A Linguistic Key to the Greek New Testament—Volume 2* (Grand Rapids, MI: Zondervan Publishing House, 1981), p. 21.
2. M.R. DeHaan and Henry G. Bosch, *Bread for Each Day* (Grand Rapids, MI: Zondervan Publishing House, 1980), December 11.
3. *Life Application Bible Commentary—Romans* (Wheaton, IL: Tyndale House Publishers, Inc., 1992), p. 164.

Chapter 6—When You Must Make a Decision...
Pray for Faith and Wisdom!

1. Author unknown, quoted in Eleanor Doan, *Speaker's Sourcebook* (Grand Rapids, MI: Zondervan Publishing House, 1988), p. 283.
2. *Checklist for Life for Teens* (Nashville: Thomas Nelson Publishers Publishers, 2002), p. 226.
3. Doan, *Speaker's Sourcebook,* quoting Edward Payton, p. 192.

Chapter 7—When You Must Make a Decision...
Pray for Understanding!

1. Roy B. Zuck, *The Speaker's Quote Book,* quoting Charles Neilsen (Grand Rapids, MI: Kregel Publications, 1997), p. 409.
2. Ibid., p. 110.
3. Ibid., p. 110-11.

Chapter 8—The Time—and Times—of Prayer

1. Sherwood Eliot Wirt and Kersten Beckstrom, *Topical Encyclopedia of Living Quotations,* quoting Paul S. Rees (Minneapolis: Bethany House Publishers, 1982), p. 181.
2. William Law, as quoted in Terry W. Glaspey, *Pathway to the Heart of God* (Eugene, OR: Harvest House Publishers, 1998), p. 152.
3. "The Difference Prayer Makes," author unknown, in Eleanor Doan, *Speaker's Sourcebook* (Grand Rapids, MI: Zondervan Publishing House, 1988), p. 198. Note: Internet source credits Grace L. Naessens for this poem.

Chapter 9—The Place and Posture of Prayer

1. Ruth Bell Graham, "Especially for You," *Decision,* vol. 43, no. 9, September 2002, p. 42.
2. S.D. Gordon, *Quiet Talks on Prayer* (Grand Rapids, MI: Fleming H. Revell, 1980), pp. 150-58.

3. Herbert Lockyer, *All the Prayers of the Bible* (Grand Rapids, MI: Zondervan Publishing House, 1973), p. 265.
4. Sandra Goodwin, "Traveling on My Knees," as cited in Paul Lee Tan, *Encyclopedia of 7700 Illustrations* (Winona Lake, IN: BMH Books, 1979), p. 1038.
5. Sam Walter Foss (1858–1911), "The Prayer of Cyrus Brown."

Chapter 10—How Can I Learn to Pray?

1. Eleanor L. Doan, *Speaker's Sourcebook* (Grand Rapids, MI: Zondervan Publishing House, 1988), p. 191.
2. Harry Verploegh, ed., *Oswald Chambers—The Best from All His Books* (Nashville: Oliver Nelson/Thomas Nelson Publishers, 1987), p. 359.
3. Doan, *Speaker's Sourcebook,* quoting Oswald Chambers, author's emphasis, p. 192.
4. Frank S. Mead, *12,000 Religious Quotations,* quoting Thomas Benton Brooks (Grand Rapids, MI: Baker Book House, 2000), p. 337.

Chapter 11—When You Are Anywhere and at Any Time...Pray!

1. Terry W. Glaspey, quoted in Terry Glaspey, *Pathway to the Heart of God* (Eugene, OR: Harvest House Publishers, 1998), p. 133.
2. Eleanor L. Doan, *Speaker's Sourcebook* (Grand Rapids, MI: Zondervan Publishing House, 1988), p. 193.
3. Frank S. Mead, *12,000 Religious Quotations,* quoting Victor Hugo (Grand Rapids, MI: Baker Book House, 2000), p. 341.
4. Peter Marshall, as quoted in Roy B. Zuck, *The Speaker's Quote Book* (Grand Rapids, MI: Kregel Publications, 1997), p. 298.
5. Elon Foster, *6000 Sermon Illustrations* (Grand Rapids, MI: Baker Book House, 1992), p. 511.
6. Vinita Hampton and Carol Plueddemann, *World Shapers: A Treasury of Quotes from Great Missionaries* (Wheaton, IL: Harold Shaw Publishers, 1991), p. 46.
7. Roy B. Zuck, *The Speaker's Quote Book,* quoting "Our Daily Bread", p. 294, (February 21, 2004).
8. Ian Bounds, source unknown.
9. Glaspey, *Pathway to the Heart of God*, p. 133.

A Dazzling Prayer-Life

1. Elizabeth George, *Life Management for Busy Women* (Eugene, OR: Harvest House Publishers, 2002), p. 239.

My Prayer Calendar*

Jan.	Feb.	Mar.	Apr.	May	June
1	1	1	1	1	1
2	2	2	2	2	2
3	3	3	3	3	3
4	4	4	4	4	4
5	5	5	5	5	5
6	6	6	6	6	6
7	7	7	7	7	7
8	8	8	8	8	8
9	9	9	9	9	9
10	10	10	10	10	10
11	11	11	11	11	11
12	12	12	12	12	12
13	13	13	13	13	13
14	14	14	14	14	14
15	15	15	15	15	15
16	16	16	16	16	16
17	17	17	17	17	17
18	18	18	18	18	18
19	19	19	19	19	19
20	20	20	20	20	20
21	21	21	21	21	21
22	22	22	22	22	22
23	23	23	23	23	23
24	24	24	24	24	24
25	25	25	25	25	25
26	26	26	26	26	26
27	27	27	27	27	27
28	28	28	28	28	28
29	29	29	29	29	29
30		30	30	30	30
31		31		31	

* See p. 19 in chapter 1 under "Checklist for Prayer" (third checkmark section) for instructions in using this encouraging calendar.

Date I Began__________

July	Aug.	Sept.	Oct.	Nov.	Dec.
1	1	1	1	1	1
2	2	2	2	2	2
3	3	3	3	3	3
4	4	4	4	4	4
5	5	5	5	5	5
6	6	6	6	6	6
7	7	7	7	7	7
8	8	8	8	8	8
9	9	9	9	9	9
10	10	10	10	10	10
11	11	11	11	11	11
12	12	12	12	12	12
13	13	13	13	13	13
14	14	14	14	14	14
15	15	15	15	15	15
16	16	16	16	16	16
17	17	17	17	17	17
18	18	18	18	18	18
19	19	19	19	19	19
20	20	20	20	20	20
21	21	21	21	21	21
22	22	22	22	22	22
23	23	23	23	23	23
24	24	24	24	24	24
25	25	25	25	25	25
26	26	26	26	26	26
27	27	27	27	27	27
28	28	28	28	28	28
29	29	29	29	29	29
30	30	30	30	30	30
31	31		31		31

A Young Woman's Walk with God

Elizabeth George

HARVEST HOUSE PUBLISHERS
EUGENE, OREGON

Every effort has been made to give proper credit for all stories, poems, and quotations. If for any reason proper credit has not been given, please notify the author or publisher and proper notation will be given on future printing.

Italicized text in Scripture quotations indicate author emphasis.

Acknowledgment

As always, thank you to my dear husband, Jim George, M.Div., Th.M., for your able assistance, guidance, suggestions, and loving encouragement on this project.

A YOUNG WOMAN'S CALL TO PRAYER

Published by Harvest House Publishers
Eugene, Oregon 97402
www.harvesthousepublishers.com

Library of Congress Cataloging-in-Publication Data
George, Elizabeth, 1944-
A young woman's call to prayer / Elizabeth George
p. cm.
Includes bibliographical references.
ISBN-13: 978-0-7369-1463-5 (pbk.)
ISBN-10: 0-7369-1463-3 (pbk.)
1. Teenage girls—Religious life—Juvenile literature. 2. Girls—Religious life—Juvenile literature. 3. Prayer—Juvenile literature. I. Title
BV4551.3.G465 2005
248.8'33—dc22 2004020516

Printed in the United States of America

Contents

Getting Your Act Together

A Word of Welcome

Dear Friend,

Without even meeting you, I can tell you are someone very special! Why? Because you're choosing to read this book. When you consider its title, it becomes pretty obvious that you desire to love God with all your heart. This book is packed with information and how-to's that will show you how to fulfill the desire of your heart—how to grow more like Jesus! As we begin our journey together, a few things will make it even sweeter.

Open your book...and enjoy it! Everything you need is here. I've tried to make it convenient for you as a busy young woman. In my mind I've pictured you reading this book on your bed at home, in a bunk bed at camp, on your family vacation, in a lounge chair sunbathing around a pool, even in the library after you've finished your homework. Enjoy your book, carry it with you, and let God's Word instruct you.

Open your heart...to your friends. Encourage them to get books too. Then you will each be growing, which means your friendships will be growing in the right direction—in the things of the Lord. A godly woman needs other godly women as friends. So invite them to join you.

Open your heart...and look around. Are there any girls you don't know very well at school, or in the neighborhood, or perhaps where you work, who you can invite to join your study? Girls who need the Savior? Who need some guidelines for their lives? Who need a friend? Whisper a prayer to God, be bold, and reach out and invite someone you'd like to know better to get together.

Open your heart...to the topics covered in this book. They are just what every gal needs. They'll give you God's wisdom and guidelines for your thoughts, words, and deeds...and for your walk with Him.

Open your heart...to the Holy Spirit through prayer. Ask Him to illuminate God's Word, to help you understand His plan for you to enjoy His presence in you. Let Him transform your life into something amazing.

Open your heart...and dream! Dream of the woman you yearn to be—a woman who walks with Jesus every day in every way.

It is the prayer of my heart that the contents of this special book will encourage you, excite you, instruct you, and inspire you to passionately follow in Jesus' steps!

In His great and amazing love,

Elizabeth George

1

Getting It All Going

I live in the state of Washington. And never in my life would I have dreamed it, but right in my front yard is an apple tree! That means I get to watch God's process for the miraculous production of apples from start to finish each year. But believe me, I know very well the work it takes me and my husband to do our part in improving and increasing a crop of apples! We nurture, fertilize, water, prune, train, spray, and protect this tree…and our efforts have definitely paid off.

As I think about our amazing apple tree, I can't help but wonder about the fruit of our lives as Christian women, no matter what our ages. Should you and I pay any less attention to our own fruitfulness—in our case the spiritual kind—than Jim and I do to an apple tree? Shouldn't we be actively cultivating the fruit of the Spirit in our lives so we reflect the glory of God and the beauty of Christ? But what exactly can we do to get the growing of spiritual fruit going? What practical steps can we take to get it all together so we become more like Jesus?

Finding Out About the Fruit of the Spirit

Well, just as I studied to learn more about my apple tree and the fruit it produces, you and I need to study God's Word to better understand the fruit of the Holy Spirit and how it grows. Take your favorite pen in hand now and interact with these truths from the Bible. And if it's not a good time—you know, you don't have a pen, you're on the bus, or you're getting ready to turn out the light and get some much-needed sleep—then just read along for now.

✎ *A Word from God's Word About Fruit...*

- The word "fruit" is used throughout the Bible to refer to telltale evidence of what is on the inside of a person. If what's inside is good, then the fruit of that person's life will be good. But if what's inside is rotten, the fruit of that person's life will be bad. That's what Jesus taught when He said,

  Make a tree good and its fruit will be good, or make a tree bad and its fruit will be bad, for a tree is recognized by its fruit....The good man brings good things out of the good stored up in him, and the evil man brings evil things out of the evil stored up in him (Matthew 12:33,35).

  What sort of fruit have you seen in your actions lately?

- Any person who has received Jesus as Savior and Lord and has Christ living within will bear good fruit. He will be *"filled with the fruit of righteousness that comes through Jesus Christ—to the glory and praise of God"* (Philippians 1:11). How do you think exhibiting the fruit of righteousness brings glory and praise to God? And in what ways has the fruit you are bearing shown others what Jesus is like?

- The fruit of the Spirit has been described as "those gracious habits which the Holy Spirit produces in the Christian."[1] In Galatians 5:22-23, the apostle Paul lists these "gracious habits"— *"the fruit of the Spirit is love, joy, peace, patience, kindness, goodness, faithfulness, gentleness and self-control."* All nine fruit stand together and make up our walk with God. They are like a string of Christmas lights—there is one string with many lights that all light up at once when plugged into the electrical socket. But if one bulb goes out, the entire string goes out. That's how God's fruit is borne in our lives. Not one of them can be missing, and all must be evident—lit up—to be God's fruit. As you recall your actions today, were any of these spiritual habits missing? What must you do to get "plugged into God," the power source, again?

"So What Can I Do?"

I'm sure you want God's fruit to mark your life, to make you beautiful from the inside out. If that's true, you probably wonder, "So what can I do? How can I make this happen? What do I need to do to get things going, to get this business of spiritual fruit-bearing in motion?"

Well, first, here's one thing you can't do. You can't think, *Perhaps if I just try harder...* No, Jesus teaches that do-it-yourself effort isn't the answer. The fruit of the Spirit can only be produced as we yield to God and allow His Spirit to work in us as we walk through the events and encounters life brings our way each day.

Next, remember that the fruit of the Spirit act as one. They are like a watch that contains many parts. A watch can be taken apart for cleaning and repair, but each piece must be put back into place for the watch to run. In this book, we will take apart and inspect each fruit of the Spirit. Then we'll see how they all work together to present a whole, just like a watch.

Here's another thing you can do: Realize that, as a whole, the nine characteristics of the fruit of the Spirit are all produced in the same way. Everything that is said of one characteristic is true of the other eight. They are one and the same fruit, interwoven and related to one another. And they are produced as we look to God.

Finally, never for a second forget about the battle that is going on between your flesh and the Spirit. In Galatians 5:17 we learn that "the sinful nature desires what is contrary to the Spirit, and the Spirit what is contrary to the sinful nature. They are in conflict with each other, so that you do not do what you want." You and I will face this struggle—the struggle between the flesh and the Spirit—until the day we die. But, praise God, when we walk or "live by the Spirit... [we] will not gratify the desires of the sinful nature" (verse 16). We will have victory over the flesh—our body and its cravings—when we walk by the Spirit.

So, what does it mean to walk by the Spirit? In simple terms, walking by the Spirit means:

> Living each minute God's way—obeying Him.
> Seeking to please God with...
> the thoughts we choose to think,
> the words we choose to say, and
> the actions we choose to take.
> Letting God guide us each step of the way.
> Letting God work in us so we can bring glory to Him.

Discovering the Secret to Walking with God

Are you catching on? Are you getting it? It is only as we walk by God's Spirit that we show forth Christ in our lives. And it is only as we "abide" in Christ that God gives us the grace to do this. This, my friend, is the secret to walking with God: We must abide in Christ. Jesus said in John 15:4-5:

> *Remain in me, and I will remain in you. No branch can bear fruit by itself; it must remain in the vine. Neither can you bear fruit unless you remain in me. I am the vine; you are the branches. If a man remains in me and I in*

> *him, he will bear much fruit; apart from me you can do nothing.*

What's the point? Only by abiding or remaining in Him can you and I as followers of Jesus bear fruit (verses 2,4,5). To "abide" or "remain" means

> "continued fellowship with the Lord,"[2]
> "dwelling in His fellowship and being submissive to His will,"[3] and
> keeping "contact with Jesus…a constant contact."[4]

Here's where our *doing* comes in. Like all I *do* to help my apple tree along, there are a few things you can *do* that help you abide in Christ. Let's call them "fruit boosters." These four practical steps—things you can *do*—will help you remain in constant contact with Jesus, to abide in Him, to remain close to Jesus and dwell in Him as He dwells in you.

1. *Get into God's Word*—One Bible teacher explains, "Abiding cannot be maintained [without]…giving the words of Christ a…[reigning] position in the heart (cf. Colossians 3:16)."[5] So…be diligent about spending time in God's Word. Make it your habit to get into your Bible, to read it, study it, and meditate on it on a regular basis. Don't merely go through the motions. Instead, work at making your time in God's Word full and meaningful.

2. *Make time for prayer*—Prayer is a must for walking with God. I read some time ago that "no blessing of the Christian life becomes continually possessed unless we are

men and women of regular, daily, unhurried, secret lingerings in prayer."[6]

Here's a question for you. Would others—your family and friends, teachers and other students—describe you as a person of "regular, daily, unhurried, secret lingerings in prayer"? Do whatever you have to do to make prayer a vital link between you and God. Through prayer you learn more about God, His heart, and His purposes. To abide in Christ and be a woman who walks with God, do all you can to develop your prayer life. (And P.S., to learn more about prayer, read my book *A Young Woman's Call to Prayer.*[7] There's nothing you can't talk about with God!)

3. *Do what God asks*—Your waking prayer each morning should be to make choices that honor God and His Word, to really love God! Jesus said, "If you obey my commands, you will remain in my love, just as I have obeyed my Father's commands and remain in his love" (John 15:10). In other words, in keeping His Father's commandments, Jesus stayed close to His Father and gave us a model for obeying God's commands.

4. *Give your heart to Jesus*—Before anything…or anyone… can grow, it must be alive. Therefore ask yourself a simple question: Am I alive spiritually?

We read in Romans that

—"*all have sinned*" (3:23), that
—"*the wages of sin is death*" (6:23), and that
—"*God demonstrates his own love for us in this: While we were still sinners, Christ died for us*" (5:8).

What this means is that you and I are sinners (there's no doubt about it!), which earned us the death penalty, but Jesus took on our sin and died in our place. As the words to one hymn ask, "Amazing love! How can it be, that Thou, my God, shouldst die for me?"[8] Think about it!

Getting It All Together

Here's another question for you as you move toward getting it all together—Have you accepted the wonderful truth of Christ's death on your behalf and named Jesus *your* Savior and the Lord of your life? Have you given Jesus your heart? As the Bible instructs, "If you confess with your mouth, 'Jesus is Lord,' and believe in your heart that God raised him from the dead, you will be saved" (Romans 10:9). Before you can experience any spiritual growth, this seed of faith in Jesus must take root in your heart and life.

So...are you alive?

Only three answers are possible—*no, I'm not sure,* and *yes*.

Answer #1: No—If you answered no—if you have not accepted Jesus as Lord and Savior—you can set foot on the path of walking with God and growing in Him right now by earnestly praying words like these from your heart. This is Step 1 toward getting your life together:

> Jesus, I know I am a sinner. I want to repent of my sins and turn and follow You. I believe You died for my sins and rose again victorious over the power of sin and death, and I want to

> accept You as my personal Savior. Come into my life, Lord Jesus, and help me obey You from this day forward.

Answer #2: I'm not sure—If you aren't sure if the seed of faith has taken root in your heart, you may want to say a prayer of recommitment. You could pray words like these:

> Jesus, I know that in the past I asked You into my life. I thought at that time that I was Your child, but my life hasn't shown the fruit of my belief. As I again hear Your call, I want to make a real commitment to You as the Lord and Master of my life.

Or perhaps the following prayer better fits your circumstances:

> Dear Lord Jesus, I know that in the past I asked You into my life. I want to be Your child, I think and hope that I am Your child, but I want to *know* that I am Your child. Lord, give me the reassurance that I have eternal life through You because of Your death on the cross for my sin.

Whatever you do, if you're not sure where you stand with God, let Him know right now in a very personal prayer. Don't worry about the words. Just share your heart with Him. After all, God loves you, and He already knows your heart. He wants to be close to you.

Answer #3: Yes—Finally, if you answered—or can now

answer—"Yes! I know I'm alive in Christ now and forever!" take a few moments to thank God and praise Him for all that Jesus has done for you. Make a fresh commitment to walk with Jesus in obedience, to walk down the path of greater growth.

Heart Response

It's the prayer of my heart that God would use what's in this book to inspire you to grow in God's grace so that you are truly changed. Is that the desire of your heart too? Then I pray that you are moved to give yourself totally to Christ. May you seek nothing other than to follow Him, to walk with God.

Things to Do Today to Get It Going

In the chapters that follow you'll be given a list of "Things to Do Today" for getting started or improving on each fruit of the Spirit. In this chapter make your own list. Glance back through this chapter and write down three things you can do today to accelerate your walk with God. Be sure to write out exactly when you will do these things.

1.

2.

3.

Would You Like to Know More About Walking by the Spirit? Check It Out!

✓ What is God's call to you in Galatians 5:16?

What will be the result if and when you follow this instruction?

✓ According to Galatians 5:17, what conflict do believers live with?

Give one or two specific examples of your struggle in this area.

✓ Make a list of the "acts of the sinful nature" listed in Galatians 5:19-21.

Check the ones you struggle with most.

✓ Now list the fruit of the Spirit named in Galatians 5:22-23.

How do they differ from the "acts of the sinful nature"?

✓ Read John 15:1-8. Then review the section entitled "Discovering the Secret to Walking with God" and make a plan of action for how you will abide in Christ this week. Don't forget to be specific about when and how you will follow-through on your plan.

Getting the Right Attitudes

2

A Loving Heart

The fruit of the Spirit is love.
Galatians 5:22

I don't think anyone—at least any female!—ever forgets a wedding. I can still clearly remember my daughter Courtney's marriage ceremony. After a whirlwind of busyness, family and friends joined me in watching a radiant and confident Courtney regally walk down the aisle in our church on her dad's arm. Soon Jim switched his dad hat to his minister's hat and summoned Courtney and her Paul to make a sober commitment to love each other for the rest of their days, to love one another with Christ's love.

Yes, I thought as I sat in the pew, *that's what God intends this wedding and all of life to be about—Christian love. He calls for a bride and groom to love one another. And He also calls each of His children to love parents and grandparents, brothers and sisters, uncles and aunts, and friends and enemies.*

Finding Out More About Love

We can't read very far in the New Testament without realizing that love is important to God. Grab your pen and note what you learn about love from these scriptures.

✎ *A Word from God's Word About Love...*

- "Live a life of love"—Ephesians 5:2

- "Love each other"—John 15:12

- "Love our neighbor"—Matthew 22:39

- "Love our enemies"—Luke 6:27

As a child of God, you are to love others in the way you see it modeled by God and His Son. Exactly how has Jesus loved you? And what does the kind of love you're supposed to give to others look like? The Bible comes to your rescue and gives you principles that help you understand Christian love. Look now at five of these.

Principle #1: Love is an act of the will

Every fruit of the Spirit requires decisions, and love is no different. It's hard to love under stressful conditions, yet that's exactly where most of life is lived, isn't it? For instance, I don't know about you, but I especially need love when I'm tired, when I'm suffering in some way, when I'm hurting, or when I'm feeling burdened. At times like these, I usually don't feel up to loving other people. That's when—I'm learning—it's necessary to activate the will if I am to show love toward others. Christian love, you see, is an act of the will—a deliberate effort that we can make only by the grace of God. So we choose to...

- give love when we want to withhold,
- reach out to others when we are tired and want to rest,
- serve when we want to be served, and
- help others when we ourselves are hurting.

Thank the Lord for God's grace! This kind of love comes only from God, which He gives us to pass on to others. Think for a minute about these willful acts of love. In fact, get out your pen and jot down your thoughts about the instances that follow.

✎ A Word from God's Word About Love...

- "*God so loved the world that he gave his one and only Son*" (John 3:16);

- "*The Son of Man did not come to be served, but to serve, and to give his life*" (Matthew 20:28);

- Jesus *"resolutely set out for Jerusalem"* (Luke 9:51) where He would die for us.

Giving, serving, heading for Jerusalem, dying on a cross. These acts of love are acts of the will, not something done out of emotion. We have to remember that it is only as we look to God for His love that we can get the right attitude—a God attitude—and show hearts of love.

Principle #2: Love is action—not just words

Love is also something we do, not just the words we say. We are supposed to walk the walk, not just talk the talk. Yet acting in love is not always easy. As any woman—young or old—knows who gets tired and still has work or homework to do, who still needs to give a helping hand at home, watch over younger brothers and sisters, do some laundry, or go to a part-time job, love means that even when you and I are exhausted and can't wait to sit down and do nothing, we do our work, we serve, and we help others. You see, love has work to do, and love does that work. Love takes action—even when doing so requires strenuous effort. We are called to love, not with word or with tongue only, but "with actions and in truth" (1 John 3:18).

Do you realize every one of your family members gives you an opportunity to put on the work clothes of love and to serve? And love has work to do at school as well…or at your job…or at church…or anywhere there are people! So roll up your sleeves and challenge yourself to do the work of love. Show forth God's love not only by your words and attitudes but by your actions.

Principle #3: Love reaches out to the unlovely

Don't you find it's easy to love "the lovely"—nice, sweet people who say "thank you!" when you do something for them? Who appreciate you? Who are kind to you? But it's much harder to love "the unlovely." People who are mean and a pain are a real challenge when it comes to love.

Yet this is exactly what Jesus calls you to do. He said, "Love your enemies and pray for those who persecute you." When you do, you become like our "Father in heaven. He causes his sun to rise on the evil and the good, and sends rain on the righteous and the unrighteous" (Matthew 5:43-45).

Do you see it? God expects you to love the unlovely just as He does (like He does when He loves you and me!). God's love is never deserved—it simply is. And that's the kind of love you are to show to your enemies as well as to your friends, to the unlovely as well as to the lovely. Only the Holy Spirit at work in your life can help you to love like Jesus. Now that's the right attitude!

Principle #4: We need God to help us love

We need God's help for each of the fruit of the Spirit and love is no different. We rely on God for love. And do we ever need it for the tough ones—for the people who are unlovely! It's like this: Jesus said it's natural to love those who love us (Luke 6:32-33). But to love those who hate us is *super*natural. It's natural to hate our enemies, but as Christians we are called to the *super*natural—to love our enemies (Luke 6:35).

Think about this: Love "means that no matter what a man may do to us by way of insult or injury or humiliation we will never seek anything...but the best even for those who seek the worst for us."[1] Friend, only God can help us serve the very person who insults, snubs, or hurts us. And His love is right there, ready for you to give. (And remember, those who are hardest to love are the ones who usually need it most!)

Principle #5: Love expects nothing in return

Do you find that when you're nice to someone, you expect that person to be nice back to you? But Jesus tells us to do good to others "without expecting to get anything back" (Luke 6:35). To love as God loves is to love without any thought of payback or reward. It is to love as Jesus loved us—"A new command I give you: Love one another. As I have loved you, so you must love one another" (John 13:34).

Defining Love—Love Is "the Sacrifice of Self"

As these five principles of biblical love clearly reveal, love is *the sacrifice of self.* This simple definition crystalizes what the Bible teaches about love. As love has been explained, "Love is not an emotion. It is an act of self-sacrifice. It is not necessarily feeling loving toward a particular person. It may not have any emotion connected with it (Romans 5:8). God always defines biblical love in terms of self-sacrifice."[2] It's obvious then that since love is the sacrifice of self,

> Love involves effort, not merely emotion.
> Love demands action, not just feelings.
> Love is something we do, not something we only feel or say.

How are you doing when it comes to loving others by giving up something of yourself? As you look to God's Spirit to empower you to give His kind of love, pray along with St. Francis of Assisi, "O Divine Master, grant that I may not so much seek to be loved…as to love."

Living Out Love

When it comes to love, it helps me to see my call to live out love as an assignment from God to love anyone and everyone He puts in my path. It's sort of like the care I give to the flowers beside my front door. They are the first thing I see every morning when I open my door, and they are usually drooping and slumped over on the porch. One look tells me they need water in the worst way. So every day I get out my watering bucket, go to the faucet, fill up the bucket, and carry water to these poor little flowers. You see, if they don't get water, they'll die.

Through the years I've kept up what I call my "bucket brigade." I know that if I don't fill my bucket at the faucet and give my flowers life-giving water, they will die. I don't necessarily feel like watering them, but I do it anyway. I act on my will, not my feelings. I make the decision and put forth the effort to give the flowers water and keep them alive.

You and I can view the challenge of loving the people God puts in our path in the same way as I view caring for my flowers. We may not necessarily feel like loving them. But when we allow God to fill us up with His life-giving love, we can then carry His love to others and pour it out into their lives. The love is not ours—it's God's. But when we present our empty selves to Him—the Source of love—and are filled by Him, then we are able to share His love with thirsty, needy people. God is then able to pass on His love to others through us.

And I confess—I have my hard days! But on the hard days, when I frequently run dry, I go back to God over and over again so He can fill me again and again with His love for the people I encounter. For instance, when I offer a friendly greeting to a woman who doesn't respond, my flesh says, "Well, if that's what I get for being nice, forget it!" But I know that's exactly when I need to run to God and have Him fill me afresh with His love for that woman so I can share it with her. She is someone God wants to show His love to, and I can let Him do so through me. I can let myself be the vessel that carries His love to her! It's amazing isn't it?

Heart Response

Please be sure and spend some time praying to the God of love. Confess to Him all your unlovely thoughts about any unlovely people He has put in your life. Admit any wrong attitudes toward others. And ask for His help in getting the right attitude—an attitude of love...His love! Ask God to enable you to "love your enemies, do good to those who hate you, bless those who curse you, pray for those who mistreat you" (Luke 6:27-28). God wants to do that for you. You just need to open yourself up to receive from Him His endless supply of life-giving, life-changing love.

Things to Do Today to Walk in Love

1. Begin loving the people God puts in your path by first loving those people at home. As the saying goes, "What you are at home is what you are!" So be a woman who walks in God's love...at home.
2. Go to God throughout the day for a fresh supply of His love to share. At the first hint of decreasing love, look to the Lord of love.
3. Remember that your assignment from God is to serve (Galatians 5:13).
4. Remember Jesus, who "did not come to be served, but to serve, and to give his life as a ransom for many" (Matthew 20:28).

Would You Like to Know More About Walking in Love? Check It Out!

✓ Read 1 Corinthians 13:4-8a. Which part of love is most difficult for you to live out?

Because fruit-bearing involves some effort on your part, what steps will you take this week toward overcoming that difficulty?

✓ According to 1 John 4:7-8, who is the source of love?

What do verses 20 and 21 of that chapter say about how we can know if someone loves God?

✓ What does Romans 5:5 teach about love?

And Romans 5:8?

✓ Who in your life is hardest to love and why?

As you think about that person, read Jesus' words in Luke 6:27-28. What specific instructions about the person you have in mind does Jesus give you here?

What will you do this week to obey each of Jesus' commands? Don't forget to be specific!

3

A Happy Heart

The fruit of the Spirit is...joy.
Galatians 5:22

One day my daughter Katherine received an unusual phone call from a business student at her college. He had started a little business of selling engagement rings to the guys on campus, and he was making a video catalog of diamonds and diamond rings. Steve had everything he needed to create his catalog—the diamonds, a studio, a camera, the lights. But he needed one more thing—a pair of hands. So he called to ask Katherine if she would come to the studio and model his rings.

So off Katherine went on the appointed taping day. When she arrived at the studio, Steve set up his camera and lights. Then he opened his jewel case and pulled out a piece of black velvet to serve as a backdrop for the diamonds. After turning on his studio lights, he removed the diamonds from his case, one by one for Katherine to model.

Next Steve instructed Katherine to slowly lift her hand up off the dark background toward the light as she modeled each ring. Steve explained, "When a diamond is placed against a dark background, the darkness makes it seem more brilliant. And when the diamond is lifted toward a light, all of its facets are revealed and allowed to sparkle." He said, "A diamond is pretty all by itself, but putting it against a black background and lifting it up to the light enhances its radiance and glory."

Oh, wow! What a perfect picture of joy! This is something we don't like to hear, but true spiritual joy shines brightest against the darkness of trials, tragedy, and testing. And the blacker the background, the greater the brilliance. In the same way, life's dark struggles make Christian joy more intense and our praise more glorious. As a poet reflected, God "sets in pain the jewel of His joy."

Finding Out More About Joy

Are you familiar with the book of Philippians in the Bible? It's a sparkling little epistle of joy. Just read it once and you'll notice its many references to joy, the next grace gift on God's list of the fruit of the Spirit. What do we learn about joy from the Bible, especially from the more than 70 New Testament references to it? It's pen or pencil time again. You'll be excited as you make notes while reading these truths and finding out more about joy!

✎ A Word from God's Word About Joy...

- *Joy is important to Jesus*—Shortly before His crucifixion, Jesus described the special relationship He would have with His disciples if they would abide in Him and His love. He ended His talk by saying, *"I have told you this so that my joy may be in you and that your joy may be complete"* (John 15:11). Jesus wanted His disciples to know the joy of fellowship with Him, joy to the fullest.

- *Joy is an expression of godliness*—You see, joy is a sure sign of the presence of God in our lives. Put differently, our joy is "the joy of God passing through a Christian,"[1] "a joy whose foundation is God."[2] As children of God, we have some great reasons to be joyful.

- *Joy is experienced anywhere and at any time*—How is this true? Because, as Philippians 4:4 tells us, we are to *"rejoice in the Lord always."* The phrase "in the Lord" points out the sphere in which our joy exists. "In the Lord" is a sphere that has nothing to do with our situation. No, instead it has everything to do with our relationship with Jesus. Because we take our relationship with Jesus everywhere we go, we can experience joy in

Him anywhere, anytime, no matter what's happening to us.

Discovering Three Good Reasons to Be Joyful

If this isn't enough to convince you about the importance of joy, look at these three reasons to be joyful. Keep your pen handy for making encouraging notes to yourself about how to have a happy heart, a more joyful life...or week...or day!

✎ *A Word from God's Word About Joy...*

- *Reason #1: Your joy is permanent*—Because your joy is rooted in your unchanging God, your joy is permanent. In John 16:22, Jesus says that *"no one will take away your joy."* However, one thing that can rob you of the joy God provides is your failure to walk with God. Therefore you are to *"live by the Spirit"* (Galatians 5:16). The Holy Spirit produces joy in your life as you abide in Christ and walk in obedience to His ways—as you walk by the Spirit.

- *Reason #2: Your joy is always available*—Since it's rooted in your faithful and ever-present God, your joy is always available. That's why you can *"rejoice in the Lord always"* (Philippians 4:4). Whatever the circumstances of your life, you have ready access to the source of true joy anytime you turn to God.

- *Reason #3: Your joy is also inexpressible*—That's how Peter described our joy in Jesus in 1 Peter 1:8: *"Though now you have not seen him, you love him; and even though you do not see him now, you believe in him and are filled with an inexpressible and glorious joy."* Joy in the Spirit is "joy beyond speech,"[3] "a foretaste of the joy of heaven,"[4] something which cannot be fully expressed or articulated.[5]

There is simply no way to explain why we experience joy when nothing in our life suggests we should be joyful!

Defining Joy—Joy Is "the Sacrifice of Praise"

It helps me to cultivate joy in my life by thinking of joy as *the sacrifice of praise.* Let me explain. When life is good, praise and thanksgiving flow freely from my heart and lips. But when life turns black, praise and thanksgiving don't flow quite so easily. Instead, I have to deliberately *choose* to follow God's advice and "give thanks in all circumstances, for this is God's will for you in Christ Jesus" (1 Thessalonians 5:18). Although I don't *feel* like praising the Lord or thanking

Him, I *do* what God says, and that effort makes my praise a sacrifice.

At times when I'd rather bask in self-pity or stay stuck in my depression, choosing to look beyond my pain makes my praise to God sacrificial. When I do lift such a sacrifice of praise to God out of the darkness of my trials, I find the Spirit's joy enlarged in my life—just as lifting a diamond to the light against a black background enhances its brilliance.

Caution! Joy Is Not an Emotion

Here's something else you must understand about true spiritual joy—It is not happiness. No, "happiness" is an emotion, a state of good fortune and success related to our circumstances. If all is going well, we are happy, but as soon as some dark cloud or irritation enters our life, our feeling of happiness vanishes.

I'm sure you're aware that pain is a fact of life. Contrary to our wishes, easy circumstances are not life's norm. Jesus warned, "In this world you will have trouble" (John 16:33). Paul explained, "Everyone who wants to live a godly life in Christ Jesus will be persecuted" (2 Timothy 3:12). In the midst of the reality of pain and sorrow, God's joy is a grace gift. He gives His joy to us as we encounter the hardships, tribulation, problems, and persecutions of life. Amazingly, this supernatural joy, given through God's Spirit, transcends all of the tough conditions of life.

As God's child through the new birth, you can experience and enjoy God's joy—regardless of what life offers you. You can be truly and genuinely happy...no matter what's going on around you. That's because your joy as a Christian...

- is not dependent on circumstances, but on the spiritual realities of God's goodness, His unconditional love for you, and His ultimate victory over sin and darkness.
- is not based on your efforts, accomplishments, or willpower, but rather on the truth about your relationship with the Father through the Son.
- is not merely an emotion, but the result of choosing to look beyond what appears to be true in your life to what is true about your life in Christ.

By now I'm sure you can see that your spiritual joy is not an experience that comes from favorable circumstances but is a sense of well-being that abides in the heart of the person who knows all is well between himself and the Lord.[6]

The Sources of Joy

Just as we take our empty self to God to be filled with His love, we also go to Him—the source of true joy—when we feel empty of Christian joy. Here are five reasons you can have that joy from Him. As you look through them, take your pen in hand and respond from your heart to the questions.

Reason #1: God Himself is a primary source of your joy—The psalmist reveals his heart's desire to "go to the altar of

God, to God my joy and my delight" (Psalm 43:4). Do you think of God as your "exceeding joy"? Do you turn to Him who lives in your heart for joy? God—the only source of true joy—wants to give you His joy. You need only to turn to Him to receive it. What can you do to turn to Him?

Reason #2: God's salvation—I'm sure you've noticed that when people share how they became Christians, they can't help but tell their story joyfully. Isaiah, for instance, could not contain his joy when he thought about all that God had done for him. He wrote, "I delight greatly in the LORD; my soul rejoices in my God. For he has clothed me with garments of salvation and has arrayed me in a robe of righteousness" (Isaiah 61:10). Now think of all that God has done for you. He paid a great price to obtain your salvation through His Son's death. There can be no greater joy than knowing you will live with God forever! Feel free to express your praise now.

Reason #3: God's promises—When my daughters were growing up, our family had a little plastic container shaped like a loaf of bread on our breakfast table. Each of the cards in that box had one promise from the Bible printed on it. Every morning one of us would close our eyes, reach over, pick a promise, and then read it as a part of our family devotions. Later that night at dinner, we would talk about that promise for the day again and how we had seen God be true to His Word since breakfast time.

Did you know that your Bible is like that plastic loaf of bread? It is filled with promises—as many (according to one calculation) as 8,000![7] Jot down one or more of your favorite promises. How often do you remember them, refer to them, use them to encourage your heart? And how does recalling them bring joy to your heart? If you are struggling with something right now, turn to the treasure of God's precious promises. Find joy in them.

Reason #4: Christ's kingdom—The fact that we who name Jesus as Savior and Lord have been welcomed into His kingdom brings great joy to the angels: "There is rejoicing in the presence of the angels of God over one sinner who repents" (Luke 15:10). Hearing others coming to Christ should evoke joy in you as well. Paul and Barnabas went from town to town describing the salvation of the Gentiles. The result? It caused great joy to all the brethren (Acts 15:3).

Do you need a dose of joy? Spend a few minutes recalling your own entrance into the kingdom of God. Share a few of the details of that wonderful day here. And if you have not yet tasted this heavenly joy, look again at pages 16 through 18. Perhaps today you will want to pray one of the prayers there from your heart.

Friend and sister, the joy of the Lord is available to you 24/7—24 hours a day, 7 days a week—any and every day, no matter what you're dealing with! Want joy? All you have to do is focus on God—not on your gloom, your tough life, the hard time someone gave you, your next exam. Just focus on God, on the eternal not the temporal. You experience the joy *of* the Lord when you go *to* the Lord and find your joy *in* the Lord. True joy—spiritual joy—is found only in the things of God. Ask God for His grace. Ask Him to help you remember to go to Him in your times of need to be filled with His joy.

Heart Response

Here's a fact of life: Until we are with the Lord, there will always be suffering. So...what trial is causing you the greatest grief, the sharpest pain, the deepest sorrow today? Is it a disappointment, a dashed dream, a disaster, a disability? Is it ridicule or persecution? A difficulty within your family? A strained relationship or an unknown future as you look down the road of life?

Whatever your greatest trial is today, let it cause you to turn to God for His joy. Let it cause you to offer Him a sacrifice of praise and allow you to be touched by Him, the only source of true joy. Your heart can be filled with genuine joy—spiritual joy—when you walk with God through your trials, praising Him with every step and breath. That's an attitude of joy!

Things to Do Today to Walk in Joy

1. Identify the trial that causes you the greatest grief. Name it here:

2. Copy Hebrews 13:15 from your Bible. Then offer to God the sacrifice of your praise concerning your heartbreaking situation…even if it is offered with tears.

3. Read James 1:2-4 and Romans 5:1-5. Then follow James' advice and consider that trial a joy. Write down what you think God is teaching you through this trial. What good has already come into your life as a result of it?

Would You Like to Know More About Joy? Check It Out!

✓ Read 1 Samuel 1:9-18. List some of Hannah's problems.

What made the difference in Hannah's attitude, and how was it changed?

✓ Read 1 Samuel 1:19–2:1. How did Hannah fulfill her vow?

Write out Hannah's sacrifice of praise in 2:1.

What was her source of joy?

What circumstances in Hannah's life could have caused her to be sorrowful?

What do you learn about joy from Hannah?

✓ Read Acts 16:22-25. List some of Paul's problems.

What did Paul do to experience and show His joy in the Lord?

✓ List some of your problems.

As you think about Hannah and Paul, what can you do right this minute...and this week...to experience the joy of the Lord?

4

A Quiet Heart

The fruit of the Spirit is...peace.
Galatians 5:22

A famous newspaper columnist and counselor, Ann Landers, was once asked if any one problem stood out in the more than 10,000 letters she received in the mail each week. Her answer? Fear.

Doctors also know the results of fear in their patients. The first symptom of illness is not always a cough or chest pain, but fear, which sooner or later shows up as a clinical symptom.

Causes for fear surround us on every side. But here's good news for us as Christians: We have a built-in resource for handling fears. That resource is the peace of God. And what a refreshing fruit God's peace is in a mad, mad, mad, mad world! Life is like a roller coaster, but we can experience God's peace—no matter what is happening in our lives—when we walk by His Spirit. We are blessed with "the peace of God, which transcends all understanding" (Philippians 4:7) right in the very middle of our trials when we look to God for it.

Finding Out More About Peace

Many people think of peace as the absence of problems. They equate peace with the feeling they experience when all is well, when there are no issues or problems or pains. But the peace of the Lord is not related to circumstances at all. In fact, God's peace comes to us and endures...regardless of life's circumstances.

Peace is like this. Our daughter Courtney and her husband, Paul, lived on Kauai, Hawaii, the island that experienced the fierce Hurricane Iniki. When Jim and I drove around the island on a visit there, we saw the evidence of destruction. In fact, you can still see it there today. But we also saw the huge warning sirens on every beach and in every town. We could well imagine the fear the islanders must have felt as those sirens wailed on the day the killer Hurricane Iniki approached. But we could also imagine the peace they must have felt when those same devices finally sounded the all-clear signal.

Now, can you imagine having the same perfect peace whether the sirens are signaling a storm or the hurricane is actually roaring around you? That's the kind of peace God offers to you for the many storms of life. Notice these truths about this peace that comes from God. Better yet, take pen in hand and note your thoughts and observations. Circle and underline what you like or find interesting.

- Our peace has nothing to do with our circumstances, and everything to do with knowing we have a right relationship with God.[1]

- Our peace has nothing to do with daily challenges or crises, and everything to do with knowing that our times are in God's hands.[2]

- Our peace has nothing to do with the conditions of our lives, and everything to do with knowing that God is all-sufficient.[3]

- Our peace is an inward repose and serenity of soul that indicates a heart at rest—regardless of our circumstances—as we place complete confidence in God minute by minute.

Now, keep your pen or pencil in hand as you make your way through these facts and scriptures.

✎ A Word from God's Word About Peace...

- Peace comes with knowing that your heavenly Father is continually with you—and indeed He is! God is omnipresent, everywhere at once, and fully aware of every detail of your life—at every moment and in every place. He knows your needs at all times and in every situation. In Psalm 139:7-10, David declared that *"if I go up to the heavens, you are there; if I make my bed in the depths, you are there...if I...settle on the far side of the sea, even there your hand will guide me."* Dear younger sister, you can never be any place—from the heights of heaven to the depths of the sea and everywhere in between—where God is not present with you and available to you. Therefore, the key to your peace is not the absence of conflict. No, it's the presence of God, no matter what the conflict.[4] Wow, just let that truth wash over you for a minute!

- Peace also comes with acknowledging that God will supply your every need. For instance, when Paul asked Jesus to remove the thorn in his flesh and Jesus said no, Paul learned the truth of Jesus' statement: *"My grace is sufficient for you"* (2 Corinthians 12:9). Paul learned the truth he wrote in Philippians 4:19—*"God will meet all your needs according to his glorious riches in Christ Jesus"*—and, in 2 Corinthians 9:8, that *"God is able to make all grace abound to you, so that in all things at all times, having all that you need, you will abound in every good work."* Do you realize what these promises mean? They mean that you will never have a real need that God is not able to meet. This, my friend, is another *wow!*

Defining Peace—Peace Is "the Sacrifice of Trust"

I like to think of peace as *the sacrifice of trust*. You see, you and I make the sacrifice of trust when we face pain and stress in our lives and choose to trust God instead of panicking or falling apart. When circumstances in your life might tempt you to panic, feel terrified, become a nervous wreck, or be filled with dread, you can choose to either give in to those feelings or trust in God, presenting yourself to Him to be filled with His peace. You can either trust Almighty God or succumb to the emotions of the flesh. Choosing to trust God—making the sacrifice of trust—causes you to experience His peace…even in the midst of tremendous uproar.

Here's how it works. We make the sacrifice of trust and experience God's peace…

> when we choose not to panic… but to rest in God's presence,

> when we release our terror… and trust in God's wisdom and ways, when we reject our nervousness…and remember that God is in control, and when we ignore our dread…and instead accept God's dealings.

Now imagine…taking your next exam full of peace instead of panic. Imagine…trying out for a part in a play or the pep squad or auditioning for the orchestra or choir and completely trusting God for the outcome. Imagine…giving your speech or making an announcement in front of your classmates without a worry in the world. Sister, that's peace! God's kind of peace.

Getting God's Peace

Are you wondering how to get this peaceful attitude, the attitude of a heart at rest? Well, you get it in the same way you get all the other fruit. When you are filled with the Holy Spirit and walking in God's ways, you will have the peace that comes from God—and from God alone. You will have a quiet heart.

Don't you just love receiving gifts? Well, pick up your pen again and unwrap these four gifts from God. They contain four sources for God's peace. Be sure and make your own set of notes as you read.

Gift #1: God, the Son—Before Jesus was even born, the Old Testament prophet Isaiah predicted, "For to us a child is born, to us a son is given…and he will be called…Prince of Peace" (Isaiah 9:6). That name reflects Jesus' mission.

- His death on Calvary gave believers the gift of peace with God that comes only with forgiveness for sins.
- His work on the cross paved the way for personal peace with God.
- His coming to earth accomplished salvation for those who put their trust in Christ.

As Romans 5:1 states, "Since we have been justified through faith, we have peace with God through our Lord Jesus Christ."

Gift #2: God the Father—Through the Bible, you can get to know God. You can learn all about His promises and His faithfulness so that you may trust Him in your times of need. One of those promises is found in Isaiah 26:3: "You will keep in perfect peace him whose mind is steadfast, because he trusts in you." As you know, there's no way you can avoid strife as you walk in the world, but you can know perfect peace in the midst of turmoil as you turn to God Himself instead of focusing on your difficulties.

Gift #3: God's Word—The Bible helps you know God by revealing His law, His ways, and His purposes. When you follow God's Word and walk in His ways, you experience His peace to the point that nothing causes you to stumble. "Great peace have they who love your law, and nothing can make them stumble" (Psalm 119:165). You experience the peace that comes with keeping a right relationship with God.

Gift #4: God, the Spirit—The Holy Spirit is your personal Helper, Teacher, and Comforter (John 14:26). Jesus said, "The Counselor, the Holy Spirit, whom the Father will send in my name, will teach you all things and will remind you of everything I have said to you." And what is the blessed result of this gift? "Peace I leave with you; my peace I give you. I do not give as the world gives. Do not let your heart be troubled and do not be afraid" (verse 27). The instruction, guidance, and comfort you receive from God's Spirit promotes your peace. When you abide in Christ and walk by His Spirit, this peace from God is yours.

Doesn't this make you want to pause and give thanks to God for these four gifts? Just think about it. As a Christian, you can look to God—the Father, the Son, and the Holy Spirit—and to God's Word for peace. Bless His name and thank Him profusely!

Walking on the Path of Peace

Now that you know more about God's peace, what can you do to live in such a way that you can cultivate this gift of His Spirit?

- You can *pray*. Pray first, pray often, and pray continually. When you pray and place your worries, fears, doubts, and concerns into God's hands, you'll be spending time in the presence of the Lord. You'll enjoy fellowshiping with Him, worshiping Him, learning from Him, and leaning on Him—and, yes, experiencing His peace.

- You can *pause* and turn to the Lord when a crisis or disaster comes along. When you pause to acknowledge God—His presence, His all-sufficiency, His power, His love—He will make your paths straight. And blessing upon blessing, once you've turned to Him, you will again be in touch with His tremendous peace.

- You can *peruse* the gospels (Matthew, Mark, Luke, John). Read and study Jesus' life to see the peace He experienced in stressful situations. You can learn how abiding in the Father directed Jesus' thoughts, words, deeds, responses, and reactions in difficult circumstances. You can carry Jesus' attitudes in your mind as you go to school, do your work and homework, interact with people of all kinds, and seek to live in peace with those at home. Jesus' example will help you walk in peace.

Heart Response

Are you longing for this kind of heart—a quiet heart, a heart at rest, a heart of peace? Then take an "attitude" exam. What has an outside observer seen in you this week? Are you in turmoil...or are you trusting in God and at peace? Are you running around in circles...or are you resting in the Lord? Are your words revealing a sense of panic and pressure...or are they words that help and encourage others? Are your actions reflecting the priorities God has set for you? Is your relationship with Him first...or are you too busy to sit at His feet and enjoy His presence?

Remember, your assignment from God is to get the right attitudes going in your life! And every day is a test. Are you improving?

Things to Do Today to Walk in Peace

1. Do yourself (and everybody else!) a favor and identify the issue that repeatedly causes you to stress out. For instance, what worry keeps you awake at night? What concern sets your mind churning and your heart fretting as the alarm clock jars you awake each morning? What problem weighs you down or never goes away?

2. Make the conscious decision to trust this problem to God. Pray and make the sacrifice of trust. This will allow your heart to rest in Him and enable you to experience His peace—even in this, your most difficult challenge.

Would You Like to Know More About Peace? Check It Out!

✓ Read Psalm 139. List what you learn about God.

List what you learn about God's knowledge of you, your whereabouts, and your situation.

List three things you want to remember about God the next time you are in a trying or lonely situation and in need of God's peace.

1.

2.

3.

✓ Read Luke 8:22-25 and Mark 4:35-41. Describe the scene in these passages. What was going on? Who was there?

How did the disciples react to the situation?

What was Jesus doing, and how did He respond to the situation? To the disciples?

How was Jesus' peace evidenced?

List three lessons you want to remember about trusting God in difficult times.

1.

2.

3.

5

Looking at Jesus' Attitudes

Think now for a few minutes about the three chapters on love, joy, and peace. They were about the circumstances of life that call for us, as God's women, to display these spiritual fruits. To review,

- a need for *love* is created by ill treatment, hostility, abuse, and hatred.
- a need for *joy* springs from sorrow, tribulation, tragedy, affliction, and trials.
- a need for *peace* comes as we face the events in life that evoke panic, fear, terror, dread, and anxiety.

Unfortunately these circumstances seem to come all too often. But oh, how blessed we are to be able to follow the example of Jesus, who faced these same fruit-bearing opportunities! Take a close look now at Jesus in the Garden of Gethsemane, where we see Him living out all three godly attitudes...love, joy, and peace...despite the events He faced. I found these words that help us understand all that happened that night before Jesus' journey to the cross:

> Ever and always the teacher, Jesus used even this struggle with the enemy in the garden the night before the cross to teach the disciples and every future believer another lesson in godliness, a lesson about facing temptation and severe trial. The Lord not only was preparing Himself for the cross but also, by His example, preparing His followers for the crosses He calls them to bear in His name.[1]

Now, allow Jesus to teach you as we peer into this dark night, which was also the most spiritually dark night in human history. That was the night the sinless Son of God faced death for your sins and mine in order to accomplish our salvation. Be aware as you read about this sacred scene from the Savior's life that you are truly standing on holy ground! Jesus' life on earth is nearing its end, and He faces every ugly word and evil deed ever directed at a person. Through God's provision of the four gospels, we are allowed to witness exactly how Jesus handled this hatred, sorrow, and trauma.

The Plan

Throughout His three years of teaching, Jesus often referred to God's plan for His death, which always caused bewilderment in His disciples. For instance, in John 7:6 Jesus said, "The right time for me [to die] has not yet come." But as Jesus prepared for His final Passover meal, He clearly stated the opposite: "My time is at hand" (Matthew 26:18 KJV). It was time for Him to die and to fulfill the Father's plan. All was in place. Judas, the traitor, had already been dismissed to do the evil deed of betraying his Master. As it neared midnight, Jesus prayed His high priestly prayer for and with His disciples (John 17). After they sang a hymn (Matthew 26:30), Jesus "left with his disciples and crossed the Kidron Valley. On the other side there was an olive grove, and he and his disciples went into it" (John 18:1).

The Purpose

What drove Jesus to the Garden of Gethsemane? It was His situation. It was this crossroad in His life. It was the challenge He faced during His final days. His time had finally come—and what was ahead? Betrayal by His disciples. Misunderstanding from His family and followers. Rejection from mankind. Hostility and persecution. An angry mob, angry leaders, and angry people. Verbal and physical assault. An unjust sentence. The excruciating pain of crucifixion. Death. And worst of all, momentary separation from His heavenly Father. From a human perspective, Jesus was losing all He had—His life, His family, His ministry, His friends, and His personal dignity.

Yet His heavenly Father had commanded that He die for these sinners—and Jesus obeyed. Doing so would benefit others—including you and me—because His death would be for sinners like us. So acting in love, Jesus gave Himself as a sacrifice, as a ransom for others (Matthew 20:28).

The Place

Facing the overwhelming challenge of the cross, Jesus went to Gethsemane (Matthew 26:36). This place was probably a secluded spot, walled in and containing some olive trees. Jesus had gone there often with His disciples (John 18:2) because it was quiet, a good spot for teaching, prayer, rest, and sleep. On the eve of His death, Jesus retreated to this familiar place of prayer with His little band of followers.

The People

After He entered the place called Gethsemane, Jesus did two things. First, He asked eight of the disciples to "sit here while I go over there and pray" (Matthew 26:36). Jesus left these men outside the wall or gate of the garden as lookouts. Next Jesus invited three of the disciples—Peter, James, and John—to go along with Him to pray.

The Problems

Disappearing into the black darkness, Jesus began the battle. The Father's plan caused Him deep distress, and the Bible gives us glimpses into His extensive *emotional* anguish. Jesus cried out, "My soul is overwhelmed with sorrow, to the point of death" (Matthew 26:38). He "began to be deeply distressed and troubled" (Mark 14:33), so much so that He fell upon the ground in prayer. Luke tells us that He was "in anguish" (22:44). Our Lord "offered up prayers and petitions with loud cries and tears" (Hebrews 5:7). As one scholar writes, "All the waves and the billows of distress came pouring over His soul."[2]

God's command to die also caused Jesus to suffer terrible physical stress: "Being in anguish, he prayed more earnestly, and his sweat was like drops of blood falling to the ground" (Luke 22:44).

Jesus was fighting another great battle in addition to these emotional and physical struggles, and that was the spiritual war. Knowing this, Jesus had instructed His companions to "watch and pray so that you will not fall into temptation" (Matthew 26:41). Our Lord threw Himself upon the mercy of His Father and uttered, "My Father, if it is possible, may this cup [of death] be taken from me" (verse 39). On the physical level, Jesus wanted the cup taken away. No one has ever desired to taste death, and neither did Jesus. But from the spiritual perspective, He wanted to do His Father's will and therefore added to His plea, "Yet not as I will, but as you will" (verse 39).

The Process

With this submission to God's will, we see Jesus emerge triumphant from His agonizing struggle in the Garden. How did He gain the victory? How did Jesus remain steadfast in the love, joy, and peace that compelled Him to willingly die for sinners? What kept Him from giving in to physical and emotional desires? What was the process? And what can we learn so that we, too, can grow in love, joy, and peace?

Love is the sacrifice of self. For love, Jesus looked to God, the Father, who had commanded Him to die for sinners. And in love, Jesus reached out to the Father for His sustaining and strengthening love. He offered *the sacrifice of self* and determined to do the Father's will. Jesus' love looked to the Father—and looked at us—and the Spirit enabled Him to submit to death on a cross (Hebrews 9:14). The *flesh* wanted to avoid the trial and pain ahead, but *love* turned to the Father and said, "Not as I will, but as you will" (Matthew 26:39). That decision led to severe and intense suffering... and our salvation.

Joy offers the sacrifice of praise. In joy, Jesus lifted praise to God. The Bible tells us that Jesus experienced great joy: "for the joy set before him [in the Father and by the Father, He] endured the cross, scorning its shame" (Hebrews 12:2).

Peace comes with the sacrifice of trust. For peace, Jesus left His problems with God. "The peace of God, which transcends all understanding" (Philippians 4:7) rushed to guard Jesus' heart and mind, and He got up off that holy, tear-stained, sweat-drenched ground to go on in peace, knowing His times were in the Father's hands, saying in all peace and with total trust, "Let us go!" (Matthew 26:46).

The Product

And now please note, nothing about Jesus' circumstances

changed! After agonizing in prayer, he was still going to go to the cross, still going to be crucified, still going to die. But He went to the cross sustained by God's love, joy, and peace.

And note something else: This transformation, this acceptance, this turning point, was not accomplished with a snap of Jesus' fingers, the wink of His eye, or the wave of any wand. It came because Jesus went to the Father—in agony and with blood and sweat and tears. Lying face down on the earth in literal darkness as He fought the deeper darkness that settled upon His soul, Jesus looked to His Father for the Father's love, the Father's joy, and the Father's peace.

Jesus' ultimate submission to God's will did not come easily. One time in prayer was not enough (Matthew 26:39). Two times was not enough (verse 42). No, Jesus turned to the Father three separate times (verse 44). And these three times in prayer were not the flinging of trite thoughts toward heaven! They were more like three hour-long sessions (Matthew 26:40) of agonizing, wrestling, struggling, and fighting so that He could do all that God required of Him.

When our Savior finally rose to go forward and face the cross, He did so with love, with joy, and with peace. Filled with these graces, the Son declared, "Let us go!" (Mark 14:42).

The Performance

Oh, dear younger sister in Christ! We've just seen Jesus submit to His Father's will—to death on the cross! We cannot help but stop to marvel! This is too amazing for us not to pause...and to praise...and to pray! Oh, dear Jesus, thank You!

But we must also look to ourselves and to our walk with God. How is your performance when it comes to following God's direction for your life? Speaking for myself, I know I pray so little. When something tough comes along in my day, I too often blurt out, "No way!" and go on my merry way. If something requires more than I want to give, I say, "Oh, thank you very much, but I won't be able to do that." Or I grind on, doing what I have to do—on my own, in my own flesh, and by my own power—never approaching the Father for His filling. I murmur, gripe, complain, and fret. I do my duty...but I do it grudgingly. And I do it without love, joy, and peace.

In times like these, I need to follow my Lord's example and go to my Garden of Gethsemane. I need to pray. I need to turn to the Father and fight with my flesh until I realize His fruit of love, joy, and peace. I need to spend the time—however long it takes—to allow Him to fill me with Himself until I have all of Him and He has all of me.

Heart Response

If you and I would, for one week or even one day, commit ourselves to God in this way—if we would rush to Him in prayer and remember His promises when we need love, when we need joy, and when we need peace, and stay there until we have it, however long it takes—we could indeed change our world for Christ. If we would commit ourselves to spend time in the Garden with the Father and to pay the price to walk by the Spirit, overcome the flesh, and thereby experience God's love and joy and peace…

Well, the effects are unknown, untold, and limitless! Prayer in our own garden would mean Christ in us changing our hearts, our relationships, our families, our friends, our neighborhoods, our schools, and our world. And He can do it! But without Him, we can do nothing (John 15:5). Without Him, we only go through the motions, giving so little to our family, a friend, a stranger, or a world that needs so much.

Here's my personal prayer for growth in these three attitudes of love, joy, and peace. I pray it will become yours as well as you visit the garden often as you walk along life's way, where you seek the right attitudes—Jesus' attitudes.

It is in prayer, Father,
That we press ourselves to You,
O All-Sufficient One,
That we get…in order to give,
that we petition…in order to praise,
that we wrestle…in order to rest.
We must have our time in the garden.
We must go to Gethsemane…
daily…first…often, if need be.

May we hold high in our hearts and minds
this picture of Jesus in the Garden.

Impress it upon our souls.
May we follow in His steps
    and refuse to rise until we have
    Your love...Your joy...Your peace.
We pray in Jesus' name, who has taught us
    how to pray. Amen.

Would You Like to Know More About Jesus? Check It Out!

✓ Read Matthew 20:28. According to these words spoken by Jesus, what was the purpose of His life on earth?

Write out Matthew 20:28 on a card to carry with you and to memorize. Allow its truth to permeate your heart as you walk in the steps of Jesus.

✓ What do you learn about Jesus' prayer life from...

Matthew 6:6?

Matthew 26:36 and John 18:2?

Mark 1:35?

✓ How earnest are Jesus' prayers in these verses?

Matthew 26:37-38—

Mark 14:33—

Luke 22:44—

Hebrews 5:7—

What command did Jesus give His disciples in Matthew 26:41?

How can you obey this command?

✓ Write out Jesus' prayer in Matthew 26:39. What was the attitude of His heart?

Getting Along with Everybody

6

A Time to Do Nothing

The fruit of the Spirit is...patience.
Galatians 5:22

Each day as I seek to walk with God, I (probably like you) try to design a schedule that will guarantee a devotional time with God each morning. On a really good day, when the alarm clock goes off in the morning I hop out of bed full of good intentions and solid plans and I experience Victory #1—I got up!

It feels so good to be up and in control of my day (so far, anyway!). What a blessing to enter into God's presence, to read His Word, and to linger in prayer. And then I experience Victory #2—I had my quiet time!

Next I start in on my daily chores. Usually my happy spiritual condition extends to serving others under my roof in a variety of ways—getting someone a glass of juice, helping with breakfast and clean up, making lunches while humming, and doing whatever it takes to get others out the door and off to school or work. As everyone waves goodbye for the day, I experience Victory #3—I got to help others make a good start on their day. I think to myself, *This is great! All is well! I'm on a roll. What a wonderful day this is going to be!*

But then real life—the rest of the day—begins. You know, a day of dealing with people—and all the joys and sorrows that can bring. It usually gets pretty intense! Also, in real life the phone rings (a lot!), and I have to take care of the person and the details of each call. Most calls go well, but there are those problem calls. Someone's upset with me. Or the person on the phone says something that hurts me. Sometimes the caller reports something someone else has said. I may even learn that I've been rejected in some way.

Pain comes in a variety of packages—through a letter in the mail...or a visitor to the house...or by telephone. And when the package is opened, you and I are left confused, wounded, bewildered, baffled, and hurting. We may feel used or abused, dumped on or manipulated, heart-sick or sorrowful. There was an insult, an accusation, a disagreement, an argument, a criticism, maybe even a physical blow. Now what are we supposed to do? Now what can we do to keep on walking with God? To experience more victories?

Thank God that He gives us three more graces, three more pieces of fruit—patience, kindness, and goodness (Galatians 5:22)—for managing the strain of personal relationships, for getting along with everyone—even with difficult people.

Listening to God's Call to Patience

It's good to realize up front that as Christians you and I are called by God to be patient. Get your pen out again. You may want to make notes about God's instructions.

✎ *A Word from God's Word About Patience...*

- The Bible instructs us to *"clothe [ourselves] with...patience"* (Colossians 3:12). That means we are to adorn ourselves with hearts of patience. Just as we dress our bodies every day by putting on clothes, we are to dress our spirits each morning with the godly quality of patience. Imagine how lovely and beautiful it is to be robed with God's patience! Can you think of someone who seems to be robed with patience? What do you see in his or her life?

- The Bible says Christians are to *"be patient"* (Ephesians 4:1-2). We better our relationships with other believers and promote unity when we conduct our lives with patience. How do we do this? By being patient when we see faults in other people or are annoyed by them in any way...instead of being irritated or critical or lashing out. Who is it that irritates you most and why? What can—and will—you do to be more patient with them?

- The Bible tells us the source of patience: We are to be *"strengthened with all power according to his glorious might so that you may have great endurance and patience"* (Colossians 1:11). According to this verse, what can—and will—you do to develop greater patience?

Patience isn't easy. But it is definitely a key to harmony in relationships. Patience is a practical first step to getting along with people. But before we can turn that key it will help us to understand the meaning of godly patience.

Finding Out More About Patience

If you're like me, you probably think of patience as being able to wait and wait and wait a very loooong time! But much more is involved in the kind of patience that is a fruit of the Spirit. Suppose patience were available in a can at the grocery store. What divine ingredients would be written on the label?

Ingredient #1—The first and primary ingredient in patience is *endurance.* The old King James word "longsuffering" paints the picture of patience pretty clearly for us. This ingredient of patient endurance is practiced primarily toward people and relates to our attitude toward others.[1] "It is the quality of putting up with other people, even when...sorely tried!"[2]

Ingredient #2—Next comes a very special condition that requires patience: *when injured.* You see, we need patience to endure injuries inflicted by others,[3] a patience that is characterized by longsuffering, evenness of temper, or patient endurance when injured by another.[4] As one source explains, "Patience is that calm and unruffled temper with which the good [person] bears the evils of life...[that] proceed from [others]."[5] So when your tolerance level wears thin, remember "real love...is patient, and it never gives up."[6]

Ingredient #3—Another ingredient in patience is *mercy*. God's patience is always connected with mercy[7] and bears with others for their good.[8] Patience wishes well to others and is willing to endure with them...hoping for their good.

Think about patience as you read these words: "If God had been a man, He would have wiped out this world long ago, but He has that patience which bears with all of our sinning and will not cast us off. [Therefore] in our dealings with our fellow men we must reproduce this loving, forbearing, forgiving, patient attitude of God."[9] Wow! We are actually acting like God when we are patient with people!

And why does God delay the punishment of man? The Bible explains that "the Lord is not slow in keeping his promise [to come again], as some understand slowness. He is patient with you, not wanting anyone to perish, but everyone to come to repentance" (2 Peter 3:9). In other words, the Lord is waiting to come again. He is desiring for more souls to believe and come to salvation. He's giving mankind an extended opportunity to receive Christ! Like God, we should be consumed with the same thought for others: "If I just wait long enough, maybe something good and wonderful will happen to this person!"

Ingredient #4—Finally, written in red letters across the label on our can of patience are these words: "Contains no anger or vengeance!" There is no wrath or thought of revenge or retaliation in God's kind of patience. Patience is the grace of the man who *could* revenge himself but *chooses* not to.[10] God tells us, "Do not take revenge...but leave room for God's wrath, for it is written: 'It is mine to avenge; I will repay,' says the Lord" (Romans 12:19).[11]

Patience withholds. It withholds vengeance, revenge, and retaliation...and endures instead.

Defining Patience—Patience "Does Nothing"

With these ingredients in mind, the definition of patience I use for myself is "Patience does nothing." Patience is the front end of these three fruit that relate to people—patience, goodness, and kindness—and it is the passive part of love.[12] It is love doing nothing.

Please, don't worry or wonder! Just hold on! In the next two chapters we'll move up the "action scale" of fruit-bearing when it comes to getting along with everyone. But for now,

if you want to walk in patience
when you've been hurt,
wronged, or
ill-treated,
do nothing!

Don't react! Don't do something negative and harmful and sinful. Instead, resist in patience. *Doing nothing* gives you time (even a second!) to *do something*—to pray, to reflect, to ask for advice, and to plan to respond in a good, better, or best way. First go to God for His patience...and then do nothing that will cause you to lose His precious patience. (And just a hint—this process is usually accomplished by praying!)

Waiting for the Judge

One evening while I was teaching on this fruit of the Spirit, I talked to my class about how to grow in God's patience. I told my students to remember to wait for the judge. Let me explain. (And this is a good time to pick up your pen! You'll want to note this concept well!)

✎ A Word from God's Word About Patience...

- In an encouraging passage written to a group of poor and persecuted Christians, the apostle James appealed to these saints to...

  "be patient...until the Lord's coming" (James 5:7),

  "be patient...because the Lord's coming is near" (verse 8),

  "the Judge is standing at the door!" (verse 9).

  Here's the message: When the Lord does arrive, things will most definitely change (Revelation 21:3-4)! Your suffering at the hands of others will be over. You will enjoy the continuing presence of Jesus. And He, the Judge, will also take vengeance upon your enemies. Indeed, everything will be made right as Christ brings justice and avenges the righteous. How does this encourage you in your suffering today?

- However, until our Lord, the Judge, arrives to settle things, you are to live with your adversaries and endure ill treatment from difficult people…while remaining patient and practicing self-restraint. You are not to turn to self-pity or complaining (see James 5:7-9). And you are not to judge, quarrel, criticize, gossip, or find fault. No, you are responsible for only one thing while you wait, and that is Christlike conduct. The Judge is responsible for everything else! How do you tend to react to mistreatment by others, and what better way will you put into practice?

- With this image in mind, ask yourself, "Can I wait?" James says you can! So pick the person in your life who has caused you the most personal pain. You know, the person who is hostile, mean, or ungrateful, who ignores you, insults you, slanders you, or blocks your progress. Then—through prayer and by God's grace and His help—resist every urge to retaliate or punish that person and instead do nothing. In patience, do nothing while you wait for the Judge.

Heart Response

Think about your struggles with patience for a minute. Which is easier—to give in to emotions and anger when someone has hurt you or to practice patience and hold back your wrath? To lash out with cruel words or to hold back your hateful words? Amazingly, it's no problem to let go, lose your temper, and tell your offender exactly how you feel and what you think! But much harder is the godly response—God's response!—of choosing to do nothing outwardly as you resist in patience inwardly. Believe me, it takes all of God's strength and grace to help you do nothing! You desperately need God's Spirit to fill you with His patience. (And so do I!) But once you're filled, then doing nothing as you resist in patience is how you practice patient endurance… when you're injured by others…without vengeance…and for their good! That's God's recipes for patience.

Things to Do Today to Walk in Patience

1. Train yourself in longsuffering. Proverbs 19:11 says, "A man's wisdom gives him patience; it is to his glory to

overlook an offense." In other words, learn to restrain your anger.

2. Lengthen your fuse. How long can you wait? Make that period a little longer. How many times can you wait? Make it a few more times next time. That's where prayer comes into play. Our patient God is willing to give you His patience whenever you ask for it.

3. Remove opportunities to sin. As Paul counsels, "Do not think about how to gratify the desires of the sinful nature" (Romans 13:14). And Proverbs says that "it is to a man's honor to avoid strife, but every fool is quick to quarrel" (20:3). Carefulness can keep you from sinning.

4. Follow Jesus' example. He remained absolutely sinless even under the most severe mistreatment. "He committed no sin, and no deceit was found in his mouth. When they hurled their insults at him, he did not retaliate; when he suffered, he made no threats" (1 Peter 2:22-23). Carry Jesus' response to suffering in your

heart and mind...and try to lift your own responses to a higher level of Christ-likeness.

5. Pray. This was Jesus' surefire method for enduring His suffering. He "entrusted himself to him who judges justly" (1 Peter 2:23). When you are injured by others, turn your aching soul heavenward. With God's help, be patient with others for their own good.

Would You Like to Know More About Patience? Check It Out!

✓ Read Genesis 6:3-5. What did God observe about mankind (verse 5)?

How long did He wait for the inhabitants of the earth to change their ways (verse 3)?

✓ Read 1 Peter 3:20, and write out the words that describe the patience of God.

✓ Read 1 Peter 2:22-23. Describe Jesus' perfect, sinless conduct (verse 22).

Yet how was He treated (verse 23)?

How did Jesus exhibit patience toward those who put Him to death?

✓ Read 2 Timothy 2:24-26. Write out the different words and phrases that indicate patience (verse 25).

What might be the outcome of such patience according to verses 25-26?

✓ Read 1 Thessalonians 5:14. What bottom-line principle for patience is stated here?

✓ As you review the teaching from these scriptures regarding patience, list three things you want to remember—or remember to do—to better handle your people problems.

7

A Time to Do Something

The fruit of the Spirit is...kindness.
Galatians 5:22

Several months ago when I walked into my local Wal-Mart store, my eye was immediately drawn to a large poster picturing several arrogant girls standing around with some pretty awful scowls on their faces. It was an advertisement of the latest DVD movie being offered for sale. And having my mind on this book and the fruit of the Spirit—and more specifically on "kindness"—I couldn't help but react to the title of the movie: *Mean Girls*.

Now contrast these "mean girls" with my friend Judy who helped me serve at a young woman's bridal shower. I worked kitchen duty while Judy moved among the women asking if they needed anything, patting them on the shoulder, and making sure everyone was comfortable. Graciously Judy chatted with each woman as she carried the heavy silver coffeepot around the room, refilling cups and removing dirty dishes and soiled napkins. Then, even though I was in the kitchen, I heard one guest (a mean girl!) sneer as Judy moved out of earshot, "She's too nice."

Since my encounter with the "mean girls," I've given much thought to those words, "She's too nice." What Judy did for all of us—including an ungrateful woman—was to actively live out kindness, the next fruit of the Spirit. Judy modeled the grace and ministry of kindness not only for those other women, but for me as well. As you'll soon see, the highest compliment a Christian can receive is to be described as "too nice." When people say that of you or me, we can definitely know we are truly exhibiting the Spirit's fruit!

Finding Out More About Kindness

Let's backtrack a minute and review our walk with God. In this section of our book, we're learning about the actions of patience, kindness, and goodness in dealing with the people in our lives. As we face people each day and as we experience any pain they may inflict upon us, we are to be patient, to do nothing. And this response can be achieved only when we ask God to fill us with His patience. Only God can help us do nothing.

But after asking for patience, it's time to make a move, to go into action, to get up and do something! And that "something" is kindness, the next fruit on the Lord's list—"the fruit of the Spirit is...kindness" (Galatians 5:22). And even though the fruit of kindness is borne in our lives as we walk by the Spirit, that walk involves living out several commands given to us in God's Word. Make notes and interact with the scriptures that follow to learn more about kindness.

✎ A Word from God's Word About Kindness...

- Ephesians 4:25-32 warns Christians against conduct that grieves the Holy Spirit and hurts the heart of God.[1] You'll want to get well acquainted with these verses for sure! But for now, focus on the commands in verse 32. Paul wraps up his list of meanness—bitterness, wrath, anger, clamor, and evil speaking—and tells us to instead *"be kind...to one another"* (verse 32). The Living Bible simply and bluntly says, *"Stop being mean...[and] instead, be kind to each other."*

- Another call to kindness is in Colossians 3:12. Here God tells us to *"clothe [ourselves] with...kindness."* Kindness is a basic Christian virtue that helps all relationships. Therefore we are to put on kindness—like we put on our clothes—in all our relationships.

- And how are we to act toward those who are not Christians? With kindness! *"The Lord's servant must not quarrel;*

instead, he must be kind to everyone" (2 Timothy 2:24). Kindness is an important element in Christian witnessing. Christians have been known through the ages by their love and concern for others, and that should be our goal too.

Defining Kindness—Kindness "Does Something"

My operating definition of kindness, which helps me immensely in cultivating and showing concern for others, is "kindness plans to do something." While patience does nothing sinful while resisting in patience (see chapter 6), kindness now plans to act.

Kindness, like all the other fruit of the Spirit, desires godly action and, therefore, looks for opportunities to do something. Kindness actively moves out, preparing for the actions of goodness (which we will look at in the next chapter). Kindness actively asks, "Who needs love? How can I ease someone's burden? How can I touch another person?" Kindness is tenderness and concern for other people. It is also a sweetness of disposition and a matter of the heart, "a grace that mellows all that might be harsh."[2]

Cultivating Kindness

The book I turn to each morning during my prayer time contains a sobering prompt that has helped me grow in kindness. It instructs me to pray for "greater love and compassion for others." Well, I have to tell you that whenever I see these words, I am humbled to the core as I examine my heart and soul. This call to prayer always makes me realize how much more I need this godly quality in my life! But prayer and the following aspects of kindness have helped me in this area. Here's what I've discovered.

1. *Caring is a part of kindness*—When you genuinely care about people, you find yourself paying attention to their circumstances and being concerned about their welfare. You get involved in their lives. As your love grows, the details of their lives become more and more important to you. It begins to really matter to you if they are sad or discouraged, struggling or in pain, needy or lonely. (Unfortunately that caring doesn't come nearly as easily for me when it comes to the problem people in my life.)

This is where prayer helps. If you follow Jesus' instruction to "pray for those who mistreat you" (Luke 6:28), radical changes occur in your heart. For starters, prayer causes you to become vitally and spiritually involved in the lives of those you pray for. Also, through prayer, God changes your heart and mind by softening your harshness and melting your selfishness into concern for others...including your enemies. Caring about others eliminates unfriendliness, a lack of compassion, and a judgmental spirit. So ask God to help you have greater love and compassion for others.

2. *Thinking is a part of kindness*—Another sure sign that your concern for people is growing is when you begin to think about others and the conditions of their lives. When

you find yourself looking at people and thinking, "What would help her? What would help him? What does he need? What does she need?" When you ask God, "How can I serve this person? How can I make his or her life easier? How can I touch her life and lift her burden?"

As we're learning, kindness plans to do something, and that takes a certain amount of thought and prayer. King David models this for us. When he became the king of Israel, David asked, "Is there anyone still left of the house of Saul [the previous king] to whom I can show kindness?" (2 Samuel 9:1). You see, David was *thinking* about showing kindness to the heirs of the former king. Can you think of someone you can be kind to?

To grow in kindness, ask God to give you a caring heart and a creative mind. Begin looking around to see the needs of people in your home, your neighborhood, your workplace, and your church. Hurting people are literally everywhere! One shocking statistic reports, "Ninety percent of all mental illness...could have been prevented, or could yet be cured, by simple kindness."[3] What can you think of doing today that would touch another life with kindness?

3. *Noticing is a part of kindness*—Another way to practice kindness is to notice other people's needs. All you have to do is use your God-given capacity for observation. As the Bible says, "Ears that hear and eyes that see—the LORD has made them both" (Proverbs 20:12). You can *always* be watching and listening to those around us. In fact, this is one of the ways God cares for us: "The eyes of the Lord are on the righteous and his ears are attentive to their

prayer" (1 Peter 3:12). And you can care for people in the same way God cares for you...just by paying attention and being on the lookout for people's needs.

I read this story about an evangelist's mom who practiced this sort of kindness and observation. One day he found her sitting at the table with an elderly homeless man. Apparently she had gone shopping, met the needy man along the way, and provided a warm meal for him. During their conversation the homeless man said, "I wish there were more people like you in the world." That's when his mom replied, "Oh, there are! But you must just look for them." The old man simply shook his head, saying, "But lady, I didn't need to look for you. You looked for me!"[4] Take note—when you begin to notice others, you'll soon know their wants and needs just as this kind woman did.

And here's another story about a woman who walks in kindness. It's about "a Hawaiian woman who strings a number of leis early each Sunday morning, not for anyone in particular! Then she goes to church praying, 'Lord, who needs my leis today? A newcomer? Someone discouraged. Lead me to the right people.' "[5]

These stories show us two pictures of kindness—two real women filled with God's love who go out actively looking for those in need. Two women who, in kindness, plan to do something, then keep a keen eye out and notice others.

Pray to grow in God's grace of kindness. Constantly ask God to work in your heart to help you care, think, and notice the people He places in your life. Look to God for His help with unkind emotions and thoughts about others. Then obey God's commands for kindness.

Heart Response

In our culture today, and in places like your school and even at home, being too nice may not sound very cool. But that's exactly what kindness is! Those around you may be "mean," but God is asking you to be kind.

When the book of Galatians was written—the book where the fruit of the Spirit is listed—the common slave name *chrestos* came from the same Greek root word for kindness. The first-century pagans confused *chrestos* (slave) with the word *Christos* for Christ and began calling Christians by a nickname that meant "goody-goody."[6] That's the same as being "too nice." The spelling of these two Greek words varies by just one letter, and they are amazingly similar! When you walk with God and copy Jesus, you too will be kind. You'll be "too nice"!

My friend Judy was spoken of as being "too nice." Why? Because she was kind. Because she was serving as a *chrestos*, a slave. Because she was caring, thinking, noticing, and touching. And because she is a *Christos*, a kind of Christ, a "goody-goody," Judy's kindness should be a goal for you as well.

Things to Do Today to Walk in Kindness

1. Pray every day this week for God to fill your heart with His compassion. Then write out how praying for compassion made a difference in you and in your week.

2. Live out God's command to be kind to others at home (Ephesians 4:32). Remember, what you are at home is what you are. Think of ways to help out your parents and your brothers and sisters, even your grandparents. Make it your goal to make their lives easier. What can—and will—you do today?

3. Pray for your enemies—those people who mistreat and use you (Luke 6:28). You will find you cannot hate a person you are praying for. You also can't neglect that person. Try it! You'll find it's true.

4. List several ways you can show God's kindness to your Number One problem person. Remember this thought—Kindness is the ability to love people more than they deserve.

Would You Like to Know More About Kindness? Check It Out!

✓ Read 2 Samuel 9:1-7. What question did David ask when he became king of Israel (verse 1)?

What did he do or what actions of kindness did he take when his question was answered (verses 2-7)?

✓ Read 2 Kings 4:8-10. To whom and how did the Shunammite woman show kindness?

✓ Read Acts 9:36. Describe Dorcas' many acts of kindness. What did she do for the widows in her community (verse 39)?

✓ Read Luke 9:12-13. For whom was Jesus concerned?

Contrast Jesus' actions and concerns with the disciples' behavior.

✓ What do these four examples reveal about how you show—or don't show—kindness?

8

A Time to Do Everything

The fruit of the Spirit is...goodness.
Galatians 5:22

Late one evening I crawled into bed clutching a book, hoping I could stay awake to read at least five minutes before turning out the lamp. It had been another wild and full day (you know, like the ones you have too!). I had just about had it...but I was going to give the five minutes a try anyway. The book in my hand was a treasure I had found that morning at the bookstore, and all day long I had been relishing the thought of opening this small delight. Only one copy was on the shelf at the store, and its title had caught my eye and captured my attention—*People Whose Faith Got Them into Trouble.*[1] Finally it was time—if I could just stay awake! As

I began reading this book subtitled "Stories of Costly Discipleship," the opening words of the first chapter caught my attention so completely that I read much longer than usual. Here's what I read:

> The sound of hooves at midnight—horsemen galloping into the courtyard—and the clatter of armor as soldiers surround the house wake the old man. Two officers dismount and pound on the wooden door with the butt ends of their spears. Maids in disheveled nightclothes rush upstairs and urge the white-haired fugitive to hide under the bed, in a closet…anywhere. Instead, he hushes them, drapes a cloak over his frail shoulders, descends the stairs, opens the door and invites the men who have come to arrest him inside.
>
> He instructs the maids, "Quickly, prepare hot food and something to drink. Can't you see these men have ridden hard tonight? They need refreshment; give them the best in the house."
>
> Confused by this unexpected reception, the arresting officers crowd into the room and cluster around a bronze charcoal brazier on the floor. As they warm their numb hands against the cold night of February 22, 166, Polycarp, elderly bishop of Smyrna...makes every effort to see that his guests are comfortable. He personally serves the officers and soldiers alike from the warm dishes his maids have prepared.[2]

What a powerful example of Christian goodness! A man being hunted down, a man who would soon taste death by execution at a fiery stake, was showing love to his persecutors! This man was exhibiting the Spirit's fruit:

—*patience* allowed him to graciously receive his captors,

—*kindness* thought of their needs, and then

—*goodness* followed through.

Serving them himself, the man being led to death met the needs of those leading him. This story of Polycarp offers us a vivid example of the fruit of the Spirit in action.

Reviewing Our Progress

Do you realize that just as a garden is laid out by a plan, God designs your life according to a plan? He uses the people, events, and circumstances of our lives to guide us along the path toward godliness. And He leads us step by step. Truly, He knows how to grow us to be like Him!

And speaking of gardens and growing, I was thinking about these three fruit of the Spirit that help us get along with everybody—patience, kindness, and goodness. My thoughts went something like this...

> *Patience* is like a seed hidden beneath the surface. It silently waits in the dark earth, hidden from view, doing nothing (it seems!), while it secretly, quietly, and slowly incubates life. This

> sweet fruit makes it possible for kindness and goodness to develop.
>
> *Kindness* grows from the seed of patience in the dark depths where it develops a root system. Kindness pushes its head up through the soil, wanting to break forth and do something until, at last, it cracks through the soil, visible to all.
>
> *Goodness* blossoms forth, along with its works of love blessing all who see it...which is what this luscious fruit of the Spirit is all about!

Getting a Handle on Goodness

Getting God's fruit of goodness into your life will be easier when you understand three things. These truths will help you in your conduct toward others.

1. *Goodness is spiritual in its origin*—The Bible shows us that God is good (Psalm 33:5; Nehemiah 9:25,35). From cover to cover, the Bible tells the story of God's gracious goodness. One scholar defines this goodness as "the sum of all God's attributes...express[ing] the...excellence of the divine character."[3] And yet, as God's children, we can exhibit His goodness.

2. *Goodness is active*—While kindness plans to do something good for others, goodness moves into total action. God *in* us and His presence *with* us produces *His* goodness in

us. And His goodness in us then results in kind deeds that benefit others.

3. *Goodness is a readiness to do good*—Goodness is also completely dedicated to helping others live well.[4] It is a readiness to do good,[5] up on tip-toe, ready and waiting to do good to others.

I'm sure you agree that your family and friends, your church and school—even the whole world!—need people who are actively kind. People who walk out their doors every day ready to do good—not just think about it or pray about it, but really do it. People who are devoted to making the lives of others better.

Defining Goodness

As I tried to understand goodness, it helped me to understand it as *goodness does everything!* In other words, it does everything it can to shower God's goodness upon others. Goodness follows through on the wonderful thoughts of kindness. Goodness takes the giant step from good intentions to actually doing everything it can to serve others. John Wesley, the famous preacher of several centuries ago, understood this principle of doing everything. In fact, he made it a rule for his life and put it in these words:

> Do all the good you can,
> by all the means you can,
> in all the ways you can,
> in all the places you can,

at all the times you can,
to all the people you can,
as long as ever you can.

Finding Out More About Goodness

How does God's goodness in us work itself out? It's pen time again! Make notes as you let these scriptures work in your heart.

✎ *A Word from God's Word About Goodness...*

- First there is the matter of your walk with God. You are called by God to

  —"*walk in love*" (Ephesians 5:2),

  —"*walk in Him*" (Colossians 2:6),

  —"*walk in a manner worthy of the God who calls you*" (1 Thessalonians 2:12),

  —"*walk in the same manner as Jesus walked*" (1 John 2:6), and

  —"*walk by the Spirit*" (Galatians 5:16).

- A life characterized by God's goodness *is* walking by the Spirit! Through this kind of living you can

  —*"overcome evil with good"* (Romans 12:21), and

  —not return *"evil for evil or reviling for reviling, but on the contrary blessing"* (1 Peter 3:9 NKJV).

- Any goodness borne in us is God's. As the Bible says in Romans 3:12, *"There is no one who does good, not even one."* However, as we practice obedience to God's commands, He produces His fruit of goodness in us—fruit which is by His grace and glorifies Him.

Choosing Goodness

Some of the young women in my Bible class realized that to walk with God they had to make some serious choices. Susan, for instance, was hurt by people in her school who were not Christians and who openly despised her for being one. She told me her plan of action: "I've set a goal. No matter what others at school do or say to me, I have decided I'm going to respond in goodness and be a good advertisement for Christ. And it's already working!"

Ann, too, was hurt—but by the Christians in her youth group at church. What did she do? How did she handle this? "I chose to not feel hurt when I was not invited to join them in their activities. I chose to not feel bitterness or resentment. I just need to show my love for them."

And then there is Maria. She faces a hostile, persecuting boss at her part-time job, a person she described as mean and rude. Her situation at work boiled down to a spiritual decision for her. She could react in the wrong way...or she could respond in the right way, God's way. She wrote, "I had to make a choice—give back what he is dishing out or show him the kindness and goodness of the Lord."

Examples like these could go on and on, and choices like these go on and on too. But I'm sure you're getting a picture about how to walk in goodness from these girls who are just like you. Like these young women, your walk with God requires many decisions on your part as you constantly look to God and ask Him, "What is the right thing to do?"

Walking in Goodness

Yes, walking with God (which is what this book is all about) requires that you and I make serious choices. As one fellow traveler notes, "The Spirit life includes goodness, and goodness doesn't come naturally; it always requires a decision."[6] And our relationships with others, especially with those who hurt us, call for choices. For instance, one definite choice we can make when we're hurt by someone is to walk in patience and do nothing. That gives us time to seek to do the right thing. Then, having made the choice not to blow up, not tell someone off, not to succumb to anger, not to fight back, not to take revenge, we can move to the next choice—the choice of kindness—and *plan to do something*, plan to do deeds of kindness.

This choice, my friend, is the focus of our constant battle between the flesh and the Spirit (Galatians 5:17). And it is this kind of choice that keeps you walking with God...even when provoked or hurt or confused by the treatment of others. You and I must put forth the effort of making the right choices—God's choices. And we must turn to God for His help in winning the victory over sin. Then, miracle of miracles, our lives bring glory to Him as His fruit grows and displays itself in our walk with Him!

As you and I walk through the day-in, day-out routines and responsibilities of life, we have many chances to choose goodness, especially as women. Read on—with pen in hand!—and see for yourself God's plan for goodness in your life.

✎ A Word from God's Word About Goodness...

- *God's women are to learn goodness.* In Titus 2:5 we read that the young women are taught by other women and encouraged by them to *be good* (Titus 2:5 NKJV).

- *God's women are to be devoted to goodness.* In 1 Timothy 5:10 (NKJV) women are urged to live a life that earns them a reputation *for good works*, to be devoted to *every good work*. And don't forget—your goodness begins at home with the people who live under your roof as well.

- *God's women are to adorn themselves with goodness.* In 1 Timothy 2:10 women are instructed to adorn themselves *with good deeds, appropriate for women who profess to worship God.* One scholar writes that good works "create that spiritual adornment which is the real glory of the Christian woman."[7] Good works indicate a life of selfless devotion to others, an adornment that lies not in what she puts on, but in the loving service she gives out.[8] Clearly God wants our good works to be our chief attraction. Our good works are what He wants others to notice—not our clothes and not our jewelry and not our looks. Our good works reflect our walk with God.

Heart Response

Oswald Chambers, a great saint from years past, writes this about goodness: "Christian character is not expressed by good doing, but by God-likeness. It is not sufficient to do good, to do the right thing. We must have our goodness stamped by the image and superscription of God. It is supernatural all through."[9] In other words, our goal is to grow in godliness, not just to crank out works. As you read through the "Things to Do Today" list that follows, keep in mind that in order to think about others, you must first stop thinking about yourself!

Things to Do Today to Walk in Goodness

1. Confess any thoughts or acts that are not kind or good. Augustine wrote, "The confession of evil works is the first beginning of good works."[10]

2. Take the initiative in meeting the specific needs of others. Remember, "Love means action."[11]

3. Forget your own comfort. "When God is at work in the believer, he desires to be good and to do good....It becomes clear that the good life is not comfort, but godliness."[12]

4. Actively seek to promote the happiness of others—someone in your family, a friend, a co-worker, or a teacher at school. "Kindness is a sincere desire for the happiness of others; goodness is the activity calculated to advance their happiness."[13]

Would You Like to Know More About Goodness? Check It Out!

✓ What do these verses say about doing good?

Luke 6:27-28—

Romans 2:7—

Romans 2:10—

Romans 12:21—

Galatians 6:10—

✓ Which of these verses were your favorites or the most challenging, and why?

✓ What actions did the following women take that modeled goodness—the desire to do something?

Rebekah in Genesis 24:15-20—

The Shunammite woman in 2 Kings 4:8-10—

Martha and Mary in Luke 10:38 and John 12:2—

Dorcas in Acts 9:36—

Lydia in Acts 16:15—

✓ Which of these women and their acts of goodness inspires you most to minister goodness to others, and why?

9

Looking at Jesus' Actions

Jesus, our wonderful Master and Teacher, perfectly lived out patience, kindness, and goodness. Do you remember Jesus praying in the Garden of Gethsemane? It was time for Him to die, yet He didn't rebel, panic, turn, or fall apart. Instead, He turned to His Father in prayer. Then, after a time of heartfelt and intense prayer, He rose up from the ground filled with God's love, joy, and peace—the first three fruit we studied. Strengthened after His time of prayer and thoroughly prepared, Jesus gathered His sleeping disciples and boldly walked through the garden gate...

...to face people. Jesus knew they were waiting on the other side of the gate. Exactly who was waiting for Jesus outside the garden?

The Traitor

As Jesus confidently walked toward the garden entrance, He said, "Rise, let us go! Here comes my betrayer!" (Matthew 26:46). Jesus definitely knew *what* was about to happen—and He also knew *who* was playing a role in the process. It was Judas! How Christ's heart must have ached as He looked into the face and eyes of a trusted friend. Who was Judas?

—He was one of the 12 men—the 12 disciples—chosen to help Jesus with His ministry of teaching, leading, providing for the needs of others, and working miracles.

—He was one who had been prayed for by the Savior and fed by His miraculous multiplication of loaves and fishes.

—He was one whose dirty feet had been washed by the Savior's holy hands.

—He was one who had heard the words of life and truths about God from the mouth of God Himself.

—He was the one to whom Jesus had entrusted the group's money.

—He was one of the few people who had the privileges he enjoyed on a daily basis in the presence of Jesus.

Yes, there Judas stood, filled with the darkness of hell itself and the evil of Satan. Judas—betrayer. What grief and disappointment must have filled our Lord! Judas, a friend, a disciple, an intimate companion—and now a traitor!

The Mob

And Judas was not alone. He was accompanied by "a great multitude with swords and clubs, from the chief priests and elders of the people" (Matthew 26:47). Included in this group were the officers of the temple (Luke 22:52), a company of Roman soldiers, the chief priests and elders.

Yes, Jesus had to deal with people—as many as a thousand! People who were not very nice. People who were mean and evil. For the next 18 hours, He would face a host of hostile people—people who would abuse Him physically and verbally, people who would hurl insults at Him, along with fists, whips, staves, hammers, and spears. Still to come were the high priest, Caiaphas, the scribes, the elders, and the Council of the Sanhedrin (Matthew 26:57-60).

And there would be even more! The list of Jesus' enemies continues:

- Pilate—who would call for Jesus' death (Matthew 27:2).
- The soldiers—who would strip Him, mock Him, spit on Him, and beat Him (verses 28-30).
- The two thieves crucified with Him—one of whom would insult Him (Luke 23:39-41).
- The crowd—which would hurl abuses and wag their heads in mockery (Matthew 27:39-40).
- The disciples—who would flee, leaving Jesus even more alone (Matthew 26:56).

Truly, the forces of evil had gathered for the purpose of arresting Jesus and putting Him to death.

The Fleshly Response

As soon as Judas kissed Jesus, His enemies came and laid hands on Him and seized Him (Matthew 26:50). In the seconds that followed, we see (again!) the fleshly response of Jesus' disciples in sharp contrast to His gracious response of patience, kindness, and goodness.

Think for a minute about this troubling scene of Jesus' arrest. It happened under the dark cover of night. Possibly a thousand people were involved. There was confusion and panic. Emotions ran high as the Savior of the world met its evil head on.

And in the heat of those emotions, "one of those who were with Jesus reached and drew out his sword, and struck the slave of the high priest, and cut off his ear" (verse 51). We learn from the book of John that this "one" is Peter (John 18:10). Peter showed no patience. Instead, he went into action. He grabbed a sword and swung. No graciousness was exhibited in Peter's desire to slash 'em, dash 'em, thrash 'em, and kill 'em! He also showed no kindness—the kindness of God that desires the best for others.

Peter's action caused someone to suffer. And he certainly showed no goodness—that fruit of the Spirit that does everything for the good of others. Instead, Peter hurt someone in his efforts to protect his Master. Peter most definitely responded in the fleshly way. He chose the easy response. He reacted. He evidenced "the acts of the sinful nature" (Galatians 5:19).

The Godly Response

Jesus also went into action. Notice how His response exhibited the fruit of the Spirit.

The godly response of patience—First, Jesus lived out God's perfect patience. Do you remember our definition of patience in chapter 6? Patience is endurance when injured by others, it is interested in their good, it is without vengeance, and it *does nothing.* Jesus lived every aspect of this gracious fruit. Wanting nothing done in revenge or reaction, He told Peter, "Put your sword back in its place" (Matthew 26:52). Although Jesus definitely could have avenged Himself, He rebuked Peter's puny action by asking, "Do you think I cannot call on my Father, and he will at once put at my disposal more than twelve legions of angels?" (verse 53). Instead of calling on 72,000 angels, Jesus acted in perfect patience. He did nothing and consequently was led away (verse 57) as a lamb to the slaughter (Isaiah 53:7).

The godly response of kindness—And why did Jesus let Himself be led away? Partly because of His kindness. God's kindness is concerned for the welfare of others (even one's enemies). It also desires to better their lives. And it consciously *plans to do something* for them. In kindness, Jesus had "resolutely set out for Jerusalem" (Luke 9:51) in the first place. In kindness, He had also agonized in prayer those three long hours. And now, acting in kindness, he met the mob head on instead of fleeing. In His divine kindness, Jesus planned to do something for His enemies. He planned to die for them!

The godly response of goodness—Finally, in goodness, our Jesus moved into action. Goodness is active kindness and flows out of a heart that stands ready to do good. And goodness *does everything possible* to help others live well.

So what did Jesus do? He turned to the man whose ear Peter had cut off, "touched the man's ear and healed him" (Luke 22:51). This man was one of the enemy mob. He had come to arrest Jesus, yet now he found himself on the receiving end of Jesus' goodness. He experienced a miracle of goodness. In fact, his healing was the last service Jesus rendered before being bound. Appropriately for our Savior and Lord, "the last action of that hand, while it was still free, was one of love, one of rendering service to men."[1]

Heart Response

Truly Jesus is the God of all grace who is "able to make all grace abound to you, so that in all things at all times, having all that you need, you will abound in every good work" (2 Corinthians 9:8)! Having seen our Savior's great graciousness in terrible circumstances, how can we ever again lash out at others? How could we ever again be impatient with others after witnessing the beauty and grace of our Lord's patience with His killers? How could we ever again wish evil or ill upon others after watching our Savior's kindness as He walked the lonely road to Jerusalem to die for us all? And how could we ever again strike out physically or verbally at another after seeing our Savior's healing touch for an enemy?

Becoming more like Jesus requires us to be filled with God's grace—His Spirit's gifts of patience, kindness, and goodness. To respond in His way requires looking to Him to "find grace to help us in our time of need" (Hebrews 4:16). Let's look to Him now in prayer...

It is in prayer, dear Father,
that we thank You for the people in our lives
who cause us to need Your grace so.
We acknowledge that
Your patience,
Your kindness, and
Your goodness enable us
to do nothing harmful,
to truly care, and
to act out Your love toward others.
In our pain...our tears...our suffering...
we look to You, O heart of love.
May we refuse to act or react until we have again
looked at our Savior's actions and
seen His patience...His kindness...His
goodness.
May we grow in these graces.
In Jesus' name,
who came not to be ministered to but to
minister to others...even to the point of
giving His life as a ransom. Amen.

Things to Do Today to Grow More Like Jesus

1. Read again Matthew 26:36-46. List three or four things these verses teach you about preparing to associate and to interact with people. Start carrying the list around with you. Put it on your prayer list too!

2. What are some of the ways you have responded in the past to people who have caused you pain—who were critical of you, or made fun of you, or snubbed you, or hurt you? What is your usual way of responding to such people?

3. After learning about Jesus' actions of goodness toward unkind people, how will you respond the next time you are mistreated? How will you...

   ...resist in patience?

   ...plan for kindness?

   ...give in goodness?

Would You Like To Know More About Growing Like Jesus? Check It Out!

✓ Read Matthew 26:47-68 and 27:27-44. Make a list of the people or groups of people Jesus faced. Then, across from each, list the different ways these people treated Jesus.

People or group	Treatment

✓ What could Jesus have done to defend Himself (Matthew 26:53)?

What did Jesus do instead according to 1 Peter 2:23?

What lessons can you take to heart from Jesus' conduct on that horrible night?

✓ Read again Matthew 26:51-54 and 69-75. By contrast to Jesus' behavior, write out a brief summary of Peter's fleshly behavior.

What lessons can you take to heart from Peter's conduct on that horrible night?

Getting Your Act Together

10

A Choice to Just Do It

The fruit of the Spirit is...faithfulness.
Galatians 5:22

One day while I was filing some of my husband's papers, a newspaper cartoon fell out of a manila folder. It was an old Pogo strip. And there was Pogo Possum, wearing a colonial general's hat made out of paper, holding a tiny wooden sword, and standing in a George Washington pose on top of a rock. Out of Pogo's mouth came the bubble with these famous words, "We have met the enemy—and they is us!"

"We have met the enemy—and they is us" is exactly how I feel many nights at the end of another day that began with good intentions. The discouragement comes when I realize that I, too, chose to watch the national average of 6.4 hours of TV...that I chose to eat the foods that generally move people to the "20 pounds overweight" category...that I've hardly touched the "to do" list (I can't even find it!)...or that I have failed to open my Bible. I am truly my own worst enemy when it comes to being a disciplined woman. How greatly I need the Spirit's fruit of faithfulness and self-control!

Taking Time to Review

Before we step into this final section of this book, I want us to think again about our progress. On our journey to discover the meaning of each fruit of the Spirit listed in Galatians 5:22-23, we first learned about love and joy and peace—attitudes that bloom with great sacrifice.

Next we dealt with the challenge of handling people God's way—and the way Jesus did—by looking to the Holy Spirit for His patience, kindness, and goodness.

And now it's time to move on to conquer the discipline of self. If you're cringing at the very thought, rejoice...and relax! There's hope! Faithfulness, gentleness, and self-control are grace gifts from God that make it possible for you to triumph over weakness, impulsiveness, and laziness. When you walk by the Spirit you win over procrastination, stubbornness, and unhealthy desires. So hang on! It may be a rough road to walk, but a pattern for victory through God's Spirit awaits you at the other end.

Now, first on God's list for getting your act together is faithfulness.

Finding Out More About Faithfulness

As Christians, God's faithfulness is to be part of our character. And faithfulness is critical because, as someone has said, "The final criterion God will use to judge us will not be success but faithfulness."[1] The following insights will help you to understand faithfulness and how better to walk in it.

Insight #1: The God of faithfulness—From the first page of the Bible to the last, we see God's faithfulness. First, we learn that God is faithful. The psalmist declared, "I will make your faithfulness known through all generations" (Psalm 89:1). Moses did that when he praised God, exulting, "He is the Rock!...a faithful God" (Deuteronomy 32:4). And here's a thought for you: One scholar reached this conclusion—"God is a Rock...and there should be something of the rock in us."[2]

Second, the New Testament shows us that Jesus is faithful. His very name is "Faithful and True" (Revelation 19:11). His ultimate demonstration of faithfulness is this: Because Jesus was faithful, He "made himself nothing, taking the very nature of a servant, being made in human likeness. And being found in appearance as a man, he humbled himself and became obedient to death—even death on a cross! (Philippians 2:7-8)."[3]

And here's something else we learn—God's Word is faithful. The apostle John was told to write down his visions because "these words are trustworthy and true" (Revelation 21:5). We are blessed to experience the faithfulness of the Godhead *and* the Bible!

Insight #2: The core of faithfulness—Faithfulness is defined as loyalty, trustworthiness, or steadfastness. It is characteristic of the person who is reliable, and it includes our faithfulness to God and His will, to God and His Word, as well as our loyalty to others. And it also means faithful not only in deed, but also in word.

Insight #3: The marks of faithfulness—What does faithfulness do? What does faithfulness in action look like? Well, if you were watching a woman who is walking with God by His Spirit, you would note these marks:

- She follows through...on whatever she has to do.
- She comes through...no matter what.
- She delivers the goods...whether a returned item or a school paper.
- She shows up...even early so others won't worry.
- She keeps her word...her *yes* means *yes* and her *no* means *no* (James 5:12).
- She keeps her commitments and appointments...you won't find her canceling.
- She successfully transacts business...carrying out any instructions given to her.
- She is regular at church...and doesn't neglect worship.
- She is devoted to duty...just as Jesus was when He came to do His Father's will (John 4:34).

Insight #4: The opposites of faithfulness—We can learn a lot from opposites. For instance, one of those opposites is *fickle.* You've met people who change—change their minds, change their loyalties, change their standards. Nothing seems to matter or be that important. Nothing seems to rate an authentic commitment.

Another opposite of faithful is *unreliable.* An unreliable person doesn't come through, can't be depended on, and can't be trusted with information or responsibility. As the saying goes, you may depend on the Lord—but may He depend on you?

Defining Faithfulness—Faithfulness Means "Do It!"

As I thought about faithfulness, I chose as my own definition the slogan *"Do it!"* or, to quote the Nike shoe ads, *"Just do it!"* Faithfulness means doing it...no matter what. Doing it regardless of feelings, moods, or desires—if the Lord wills (James 4:15).

"Do it!" has become my battle cry as I struggle each day with my special areas of weakness. Tiredness heads the list...followed closely by laziness. But when I make a decision to *do it* and look to God for His strength and purpose in *doing it,* He gives me the grace to have victory over both. We'll look later at more of the enemies of faithfulness, but for now let the motto *"Do it!"* move you toward greater faithfulness. Try it...for an hour, a day, a week. I think you'll amaze yourself (and others!) as they see this sturdy fruit grow in your life through the work of God's faithful Spirit.

And there's nothing like the Scriptures to help you grow! Is your pen nearby? Grab it now and make notes about how each of these verses can help you get your act together concerning faithfulness.

✎ *A Word from God's Word About Faithfulness...*

- Lamentations 3:22-23—*"Because of the* L*ORD's great love we are not consumed, for his compassions never fail. They are new every morning; great is your faithfulness."*

- Romans 3:3—*"What if some did not have faith? Will their lack of faith nullify God's faithfulness?"*

- Revelation 19:11—*"I saw heaven standing open and there before me was a white horse, whose rider is called Faithful and True. With justice he judges and makes war."*

- Revelation 21:5 and 22:6—*"He who was seated on the throne said, 'I am making everything new!' Then he said, 'Write this down, for these words are trustworthy and true....' The angel said to me, 'These words are trustworthy and true. The Lord, the God of the spirits of the prophets, sent his angel to show his servants the things that must soon take place.'"*

- 1 Corinthians 4:2—*"Now it is required that those who have been given a trust must prove faithful."*

Realizing the Need for Faithfulness

Boy, is there ever a need for faithfulness! We women, whether older or younger, have many—*many!*—assignments from God, and there's no way to accomplish them without faithfulness. Faithful diligence and discipline is needed every step of the way...and throughout the day. For instance...

Homework—Like you, I have "schoolwork" and papers to turn in as I work daily to meet my writing deadlines and turn in my book manuscripts...on top of taking care of a household—both the people and the place. My work at my desk really forces me to follow my maxim *"Do it."* I call it "the discipline of the desk" and mentally chain myself there each day to get my work done, to meet my commitments, to come through on time, to turn in my homework! I like what the great British statesman Winston Churchill said about doing his writing, his "homework." He wrote, "Shut yourself in your study...and make yourself write. Prod yourself!—kick yourself!—it's the only way."[4] That's another way of saying "Do it!" when it comes to the desk.

Devotions—I'm sure you desire the mark of God's freshness on your life. And how is that achieved? By faithfully going to God's Word on a day-by-day basis. Just as a flower needs water to flourish, so we need to drink daily from God's living Word.

Friends—You need to be a faithful friend, but first you must be sure you have the right kind of friends—friends who know and love Jesus Christ. Then be faithful to them, stand with them as together you face the challenges of school...and even the persecution that may come with your belief. And for those friends and acquaintances who don't yet know Jesus, be kind and friendly…and faithful to share Him with them.

Church—God expects you to be faithful in the church. For starters, faithful attendance promotes your spiritual growth. Church is also where you serve God's people, which calls for faithfulness.

William Carey, the father of modern missions, was faithful in his service to God in India for 41 years! When he was asked what his secret to success as a missionary was, he replied, "I can plod; I can persevere in any definite pursuit. To this I owe everything."[5] You affect the world when you are faithful to just faithfully plod on in whatever work God has called you to do!

Struggling to Be Faithful

There's no doubt that to be faithful is a natural, fleshly struggle. That's why we so need to choose to look to God for His strength! Every day we are tempted to do nothing... or as little as possible. Every day we struggle with excuses and challenges like these:

- *Tiredness*...says, "I can't do it." Tiredness moans, "I can't get up...I can't get up and catch the bus...I can't make it to church...I can't study...I'm just too tired!"

- *Laziness*...says, "I don't want to do it." Laziness whines, "I don't want to do my work chores...I don't want to get up and check on my little brother...I don't want to sign up for a ministry...I don't want to go to Bible study."

- *Hopelessness*...says, "It doesn't matter if I do it." Hopelessness asks, "Why try?" and then gives up. Hopelessness easily comes to the erroneous conclusion that "it doesn't matter if I do it."

- *Procrastination*...kills faithfulness with its attitude "I'll do it later." Procrastination announces, "I'll prepare for that class later...I'll finish my homework later...I'll clean up my room later...I'll call the members of my study group later." And exactly what do we think will happen later? Do we really think the frenzy of life will slow down, that some magical minutes will miraculously open up, that new energy will mysteriously arrive, and we'll feel like doing the task we're putting off?

- *Rationalization*...is a subtle but evil perspective on life and responsibility. Rationalization says, "Someone else will do it." Rationalization calculates, "Someone else will set up for the meeting... Someone else will make the announcement...Someone else will get ready for the group."

- *Apathy*...says, "I don't care if I do it." Apathy shrugs, "I don't care if the dishes get done...I don't care if I'm a good daughter or sister or student...I don't care if I read my Bible...I don't care if I grow...I don't care if I'm faithful."

- *Rebellion*...is the attitude that should frighten us most. Rebellion says, "I won't do it." Rebellion stubbornly states, "I won't do what the Bible says...I won't help out at home...I won't do what my parents ask...I won't do what the counselor advised." Rebellion is a hardness that we should fear because, as the Bible teaches, "A man [or woman] who remains stiff-necked...will suddenly be destroyed—without remedy" (Proverbs 29:1). There is no deadlier attitude of the heart than rebellion—whether blatant, outspoken rebellion or quiet rebellion, when you simply and silently go about life in your own way.

Are you wondering where you can get the strength necessary for all this faithfulness? Where you can get the desire? Where you can get much needed help? Well, good news! Our great God ends our struggles by making all we need to be faithful available to us through His grace.

Praise God that you and I can choose to go to Him when we are too tired, too lazy, too uncommitted, too sick, or too sorry for ourselves. We can choose to do as David, the shepherd-king of Israel, did. He "found strength in the LORD his God" (1 Samuel 30:6). David repeatedly declared, "The Lord is the stronghold of my life" (Psalm 27:1). We, too, can find in Him the strength (*His* strength), the vision (*His* vision), and the faithfulness (*His* faithfulness). Indeed, He is waiting to give us His faithfulness.

Heart Response

My friend, faithfulness is such a rarity in this world! Do you realize that if you will walk in faithfulness, you will become a "hero"—one of God's faithful heroes and a hero to others? I close this chapter with the following definition of a "hero." I pray that it will move you to choose to look to God for greater faithfulness!

> The hero does not set out to be one. He is probably more surprised than others by such recognition. He was there when the crisis occurred... and he responded as he always had in any situation. He was simply doing what had to be done! Faithful where he was in his duty there... he was ready when the crisis arose. Being where he was supposed to be...doing what he was supposed to do...responding as was his custom...to circumstances as they developed... devoted to duty—he did the heroic![6]

Things to Do Today to Walk in Faithfulness

1. Choose to call upon God in prayer. David wrote, "When I called, you answered me; you made me bold and stouthearted" (Psalm 138:3).

2. Choose to be faithful in small things. "Whoever can be trusted with very little can also be trusted with much, and

whoever is dishonest with very little will also be dishonest with much" (Luke 16:10).

3. Choose to rely on God's strength. "I can do everything through him who gives me strength" (Philippians 4:13).

4. Choose to fight self-indulgence. "I beat my body and make it my slave" (1 Corinthians 9:27).

5. Choose to eliminate laziness and idleness. "[She] does not eat the bread of idleness" (Proverbs 31:27).

6. Choose to begin at home. "She watches over the affairs of her household" (Proverbs 31:27).

7. Choose to be faithful in all things. Women must be "trustworthy in everything" (1 Timothy 3:11).

8. Choose to take a quick inventory of your own Christian walk. Then ask God for His strength to go to work on getting His faithfulness into your life...just for today.

Would You Like to Know More About Faithfulness? Check It Out!

✓ Read Matthew 25:14-30, Jesus' parable of the talents. What words did Jesus use to praise those who are reliable?

What words did He use regarding those who are not faithful?

What do you find most encouraging from Jesus' story and teaching on faithfulness?

✓ Read 1 Timothy 3:11 and list the four qualities required in a woman who serves in her church.

Why do you think faithfulness is one of the qualifications for service to others in a church?

✓ Read the following verses in your Bible, noting how each instructs you regarding faithfulness and encourages you to be faithful.

Psalm 138:3—

Proverbs 31:27—

Luke 16:10—

1 Corinthians 9:27—

Philippians 4:13—

11

A Choice to Take It

The fruit of the Spirit is...gentleness.
Galatians 5:22-23

Before I began teaching and writing about the fruit of the Spirit, I meditated on gentleness for one whole year! Needless to say, that was one entire year devoted to cultivating gentleness in my own life. Then, as I've continued my study and worked my way through this book, God has given me a second year to think about gentleness.

Here's one thing I've discovered in the process: Of all the blossoms along the path we walk with God, the flower of gentleness appears so fragile, yet as we'll soon see, it develops out of the strongest of underground root systems. So what makes the flower of gentleness bloom?

Finding Out More About Gentleness

As we move toward the finish of our journey toward what it means to walk by the Spirit, remember that to get your act together requires faithfulness. Faithfulness just "does it," whatever "it" is that lies in your path to be done. And to "do it" requires leaning on God and looking to Him for His strength and resolve. And now, with gentleness, we quickly learn that we have to depend again on God.

Exactly what is the fruit of the Spirit called gentleness? Briefly, gentleness...

- means to be gentle or meek, to be lowly or humble,
- is a form of self-control that Christ alone can give,
- expresses itself in a submissive spirit toward both God and man, and
- is the opposite of self-reliant arrogance.

And, as you'll discover, gentleness is truly grown in a hothouse—and there's a high price to pay to cultivate its bloom!

Catching On to the Meaning of Gentleness

Just why is gentleness so costly? And how is it grown in our hearts? Here are a few answers.

1. *Gentleness means trusting the Lord*—By now you definitely know that you must trust the Lord for every fruit of the Spirit—and gentleness is no different. Explaining Jesus'

words, "Blessed are the meek, for they will inherit the earth" (Matthew 5:5), one Bible scholar wrote:

> "The meek" [or gentle] describes the person who is not resentful. He bears no grudge....He finds refuge in the Lord and commits his way entirely to him....Yet *meekness is not weakness*....It is submissiveness under provocation, the willingness rather to *suffer* than to *inflict* injury. The meek [or gentle] person leaves everything in the hand of him who loves and cares.[1]

Did you catch it? Gentleness is *not* resentful, it bears *no* grudge, and it is *not* involved in reflecting on present or past injuries.

So what does the woman characterized by gentleness do instead? She finds refuge in the Lord and His ways. This enables her to endure unkind behavior and suffering in humble submission to an all-wise, caring Father, trusting totally in His love.

Are you wondering, How in the world can anyone bear such bad treatment? For me the answer boils down to one word—faith. No, make that three words—faith in God! The invisible root system of gentleness goes deep into the rich soil of faith. Faith believes that God is able to help us handle everything that happens in our lives. Our faith in the God behind this truth keeps us from struggling and fighting because faith believes God can and will enable us and fight for us (Psalm 60:12).

Now do you see why I've been at work on this fruit for two years? I have the feeling I'll be doing it for many more!

2. *Gentleness means submitting to the Master*—An expert on the Greek language paints this picture of gentleness. He writes, "The adjective gentle...is used of an animal that has been tamed and brought under control."[2] Do you realize...

- the word *tame,* which is the opposite of wild, describes one accustomed to control by another?
- the word *tame* suggests one whose will has been broken or who has allowed himself or herself to be dominated by the will of another?
- the tame person, therefore...

—has been toned down and exhibits complete dependence on another.

—has yielded all will to another's control.

—unquestioningly and humbly obeys what is ordered and accepts what is given.

—is docile and obedient and pliable, as opposed to fierce.

—is easy to work with and to be with.[3]

You (and me too!) may not be sure you like what you're reading or what gentleness implies! But it helps to think about meekness in terms of submitting to your Master, the Lord Jesus. Don't you desire to be controlled by Him? Don't you truly yearn for Him to take complete charge of your life?

To lead and guide you? To protect and care for you as you follow Him unquestioningly in faith? Don't you want to be easy to work with and be with?

I think so! So breathe a huge sigh of release and hand over to God any part of your life that you have not yet given to Him. Thank Him—as your Master and as the Master Gardener—that He is able to care for all of you.

3. *Gentleness means following Jesus' example*—I have a confession to make. As the definition of gentleness became clearer...and tougher, I felt more and more hopeless. But when I saw in God's Word that Jesus was gentle, the meaning of gentleness became much clearer and cooler.

Here's how Jesus described Himself. He called out, "Take my yoke upon you and learn from me, for I am gentle and humble in heart" (Matthew 11:29). Do you want to follow Jesus' example of gentleness? Then commit your way to Him. Jesus' gentleness was grounded in a complete trust in His loving Father. And yours can be, too, as you follow His example.

4. *Gentleness means bowing the soul*—The Old Testament gives us a lovely word picture that helped me with gentleness. Visualize this: The Old Testament term for gentleness (*anah*)[4] describes a mature, ripened shock of grain with its head bent low and bowed down. Just think about it. As wheat grows, the young sprouts rise above the rest. Their heads shoot up the highest because no grain has yet formed. In their immaturity little "fruit," if any, has appeared. But as time passes and maturity sets in, fruit develops and grows—so much of it that the heavy stalk bends and its head sinks

lower and lower. And the lower the head bows, the greater the amount of fruit there is on it.

Oh, for us to be this kind of Christian woman—one with a lowered head, seasoned and mature, well past the stages of pride! Oh, if we would only bend in need, bow the soul, and trust in God!

Putting on Gentleness

Gentleness means putting on a gentle spirit. Gentleness demands a choice from us, a choice and a decision to "put on" the clothing of gentleness (1 Peter 3:4). What individual garments make up the wardrobe of gentleness? From 1 Peter 3:1-6 we discover:

—*The garment of submission* (verse 1): All Christians are to submit themselves to others. (Christians are to submit to every human institution in government,[5] servants are to be submissive to their masters with all respect,[6] Christ submitted without a word to His tormentors,[7] and wives are encouraged to be submissive to their own husbands.[8])

—*The garment of pure and reverent behavior* (verses 1-2): This means God-fearing and blameless conduct. It's behavior that refuses to fight, refuses to give in to anger, refuses to think about revenge or payback, and refuses to assert itself.

—*The garment of a gentle and quiet spirit* (verses 3-4): Rather than being obsessed with your outward appearance, the Bible says you—as God's woman—are to focus on your inner condition, the condition of your heart, the "hidden person of the heart." Your aim is a heart that reflects a gentle and quiet spirit. "Gentle" means not causing disturbances, and "quiet" means bearing with tranquility the disturbances caused by others.[9] Only God can give you the strength not to create disturbances, cause a scene, stir up trouble...and not to react to any disturbances created by others.

—*The garment of trust* (verse 5): "The holy women" in the past "put their hope" in God. Theirs was a trust that looked to God in hope and rested in Him.[10] And nothing's changed!

—*The garment of faith* (verse 6): Sarah did not "give way to fear." Like her, you put your faith and trust in God into practice as you graciously accept the details of your life that contribute to a gentle and quiet spirit.

As a woman of God, you are to choose to put on each one of these garments of gentleness—submission, pure and reverent behavior, a gentle and quiet spirit, trust, and faith. Just like you get dressed each day and choose the clothes you put on, you must visit God's wardrobe closet each morning and choose to put on these garments that make for a put-together look—a gentle spirit. God says such a look and such a heart is rare and precious, truly beyond price (verse 4)!

✎ A Word from God's Word About Gentleness...

Before you leave the inspection of these garments that are to make up your spiritual wardrobe, read through 1 Peter 3:1-6:

> *Wives, in the same way be submissive to your husbands so that, if any of them do not believe the word, they may be won over without words by the behavior of their wives, when they see the purity and reverence of your lives. Your beauty should not come from outward adornment, such as braided hair and the wearing of gold jewelry and fine clothes. Instead, it should be that of your inner self, the unfading beauty of a gentle and quiet spirit, which is of great worth in God's sight. For this is the way the holy women of the past who put their hope in God used to make themselves beautiful. They were submissive to their own husbands, like Sarah, who obeyed Abraham and called him her master. You are her daughters if you do what is right and do not give way to fear.*

Now note which garments are the hardest for you to put on. Share why. Then share what you are going to do about each necessary garment needed for gentleness in your life.

Are there certain people you refuse to submit to?

Do you fight or get angry with others, say, your parents, brothers or sisters, certain people at school?

Would you say you spend more time on improving your outward looks or your heart?

Do you generally trust in the Lord and rest in Him?

Is it hard for you to, by faith, graciously accept the details of your life?

Defining Gentleness—Gentleness Means "Take It"

My personal definition of the woman who is practicing gentleness or meekness is that she will *take it*. And what is it she takes? Do you remember? She bears with tranquility the disturbances others create. She endures ill treatment. She remains calm in the midst of confusion. Carrying the image of Jesus and His suffering in her mind and heart, she takes it. And this cultivates the fruit of God's gentleness.

I know this can be hard to swallow, and there are obvious moral exceptions (such as physical abuse). And we should always be asking God for His wisdom (James 1:5). But please, open your heart and mind to the beauty of this fruit. God so desires this precious and rare beauty of gentleness to characterize our lives! Hear these thoughts on gentleness:

> Gentleness "is perfect quietness of heart. It is for me to have no trouble; never to be fretted or vexed or irritated or sore or disappointed....It is the fruit of the Lord Jesus Christ's redemptive work on Calvary's cross, manifest in those of His own who are definitely in subjection to the Holy Spirit."[11]

> Gentleness "is...first and chiefly towards God. It is that temper of spirit in which we accept [God's] dealings with us as good, and therefore without disputing or resisting....[It is a humble heart] which...does not fight against

> God and... struggle and contend with Him. This meekness, however, being first of all a meekness before God, is also such in the face of men...."[12]

Yes, it's true that in the eyes of others, gentleness may look like weakness. But producing this fruit calls for the greatest of strength! Indeed, gentleness has been called "the fruit of power."[13] And that's the strength and power that come from looking to God!

Heart Response

As we wrestle with the way to gentleness and how to get it into our lives, here are some things for you to think and pray about. Does your life show the fruit of gentleness? Do you know of any ways or areas you are failing to submit to God and His management of your life? Do you consider God's meekness to be weakness? Do you generally bear grudges toward others or think about revenge? Or are you mostly able to look beyond any injury caused to you by someone else…right to the God of wisdom? You may want to record your first impressions. And you may want to jot down what you will do to grow in the fruit of gentleness. In fact, you could do it right here, right now!

Things to Do Today to Walk in Gentleness

1. Trust in God—Trust that, in everything, God knows what He is doing in your life.

2. Pray for gentleness—Prayer develops the gentle habits of bowing, bending, kneeling, yielding, and submitting to God.

3. Refuse to complain and grumble—To complain, one wise believer notes, "is an accusation against God. It questions God's wisdom and God's good judgment. God has always equated complaining with unbelief...[because] to complain is to doubt God. It is the same thing as suggesting that God really doesn't know what He's doing."[14]

4. Refuse to manipulate—Let God resolve your issues for you. Put your faith in scriptures like those in the next section.

Would You Like to Know More About Walking in Gentleness? Check It Out!

✓ What does God command in the following verses?

Galatians 6:1—

Ephesians 4:2—

Colossians 3:12—

1 Timothy 6:11—

2 Timothy 2:24-25—

Titus 3:1-2—

✓ Why is gentleness so important to God?

Why is gentleness so important to your walk with God?

✓ Consider these examples from the Bible of some who learned what it meant to "take it," to look to God for His gentleness in their trying situations.

The apostles—Acts 5:40-41

Stephen—Acts 7:54-60

Paul and Silas—Acts 16:22-25

Servants to both good and harsh masters—1 Peter 2:18-21

✓ What do the following scriptures teach you about trusting God, a key step toward gentleness? And for what can you trust Him?

Psalm 60:12—

Psalm 37:6-7—

Psalm 57:2—

Psalm 138:8—

How will remembering these truths help you "take it"?

12

A Choice to Not Do It

The fruit of the Spirit is...self-control.
Galatians 5:22-23

It was Friday night. Jim and I were sitting in the second row with our two daughters and their college friends. The crowd of thousands who sat in our church were stirring in anticipation. I had heard about the speaker from my first days as a Christian and had also read his classic book *Spiritual Leadership.* And now J. Oswald Sanders was going to speak to us in person! It was one of those once-in-a-lifetime experiences. And I confess! I actually pinched myself to be sure it was real.

As Dr. Sanders mounted the five steps leading up to the pulpit, we held our breaths. That's because this saint of 92 years needed two men to help him get up the stairs. But amazingly, as he finished his greetings and opened his tattered Bible to begin teaching God's Word, strength and vigor came to him. He seemed transformed before us. We were witnessing God's power in the life of a man who had dedicated his many decades to serving and loving the Lord, a man who had walked with God for close to a century.

Do you ever wonder how you can grow to the spiritual stature of a giant like J. Oswald Sanders? I think the answer to that question is more clear when you realize which character quality he placed first in importance for spiritual life and leadership. He named it Number One in his list of "Qualities Essential to Leadership"—Discipline! He writes,

> It has been well said that the future is with the disciplined, and that quality has been placed first in our list, for without it the other gifts, however great, will never reach their maximum potential. Only the disciplined person will rise to his highest powers. He is able to lead because he has conquered himself.[1]

Conquering one's self—self-discipline—is what the Spirit's fruit of self-control is all about. This important gift from God is another key which, when chosen and turned, ignites the power that fuels the fruit of the Spirit. You see, self-control fires up the spiritual energy needed to kindle all of the Christian life. How?

Reviewing God's Fruit

Think about the importance of self-control and the fruit of the Spirit for a moment, beginning with...

...Love, joy, and peace. You can know about love and what it does. And you can have the desire to love. But God's self-control helps you live out that love. The same is true for joy and peace.

...Patience, kindness, and goodness. When every fiber of your flesh wants to be angry and blow up, or circumstances make it hard for you to be kind or good to others, only the Holy Spirit's self-control can help you extend these godly responses.

...Faithfulness and gentleness. By now you know how much of the Spirit's self-control is needed to follow through in faithfulness when laziness and selfishness come so easily. You also know that only God's self-control can give you the strength and gentleness to "take it."

And now for the final fruit on God's list, self-control. And boy, do we need this fruit! It's powerful. It's essential to the Christian life. And it's a rock-solid foundation for our journey to be like Jesus. But how, we wonder, can we ever get a grip on something this large, this important? Answer: It helps to get a grip on what self-control means.

Finding Out More About Self-Control

I love the sweetness of the fruit of the Spirit gentleness and the thought of it being like a soft, beautiful garment we wear when we're walking by the Spirit. However, the spiritual clothing of self-control seems more like armor. Indeed, to practice self-control requires putting on battle gear and getting into a warrior's mentality. You'll see why as you read on.

To begin, the root of "self-discipline" implies the self-restraint of desires and lusts.[2] The famous Greek philosopher Plato used this term to describe the person who has mastered his desires and love of pleasure.[3] Self-control is the controlling power of the will under the operation of the Spirit of God,[4] literally a holding in of one's self with a firm hand by means of the Spirit.[5] In simple terms, self-control is the ability to keep one's self in check.[6]

Did you notice the two repeated topics in these definitions? One is the control of the self—as in *self*-restraint, *self*-government, and *self*-command.[7] The second common thread is the object of control—our passions, appetites, pleasures, desires, and impulses.[8] In other words, all that is physical, sensual, and sexual. Think about it! This includes everything we see, hear, touch, think about, and hunger for. God took pains to list the works of the flesh for us in Galatians 5, among them, immorality, impurity, sensuality, drunkenness, and carousing. Surely no child of God would want to live a life marked by these deeds! But only the Spirit's self-control can help us avoid them.

Gaining Victory Through Self-Control

When you're walking by the Spirit, God's self-control is evident in your life. That's when you reflect these strengths that win victory over sin:

- Self-control controls and checks the self.
- Self-control restrains the self.

- Self-control disciplines and masters the self.
- Self-control holds in and commands the self.
- Self-control says *"No!"* to self.

Here's what a friend of mine did to gain a victory. She wrote this list on a 3" x 5" card and taped it on the bathroom mirror to help her with her problem of overeating. I think her list is a great idea. And you know what? Because the list applies to any and all problems, you might want to make one for yourself. And be sure you put the list in your prayer notebook. These steps will remind you often of God's pattern for self-control.

Defining Self-Control—Self-Control Means "Don't Do It!"

So far in this section about getting your act together, we've learned that faithfulness means—"Do it!" and gentleness means—"Take it!" And now for our understanding, self-control means—"Don't do it!" In times of temptation we are to call on God for His strength and then choose to *don't do it!* In other words, don't give in to emotions, to cravings, to urges. Don't think or do what you know is against God's Word. Don't pamper yourself. Don't make the easy choices. Don't rationalize....And a thousand other "don't do its"! As one pastor explained,

> The word *self-control* means "the ability to say no." It is an evidence of willpower that sometimes expresses itself in "won't power." It is the

> ability to say yes at the right time; yes to certain things, and no to others. It is that kind of inward strength that takes all the circumstances and experiences of life and subjects them to evaluation and then decides, "This is right, this is in the will of God," or, "This is wrong, I will put it aside."[9]

God's message to you? Don't do what you could—do what you should!

Struggling for Self-Control

As I was thinking about the struggle for self-control, I made a list of the areas that challenge women—both young and old—most and cause them to need to turn to God for help. (And by the way, these struggles don't go away with age!) It's like a fellow believer observed, "To a greater or lesser degree, if you are alive you are tempted!"[10] That means you (and me too!) need God's self-control every minute of every day in every area of life! Every which way we turn, we face temptation. Therefore we need the Spirit's help to resist in the common areas of life...

Food. Life would definitely be easier if we didn't have to be around food. God created our body to need fuel, but somehow the natural need and desire for food can get out of hand. For instance, because I'm writing about food, my mouth and mind are suddenly yearning to eat something—anything!—but it isn't time to eat. I don't *need* to eat because I just ate lunch. I just *want* to eat! So I'm forcing myself to sit here and keep on writing. I'm thinking, "Elizabeth, just say no. Don't do it. Don't get up and go to the pantry. Fight it. You can have this victory with God's help. Stay seated, keep your mind on the Lord, and work on!"

Now, could I have something to eat? Of course. Would it hurt me to eat? Of course not—well, not now, but maybe in the morning when I got on the scales! But what would the blessings of not giving in to the flesh be? Well, for one thing, I'll make some progress on this chapter as I keep on writing. And here's another—I can have God's victory in this small thing. Plus, by saying no I build a track record with God and gain experience that will help me later when I face a larger thing.

Thoughts. Every woman struggles with her thoughts. You know how easy it is to go into daydream mode and start thinking about things—things that are real or not—such as that cute guy in your English class...and how he did or didn't speak to you. Your thoughts might be innocent enough, but what if they turn into impure thoughts? Or what if you start thinking about the ugly remark someone made about you in the hall between classes? If you're not careful, your thoughts can slide into a state of bitterness and a desire to "get even"...and, well, you know the rest of the scenario all too well!

Money and possessions. These two struggles go hand in hand. Almost every waking minute of every day you're faced with TV ads, billboards, radio commercials, the label on someone's shirt or shoes, all tempting you to desire something and spend your money to get it. And the truth is, most of the stuff being promoted is what you don't need. I'm not saying it's wrong to have nice or cool things. But I am saying this is where self-control comes to your rescue. You have to start telling yourself, "Don't do it! Stop thinking you've just got to have that new and more stylish pair of shoes or jeans!" You need to look to God for His help in curbing yourself, holding yourself back, and controlling your desires. The Spirit can give you the strength to resist the temptation to love the things in the world (1 John 2:15), if you will walk by the Spirit.

Sexual struggles. I've saved this struggle for last, not because it's less important, but because it's vitally important! Maybe your youth pastor has shared the statistics that speak of the sexual activity of even 9- to 12-year-old girls. Sexual purity is an area where you absolutely need God's self-control. Our society tends to overlook and accept sex outside of marriage. In fact, many people expect it! But is this what God wants for His young women? You know the answer—and it's *No!* So how are you going to resist the strong temptation of sexual impurity? This battle, like each of the other struggles we've addressed and along with a lot of other allurements, is won in the same way, my dear young friend. It's fought—and won—when you call upon God, rely on His gift of His self-control, obey Him, and say, *No!* And so it goes. Over and over you look to Him, ask Him for fresh strength and self-control to say again, "Don't do it!" This is the key to winning sexual struggles and cultivating God's self-control in your life.

And now it's pen time! Take a look at these scriptures and

make notes to yourself about how to gain self-control in your areas of struggle.

✎ A Word from God's Word About Self-Control...

- For all your battles—The two things you must always remember in your struggle for self-control are:

  —*"Live by the Spirit...[and] you will not gratify the desires of the sinful nature,"* and

  —*"the Spirit...is contrary to the sinful nature"* (Galatians 5:16-17).

- Food—Do you need help? Here's what 1 Corinthians 10:31 says: *"So whether you eat or drink or whatever you do, do it all for the glory of God."*

- Thoughts—Don't give in to sinful thoughts or harmful thought patterns! Instead, *"whatever is true, whatever is noble, whatever is right, whatever is pure, whatever is lovely, whatever is admirable—if anything is excellent or praiseworthy—think about such things"* (Philippians 4:8).

- Money and possessions—Take this advice to heart: *"Do not love the world or anything in the world. If anyone loves the world, the love of the Father is not in him. For everything in the world—the cravings of sinful man, the lust of his eyes and the boasting of what he has and does—comes not from the Father but from the world. The world and its desires pass away, but the man who does the will of God lives forever"* (1 John 2:15-17).

- Sexual struggles—Pay attentions to the do's and don'ts in the Bible!

  —Don't give in! Instead, *"flee from sexual immorality. All other sins a man commits are outside his body, but he who sins sexually sins against his own body. Do you not know that your body is a temple of the Holy Spirit, who is in you, whom you have received from God? You are not your own; you were bought at a price. Therefore honor God with your body"* (1 Corinthians 6:18-20).

  —Do walk by the Spirit! *"It is God's will that you should be sanctified: that you should avoid sexual immorality; that each of you should learn to control his own body in a way that is holy and honorable, not in passionate lust like the heathen, who do not know God"* (1 Thessalonians 4:3-5).

Heart Response

Dear sister, the good news for you and me is that we can claim God's power, walk by His Spirit, exercise self-control, and win the battle over fleshly temptation. Then we will wondrously display the beauty of Christ as we walk with Him through everyday life. We'll truly have our lives together! What a wonderful God we have who makes the storehouse of His grace—His self-control—available to us!

Almost every Christian enjoys the warm but strong exhortations of author and pastor Max Lucado. Here's his encouragement—from his heart to yours—to choose self-control!

I choose self-control...

I am a spiritual being.
After this body is dead, my spirit will soar.
I refuse to let what will rot rule the eternal.
I choose self-control.
I will be impassioned only by my faith.
I will be influenced only by God.
I will be taught only by Christ.
I choose self-control.[11]

—Max Lucado

Now, my friend, may you, too, choose self-control.

Things to Do Today to Walk in Self-Control

1. Begin with Christ. Is He your Lord and Master? Self-mastery begins with being mastered by Christ.

2. Monitor your input. Regulate what you eat, where you go, what you see. Follow David's advice: "I will set before my eyes no vile thing" (Psalm 101:3).

3. Stay busy. Make a schedule...and keep it! Volunteer to help others. Do whatever it takes to stay busy. By doing so, you will refuse to eat "the bread of idleness" (Proverbs 31:27), and you'll find yourself with less time to be tempted.

4. Say "No!" Solomon wrote, "Like a city whose walls are broken down is a man who lacks self-control" (Proverbs 25:28). Echoing that truth is this thought: "The word *No* forms the armament and protective walls of the spiritual city....Sometimes *No* can be a hard word to say, but it is the key to self-control, the word that the Lord blesses."[12]

5. *Pray.* Pray about every aspect of your life! Nothing should be too small to bring before the Lord. Ask for His wisdom to discern good from evil and His strength to say *yes* to the good and *no* to the evil.

Would You Like to Know More About Walking in Self-Control? Check It Out!

✓ Look at these scriptures in your Bible and note God's message to you about self-control.

Romans 6:12—

Galatians 5:16—

Romans 6:13—

1 Corinthians 10:31—

Galatians 5:24—

✓ What lessons do you learn from these people about self-control or the lack of self-control?

Joseph and Potiphar's wife—in Genesis 39:7-10.

Moses—Numbers 20:2-11.

Achan—in Joshua 7:21.

David—in 1 Samuel 24:3-7 and 26:7-9.

What reason was behind David's self-control according to 1 Samuel 24:8-15 and 26:10?

David—in 2 Samuel 11:1-4.

13

Looking at Jesus

As we've moved through God's fruit of the Spirit, we have definitely learned more about how to get them into our lives! All along the way Jesus has shown us what each of them looks like lived out by God's grace. And now I want you to look with me at His life again. I want you to look at these final three fruit that deal with the discipline of self—with getting your act together—faithfulness, gentleness, and self-control. As we look at Jesus now, see how many times and in how many ways you witness Him being faithful and "doing it" (like going to the cross), "taking it" (like not talking back), and "not doing it" (like not lashing out or fighting back).

Do you remember when we last observed Jesus? We saw Him arrested and led away for His trial and crucifixion. Do you ever wonder, How did Jesus handle all of this, and what was His mind-set as He faced the cross?

Peter, who watched these awful events unfold, answers these questions for us. Although he denied any tie with Jesus when questioned by others (saying, "I don't know the man!"—Matthew 26:72), Peter continued to follow his Master at a distance. And with a few brief strokes of his pen, Peter summarized our Lord's behavior so that we may follow in His steps, so that we may successfully "do it," "take it," and "don't do it" at the right time and in the right situations. Peter tells us,

> *He committed no sin,*
> *and no deceit was found in his mouth.*
> *When they hurled their insults at him,*
> *he did not retaliate;*
> *when he suffered, he made no threats*
> (1 Peter 2:22-23).

Jesus Committed No Sin

Here's something you should never forget: Throughout His earthly existence—and including His final days—Jesus committed no sin! You've probably had moments when you didn't commit any sin—you know, when all is well and life is good. But let's face it, these times are not the norm.

But now, for a moment, picture the worst of circumstances, the kind Jesus experienced on the way to the cross—the kind packed with betrayal, lying, false charges, unjust punishment, brutality, physical abuse, fists, clubs, rods, whips, nails, and a spear! Then try to imagine committing no sin in that kind of environment! To not sin in such circumstances would definitely be the work of the Holy Spirit. Only He can enable us to walk through difficult situations without sinning!

But why was Jesus suffering? Why was He being so harshly mistreated? All His life He had...

> done well,
> done the right thing,
> done all that God asked and required of Him, and
> successfully carried out the Father's will for His life.

Jesus had...

> taught God's truth,
> healed God's creation,
> fed God's people, and
> taken light into darkness.

Jesus had also...

> preached the gospel to the poor,
> proclaimed freedom for the prisoners,
> restored the sight of the blind, and
> released those who were oppressed (Luke 4:18).

Yet Jesus suffered for doing what is right (verse 29). As the holy Son of God, He never in a single instance sinned. He lived His entire life without sin (Hebrews 4:15). Jesus, of all people, did not deserve to suffer in any way!

And here's something else—Even those who condemned Jesus knew He hadn't sinned. He was 100 percent not guilty. For instance, Pilate told the chief priests and the multitudes, "I find no basis for a charge against this man" (Luke 23:4). After Jesus returned from Herod's court, Pilate repeated to the chief priests and the rulers of the people, "I have examined [Jesus] in your presence and have found no basis for your charges against him" (verse 14). Pilate went on to say, "Neither has Herod, for he sent him back to us; as you can see, he has done nothing to deserve death" (verse 15). One final time Pilate asked the Jewish leaders, "Why? What crime has this man committed? I have found in him no grounds for the death penalty" (verse 22).

No, our Jesus committed no crime. He committed no sin.

Do you realize that, like Jesus, you can call upon God to help you make the right choices in life? You can experience victory over sin? You can make choices that say *no* to sin, choices that may require you to *do it, take it,* or *don't do it,* whatever the case may be? Scottish devotional writer Thomas Guthrie warned,

> Never fear to suffer; but oh! fear to sin. If you must choose between them, prefer the greatest suffering to the smallest sin.[1]

Can you make this the perspective of your heart too? When you turn to God for help, He will help you choose not to sin.

Jesus Spoke No Sin

Not only was Jesus sinless in deed, but He was also sinless in word. Peter tells us, "No deceit was found in his mouth" (1 Peter 2:22). Even after careful examination, Jesus' accusers found no craftiness or trickery.[2] Jesus always spoke the truth—100 percent of the time. He always spoke and acted with pure motives. Nothing of deceit or guile could be uncovered...because it just wasn't there!

And here's something else—Jesus didn't talk back. He refused to answer at His trial. When falsely accused by the chief priests and elders, "he gave no answer" (Matthew 27:12). When questioned by Pilate, Jesus "made no reply, not even to a single charge" (verse 14). When Caiaphas and the Sanhedrin challenged Him—"Are you not going to answer? What is this testimony that these men are bringing against you?" (Mark 14:60)—Jesus "remained silent and gave no answer" (verse 61). Instead of verbally pressing His case to people who did not have ears to hear, Jesus silently submitted to harsh treatment and a cruel death that He did not deserve.

Jesus Did Not Resist

Jesus also did not resist His accusers and enemies. He absolutely refused to fight verbally or physically. We read, for instance, that while being insulted, He did not retaliate (1 Peter 2:23). To be insulted or reviled means to be harshly cursed with a string of sharp, abusive words.[3] And that's the treatment our Jesus, the sinless Lamb of God, suffered!

What did Jesus do when He was attacked verbally and physically? The Bible says that "when he suffered, he made no threats" (1 Peter 2:23). Here, "suffered" means buffeted, struck with fists (Matthew 26:67). Peter is remembering the blows inflicted upon Jesus by the servants, the scorn of the high priest, the stripes, the cross...and the silent submission of Jesus. As one scholar explains, "Under sustained and repeated provocation, never once did [Jesus] break the silence. All the time during which He was physically beaten, He was not reviling back. All the time during which He was suffering, he was not resorting to threats."[4] Even "continuous suffering at the hands of the mob did not elicit from our Lord any retaliatory words."[5]

Of course sinful, scornful, harsh words wouldn't fit the picture of Jesus' perfect godliness! Reacting is something you and I might do...but not Jesus. When He was unfairly treated, He did not utter threats, condemn His oppressors, or call down judgment upon them. No, He kept His mouth closed. In the words of Isaiah, "He was oppressed and afflicted, yet he did not open his mouth; he was led like a lamb to the slaughter, and as a sheep before her shearers is silent, so he did not open his mouth" (Isaiah 53:7).

Heart Response

Oh, how precious is our Jesus! And oh, to be like Him!

I'm sure your heart hurts as you think about this scene of horror and evil. The Savior's response is sobering. It should make you think (and purpose!) that surely...if He exhibited such graciousness—such faithfulness, gentleness, and self-control—in these evil circumstances, then you can do the same in your much quieter sphere of life and service. And surely...if He bore with tranquility the pain and suffering caused by His killers, you can quietly endure the ill treatment you receive from others. And surely...if He kept His mouth shut when He was innocent, you can do the same.

But by now you should also know that you can only do these things and give these responses by the power of God's Spirit. He is the one who fills you with His faithfulness, gentleness, and self-control. My dear traveling friend, don't fail to look to God for His help in being more like Jesus.

And now...a final prayer of thanksgiving...

It is with overflowing hearts, O Father,
That we whisper yet another "Thank You"—
This time for the grace of Your Son
Who demonstrated complete faithfulness to You,
Who accepted in gentleness such unjust mistreatment, and
Who exhibited self-control
in the harshest of circumstances
As He walked to the cross to die for us.
May we receive Your grace...that we may
Faithfully do all that You ask of us,
Gently and quietly suffer what comes our way, and,
In control of ourselves, do nothing that dishonors Your worthy Name.
In Jesus' name, our Model and Savior and Lord.
Amen.

Things to Do Today to Grow More Like Jesus

1. Reflect on your life—Pause and pray about your conduct or lifestyle as you consider your Savior and your call to follow His example. Do any glaring areas of sin leap to your mind and heart?

2. Confess any sin areas now—Follow up by determining what you will do to deal with them, eliminate them, to "don't do it!" Remember, "He who conceals his sins does not prosper, but whoever confesses and renounces them finds mercy" (Proverbs 28:13).

3. Rejoice that you have forgiveness in Jesus—"If we confess our sins, he is faithful and just and will forgive us our sins and purify us from all unrighteousness" (1 John 1:9).

Would You Like to Know More About Growing Like Jesus? Check It Out!

✓ Read 1 Peter 2:22. Note in the blank below the first of the two facts written about Jesus' conduct and behavior.

Jesus ______________________________________.

What do these scriptures relate about the truth of this fact?

Acts 3:13-15—

Hebrews 4:15—

Hebrews 7:26—

1 John 3:5—

✓ Read 1 Peter 2:22 again and note in the blank below the second of the two facts written about Jesus' conduct and behavior.

Jesus ____ .

What do these scriptures relate about the truth of this fact?

Isaiah 53:7—

Mark 14:60-61—

Mark 15:4-5—

Luke 23:8-9—

✓ Read 1 Peter 2:23 and note two additional facts written about Jesus' conduct and behavior.

First, Jesus ______________________________ .

Second, Jesus ______________________________

but ______________________________ .

What do these scriptures relate about Jesus' treatment by His enemies?

Matthew 26:67-68—

Matthew 27:26—

Matthew 27:27-32—

Matthew 27:39-40—

Matthew 27:41-43—

Matthew 27:44—

What did Jesus do instead, according to Luke 23:34 and 46?

Getting the Most Out of Your Life

Whew! We made it! You and I have completed our walking tour of the fruit of the Spirit! Together we strolled along the path, moving from group to group, from fruit to fruit. With God's Word as our guide, we read about each grace—each fruit—what each one is and how it can be cultivated as we walk with God. I'm glad for the time we had to study, to enjoy each fruit. We've seen and tasted them all. And we now know more about bearing God's fruit in our lives.

As we leave these pages and one another, I want you to take God's message with you into your daily life. I want you (and me too!) to get your act together, get along with everybody, get the right attitudes, get it all going, and get the most out of your life. It's one thing to talk about spiritual fruit, but God wants you to live it out. He wants you to walk the walk! As you've seen, His Word describes exactly what He wants your life to look like and what He wants others to see in you as you bear the fruit of His Spirit in real, everyday life.

A Story

Let me tell you a story about someone who walked with God and lived out the fruit of the spirit...and its impact on a young woman. His name is Sam Britten. Sam was an elder and a servant at my former church. He was also the director of the Center of Activities of the Physically Disabled at California State University at Northridge. I have known Sam for decades, but one of the students on campus helped me appreciate him even more.

Judi had heard about the remarkable things going on in the center for the physically disabled, which was just down the hall from one of her classes. So one afternoon, out of curiosity, she entered the room and stood silently watching. What she saw was Dr. Britten, down on his knees, helping and encouraging one of his disabled students.

Judi, who was not a Christian but who had heard of Jesus, said: "As I stood there watching Dr. Britten and saw his love and kindness and patience and gentleness with that student, I thought, 'This must be what Jesus was like!'" Daily Judi was drawn to Dr. Britten's room. And again and again she saw this same scene. "Some days," she confessed, "I had to leave the room and go out into the hall so that I could weep. It was so moving to watch this man!"

Approaching Margie, one of Sam's assistants, Judi asked if she knew what made Sam like Jesus. Margie answered, "Oh, he's a Christian. He knows Jesus, and he reads his Bible a lot and prays. In fact, we all pray together every day before the people arrive for treatment." Well, you guessed it. Soon Judi had bought herself a Bible. She began reading it and praying. She also found a church, and within a year Judi had given her heart to Jesus.

Dear reader and friend, this picture of Sam Britten is what this book is all about—Jesus in you, Jesus visible to others as you walk by the Spirit, Jesus loving and serving others through you, Jesus on display in you just as He is displayed in Sam Britten. When you get it together spiritually and walk by the Spirit, you behave as Jesus did. Filled with His Holy Spirit, you can model Him to a needy world.

A Comment

The apostle John wrote about this kind of Christlikeness saying "When he appears, we shall be like him" (1 John 3:2). Then, in the next verse, he tells us how we can become like Jesus now: "Everyone who has this hope fixed in him purifies himself, just as he is pure" (verse 3). And how does this purification happen, and how can we help it happen?

To wrap up our precious walk with God through this book, read these comments by British preacher Dr. John Blanchard. He also gives us some steps we can take:

> Everyone who truly believes that he will one day be like Christ...surely purifies himself and relentlessly pursues godliness as a number one priority. This is the mark of the true child of God. We are to feast our eyes upon Christ, upon as much of Christ as we can find in the

> sacred Scriptures. We are to do everything that we possibly can: We are to wrestle and fight and pray and be disciplined in order that more and more we become like Christ—whatever the cost—knowing that every sin that is overcome, every temptation that is resisted, every virtue that is gained is another step, another step, another step, another step toward that moment when we shall be like Him.

A Prayer

When Dr. Blanchard finished his sermon, he prayed the following prayer—a prayer for you and for me as we, God's women, seek to walk with God and model Jesus to a needy world. Make this prayer your own!

> We can bless You for all of Your goodness *to* us, for the enabling of the Holy Spirit *in* our lives, for every word of Scripture that has come to burn in our hearts, for every step of progress that has been made, for every victory that has been gained, for every temptation that has been resisted. And we can and do praise You as well, knowing that it is only by Your grace and power that these things were achieved.[1]

Becoming More Like Jesus

Look back through your book and write out the short slogan or motto for each fruit of the Spirit. Remembering, for instance, that "love is the sacrifice of self" will help you respond to the events of your day—and life—in a godly way, to be more like Jesus. Review this list often.

1. Love...

2. Joy...

3. Peace...

4. Patience...

5. Kindness...

6. Goodness...

7. Faithfulness...

8. Gentleness...

9. Self-control...

Notes

Chapter 1—Getting It All Going

1. Merrill E. Unger, *Unger's Bible Dictionary* (Chicago: Moody Press, 1972), p. 382.
2. Alfred Martin, *John, Life Through Believing* (Chicago: Moody Bible Institute, 1981), p. 92.
3. Everett F. Harrison, *John, The Gospel of Faith* (Chicago: Moody Press, 1962), p. 91.
4. William Barclay, *The Gospel of John,* vol. 2, rev. ed. (Philadelphia: The Westminster Press, 1975), p. 176.
5. Harrison, *John, The Gospel of Faith,* p. 91.
6. Albert M. Wells, Jr., ed., *Inspiring Quotations Contemporary & Classical* (Nashville: Thomas Nelson Publishers, 1988), p. 158.
7. Elizabeth George, *A Young Woman's Call to Prayer—Talking with God About Your Life* (Eugene, OR: Harvest House Publishers, 2005).
8. Charles Wesley, "And Can It Be that I Should Gain," *Psalms and Hymns* (1738.)

Chapter 2—A Loving Heart

1. William Barclay, *The Letters to the Galatians and Ephesians,* rev. ed. (Philadelphia: The Westminster Press, 1976), p. 50.
2. John MacArthur, Jr., *Liberty in Christ* (Panorama City, CA: Word of Grace Communications, 1986), p. 88.

Chapter 3—A Happy Heart

1. John MacArthur, Jr., *Liberty in Christ* (Panorama City, CA: Word of Grace Communications, 1986), p. 90.
2. William Barclay, *The Letters to the Galatians and Ephesians,* rev. ed. (Philadelphia: The Westminster Press, 1976), p. 50.
3. William Barclay, *The Letters of James and Peter,* rev. ed. (Philadelphia: The Westminster Press, 1976), p. 178.
4. H.D.M. Spence and Joseph S. Exell, eds., *The Pulpit Commentary,* vol. 22 (Grand Rapids, MI: William B. Eerdmans Publishing Company, 1978), p. 6.
5. W.H. Griffith Thomas, *The Apostle Peter* (Grand Rapids, MI: Kregel Publications, 1984), p. 162.
6. John MacArthur, Jr., *The MacArthur New Testament Commentary, Galatians* (Chicago: Moody Press, 1987), p. 166.
7. Herbert Lockyer, *All the Promises of the Bible* (Grand Rapids, MI: Zondervan Publishing House, 1962), p. 10.

Chapter 4—A Quiet Heart

1. Kenneth S. Wuest, *Wuest's Word Studies in the Greek New Testament,* vol. 1 (Grand Rapids, MI: William B. Eerdmans Publishing Company, 1973), p. 160.

2. William Barclay, *The Letters to the Galatians and Ephesians,* rev. ed. (Philadelphia: The Westminster Press, 1976), p. 50.
3. Howard F. Vos, *Galatians, A Call to Christian Liberty* (Chicago: Moody Press, 1971), p. 107.
4. Albert M. Wells, Jr., ed., *Inspiring Quotations Contemporary & Classical* (Nashville: Thomas Nelson Publishers, 1988), p. 152.

Chapter 5—Looking at Jesus' Attitudes

1. John MacArthur, Jr., *The MacArthur New Testament Commentary, Matthew 24–28* (Chicago: Moody Press, 1989), p. 167.
2. William Hendriksen, *New Testament Commentary, Matthew* (Grand Rapids, MI: Baker Book House, 1973), p. 917.

Chapter 6—A Time to Do Nothing

1. Charles F. Pfeiffer and Everett F. Harrison, eds., *The Wycliffe Bible Commentary* (Chicago: Moody Press, 1973), p. 1297.
2. Alan Cole, "The Epistle of Paul to the Galatians," *Tyndale New Testament Commentaries* (Grand Rapids, MI: William B. Eerdmans Publishing Company, 1965), p. 167.
3. John MacArthur, Jr., *The MacArthur New Testament Commentary, Galatians* (Chicago: Moody Press, 1987), p. 167.
4. Howard F. Vos, *Galatians, A Call to Christian Liberty* (Chicago: Moody Press, 1971), p. 108.
5. Merrill F. Unger, *Unger's Bible Dictionary* (Chicago: Moody Press, 1972), p. 829.
6. George Sweeting, *Love Is the Greatest* (Chicago: Moody Press, 1974), p. 53.
7. John MacArthur, Jr., *Liberty in Christ* (Panorama City, CA: Word of Grace Communications, 1986), p. 92.
8. H.D.M. Spence and Joseph S. Exell, eds., *The Pulpit Commentary,* vol. 20 (Grand Rapids, MI: William B. Eerdmans Publishing Company, 1978), p. 287.
9. William Barclay, *The Letters to the Galatians and Ephesians,* rev. ed. (Philadelphia: The Westminster Press, 1976), p. 51.
10. Ibid., p. 51.
11. D.L. Moody, *Notes from My Bible and Thoughts from My Library* (Grand Rapids, MI: Baker Book House, 1979), p. 323.
12. Spence and Exell, eds., *The Pulpit Commentary,* vol. 20, p. 294.

Chapter 7—A Time to Do Something

1. William Barclay, *The Letters to the Galatians and Ephesians,* rev. ed. (Philadelphia: The Westminster Press, 1976), p. 158.
2. John MacArthur, Jr., *The MacArthur New Testament Commentary, Colossians and Philemon* (Chicago: Moody Press, 1992), p. 155.
3. John M. Drescher, *Spirit Fruit* (Scottdale, PA: Herald Press, 1974), p. 210.
4. Ibid., p. 206.
5. Anne Ortlund, *Disciplines of the Beautiful Woman* (Waco, TX: Word, Inc., 1977), pp. 96, 98.

6. Alan Cole, "The Epistle of Paul to the Galatians," *Tyndale New Testament Commentaries* (Grand Rapids, MI: William B. Eerdmans Publishing Company, 1965), p. 167.

Chapter 8—A Time to Do Everything

1. John W. Cowart, *People Whose Faith Got Them into Trouble* (Downers Grove, IL: InterVarsity Press, 1990).
2. Ibid., pp. 13-14.
3. Merrill F. Unger, *Unger's Bible Dictionary* (Chicago: Moody Press, 1972), p. 420.
4. John MacArthur, Jr., *The MacArthur New Testament Commentary, Galatians* (Chicago: Moody Press, 1987), p. 168.
5. Kenneth S. Wuest, *Word Studies in the Greek New Testament,* vol. 1 (Grand Rapids, MI: William B. Eerdmans Publishing Company, 1974), p. 160.
6. Howard F. Vos, *Galatians, A Call to Christian Liberty* (Chicago: Moody Press, 1973), p. 108.
7. William Hendriksen, *Exposition of the Pastoral Epistles, New Testament Commentary* (Grand Rapids, MI: Baker Book House, 1976), p. 188.
8. Ibid., p. 107.
9. William Hendriksen, *Exposition of the Bible According to Luke, New Testament Commentary* (Grand Rapids, MI: Baker Book House, 1978), p. 558.
10. Oswald Chambers, *Studies in the Sermon on the Mount* (Fort Washington, PA: Christian Literature Crusade, 1960), p. 53.
11. Albert M. Wells, Jr., ed., *Inspiring Quotations Contemporary & Classical* (Nashville: Thomas Nelson Publishers, 1988), p. 82.
12. Neil S. Wilson, ed., *The Handbook of Bible Application* (Wheaton, IL: Tyndale House Publishers, Inc., 1992), p. 369.
13. Dan Baumann, *Extraordinary Living for Ordinary People* (Irvine, CA: Harvest House Publishers, 1978), pp. 83-84.

Chapter 9—Looking at Jesus' Actions

1. William Hendriksen, *Exposition of the Gospel According to Luke, New Testament Commentary* (Grand Rapids, MI: Baker Book House, 1978), p. 989.

Chapter 10—A Choice to Just Do It

1. Albert M. Wells, Jr., ed., *Inspiring Quotations Contemporary & Classical* (Nashville: Thomas Nelson Publishers, 1988), p. 69.
2. H.D.M. Spence and Joseph S. Exell, eds., *The pulpit Commentary,* vol. 20 (Grand Rapids, MI: William B. Eerdmans Publishing Co., 1978), p. 287.
3. John MacArthur, Jr., *The MacArthur New Testament Commentary, Galatians* (Chicago: Moody Press, 1987), p. 169.
4. Richard Shelley Taylor, *The Disciplined Life* (Minneapolis: Dimension Books, Bethany Fellowship, Inc., 1962), p. 37.
5. Vanita Hampton and Carol Plueddemann, eds., *World Shapers* (Wheaton, IL: Harold Shaw Publishers, 1991), p. 17.

6. Richard C. Halverson, "Perspective" newsletter, 10/26/77.

Chapter 11—A Choice to Take It

1. William Hendriksen, *Exposition of the Gospel According to Matthew, New Testament Commentary* (Grand Rapids, MI: Baker Book House, 1975), pp. 271-72.
2. William Barclay, *The Letters to the Galatians and Ephesians*, rev. ed. (Philadelphia: The Westminster Press, 1976), p. 52.
3. *Webster's New Dictionary of Synonyms* (Springfield, MA: G. & C. Merriam Company, Publishers, 1973), p. 812.
4. Merrill F. Unger, *Unger's Bible Dictionary* (Chicago: Moody Press, 1972), p. 709.
5. 1 Peter 2:13.
6. 1 Peter 2:18.
7. 1 Peter 2:21-25.
8. 1 Peter 3:1.
9. Robert Jamieson, A.R. Fausset, and David Brown, *Commentary on the Whole Bible* (Grand Rapids, MI: Zondervan Publishing House, 1973), p. 1475.
10. Kenneth S. Wuest, *Wuest's Word Studies from the Greek New Testament*, vol. 2 (Grand Rapids, MI: William B. Eerdmans Publishing Company, 1974), p. 81.
11. Albert M. Wells, Jr., ed., *Inspiring Quotations Contemporary & Classical* (Nashville: Thomas Nelson Publishers, 1988), p. 92.
12. W.E. Vine, *An Expository Dictionary of New Testament Words* (Old Tappan, NJ: Fleming H. Revell Company, 1966), pp. 55-56.
13. Ibid., p. 56.
14. Don Baker, *Pain's Hidden Purpose* (Portland, OR: Multnomah Press, 1984), pp. 86-89.

Chapter 12—A Choice to Not Do It

1. J. Oswald Sanders, *Spiritual Leadership*, rev. ed. (Chicago: Moody Press, 1980), pp. 71-72.
2. Robert Jamieson, A.R. Fausset, and David Brown, *Commentary of the Whole Bible* (Grand Rapids, MI: Zondervan Publishing House, 1973), p. 1275.
3. William Barclay, *The Letters to the Galatians and Ephesians*, rev. ed. (Philadelphia: The Westminster Press, 1976), p. 52.
4. W.E. Vine, *An Expository Dictionary of New Testament Words* (Old Tappan, NJ: Fleming H. Revell Company, 1966), p. 114.
5. Charles F. Pfeiffer and Everett F. Harrison, *The Wycliffe Bible Commentary* (Chicago: Moody Press, 1973), p. 1297.
6. John MacArthur, Jr., *Liberty in Christ* (Panorama City, CA: Word of Grace Communities, 1986), p. 96.
7. H.D.M. Spence and Joseph S. Exell, eds., *The Pulpit Commentary*, vol. 20 (Grand Rapids, MI: William B. Eerdmans Publishing Company, 1978), p. 287.

8. Kenneth S. Wuest, *Wuest's Word Studies from the Greek New Testament* (Grand Rapids, MI: William B. Eerdmans Publishing Company, 1974), p. 160.
9. Dan Baumann, *Extraordinary Living for Ordinary People* (Irvine, CA: Harvest House Publishers, 1978), pp. 118-19.
10. Bruce Wideman, *Presbyterian Journal,* July 30, 1975, p. 7.
11. Quoted in Luis Palau, *Heart After God* (Portland, OR: Multnomah Press, 1978), p. 70.
12. John H. Timmerman, *The Way of Christian Living* (Grand Rapids, MI: William B. Eerdmans Publishing Company, 1987), pp. 147-48.

Chapter 13—Looking at Jesus

1. D.L. Moody, *Notes from My Bible and Thoughts from My Library* (Grand Rapids, MI: Baker Book House, 1979), p. 362.
2. Kenneth S. Wuest, *Wuest's Word Studies from the Greek New Testament,* vol. 2 (Grand Rapids, MI: William B. Eerdmans Publishing Company, 1973), p. 67.
3. Ibid., pp. 67-68.
4. Alan M. Stibbs, *The First Epistle General of Peter, The Tyndale New Testament Commentaries* (Grand Rapids, MI: William B. Eerdmans Publishing Company, 1976), p. 118.
5. Wuest, *Wuest's Word Studies,* pp. 67-68.

Getting the Most Out of Your Life

1. John Blanchard, "The Most Amazing Statement in Scripture" (Grace to You, P.O. Box 4000, Panorama City, CA 91412).

Personal Notes

Personal Notes

Personal Notes

Personal Notes

Personal Notes

Books by Elizabeth George

- Beautiful in God's Eyes
- Finding God's Path Through Your Trials
- Life Management for Busy Women
- Loving God with All Your Mind
- A Mom After God's Own Heart
- Powerful Promises for Every Woman
- The Remarkable Women of the Bible
- Small Changes for a Better Life
- A Wife After God's Own Heart
- A Woman After God's Own Heart®
- A Woman After God's Own Heart® Deluxe Edition
- A Woman After God's Own Heart®—A Daily Devotional
- A Woman After God's Own Heart® Collection
- A Woman's Call to Prayer
- A Woman's High Calling
- A Woman's Walk with God
- A Young Woman After God's Own Heart
- A Young Woman After God's Own Heart—A Devotional
- A Young Woman's Call to Prayer
- A Young Woman's Walk with God
- Walking with the Women of the Bible

Children's Books

- God's Wisdom for Little Girls
- A Little Girl After God's Own Heart

Study Guides

- Beautiful in God's Eyes Growth & Study Guide
- Finding God's Path Through Your Trials Growth & Study Guide
- Life Management for Busy Women Growth & Study Guide
- Loving God with All Your Mind Growth & Study Guide
- A Mom After God's Own Heart Growth & Study Guide
- The Remarkable Women of the Bible Growth & Study Guide
- Small Changes for a Better Life Growth & Study Guide
- A Wife After God's Own Heart Growth & Study Guide
- A Woman After God's Own Heart® Growth & Study Guide
- A Woman's Call to Prayer Growth & Study Guide
- A Woman's High Calling Growth & Study Guide
- A Woman's Walk with God Growth & Study Guide

Books by Jim & Elizabeth George

- God Loves His Precious Children
- God's Wisdom for Little Boys
- A Little Boy After God's Own Heart

Books by Jim George

- The Bare Bones Bible™ Handbook
- The Bare Bones Bible™ Bios
- A Husband After God's Own Heart
- A Man After God's Own Heart
- The Remarkable Prayers of the Bible
- The Remarkable Prayers of the Bible Growth & Study Guide
- A Young Man After God's Own Heart